DERBY OUR CITY

Nicola Rippon

breedon **books**

P U B L I S H I N G

First published in Great Britain in 2001 by
The Breedon Books Publishing Company Limited
Breedon House, 3 The Parker Centre,
Derby, DE21 4SZ.

Dedication

To Mr Peter Odell. The very best kind
of teacher, he made learning fun.

ISBN 1 85983 245 8

Printed and bound by Butler & Tanner, Frome, Somerset, England.

Cover printing by Green Shires, Leicester, England.

CONTENTS

Introduction 7

Bleak yet beautiful 8

Hippos, hyenas and bears 9

The first Derbeians 10

The Romans build a fort 11

The English arrive 15

Viking Derby 17

The last invasion 21

The Black Death in Derby 30

Reformation and Dissolution 33

The Civil War 39

John Flamsteed – first Astronomer Royal 46

The Glorious Revolution 50

The centre of the universe? 51

Industry, endeavour, enlightenment 55

The most original man – Erasmus Darwin 60

An elegant mind – John Whitehurst 65

Key industrialists – Strutt and Evans 67

Joseph Wright of Derby 69

Pickford's Derby 71

American connections 74

Riots and strikes 78

Transport by canal 80

A railway town 82

Crime and punishment 85

Lessons for life 92

Thoroughly modern Derby 99

A place of trees – Derby Arboretum 103

Entertaining Derby 106

This sporting life 113

Into a modern era 119

A skilled workforce 123

Derby and the Great War 128

Derby and the General Strike 135

A town of some importance 138

At war again 144

Derby against the elements 153

A princess comes to town 157

The King is dead... 159

...Long live the Queen 162

Derby in the Fifties 165

A plan to change the face of Derby 168

A city for the Seventies 171

The Pride of Derby 175

Bibliography 182

Index 183

Acknowledgements

The following have helped with research and illustrations: Derby Museum, Derby Local Studies Library, Derby Evening Telegraph, Public Record Office, Aerofilms, The American Philosophical Society, Lowell Historical Society, Lowell National Historical Park, W. W. Winter, Robert Astick of the Multi-Faith Centre Project, Sam Winfield Collection, Rod Jewell Collection, Don Farnsworth, EMPICS.

INTRODUCTION

HISTORY is the past, it is gone. Long lists of dates and names, and places, kings, queens and battles. For many people, history is a dry subject. But I was fortunate. My childhood was filled with stories of Romans, of Vikings, of Saxon princesses and Scottish princes. Rarely did we walk anywhere without a member of my family telling me some tale of the history of a certain place, a certain building. My paternal grandfather, who was not even a native of Derby, had a passion for what today we would probably call social history. It was infectious. He would talk of the music halls, singing the songs of those pre-war days, and he would speak of his awe as he looked up at the screen and watched his favourite film stars in the early days of cinema. My mother's father has always told wonderful stories of childhoods spent in the Arboretum clambering over the Florentine Boar, of the time he and his best friend tossed a coin over two girls they met in Darley Park and how the girl he 'won' became his wife, my grandmother; he talked of his life at Rolls-Royce during and after the war, and of his experiences in the Home Guard.

It would have been all too easy to dismiss as 'just old people talking', but the tales were always recounted with such passion, such enthusiasm, that it was as real and as relevant to me as was my own life. I was encouraged to look around, to notice the buildings and to imagine the critical events and the minutiae of history that have occurred on the streets of Derby. And now I realise that I too have lived through history and that the same has been true for all Derbeians over the past 2,000 years.

This city holds treasures and surprises at every turn, so whether you are a Derbeian or a visitor to our city, take this book, take a few spare moments and look around. Our heritage is here amongst us. It is in the very fabric of the buildings that surround us. The bricks and mortar, the stone and ashlar of our city hold in their atoms the experiences and memories of generations of Derbeians. Perhaps this book will help to unlock some of those secrets.

BLEAK YET BEAUTIFUL

LONG before humankind ever stood upon this place, Nature wrought changes more dramatic and turbulent than anything that followed.

Derbyshire stands upon land in parts rich with minerals and fossils, bleak yet beautiful and riddled with caverns, elsewhere lush and green, gently undulating with ancient meandering rivers and streams, all of which provide ample evidence of millions of years of changes in climate and terrain. Once the county was enveloped in a warm sea giving rise to the barren limestone hilltops in the northwest. When that sea drained and evaporated it left behind mud and sand which formed the millstone grit in the centre of the county. The sea returned, forming a swamp, then disappeared once more leaving Derbyshire a desert. Gypsum deposits formed at what is now Chellaston, and the south of the county stands on red marl formed from the remaining mud flats.

Nestled at what is almost the southern-most tip of the county, stands the city of Derby, an historic settlement, and one which owes its very existence to the landscape that surrounds it. For Derby stands at the lowest and easiest crossing-point of the River Derwent and at the southern end of the Pennine chain. Virtually in the middle of the country, with easy access to all corners, it is a place surrounded by minerals and amply supplied with water with which to feed and drive industry.

But the kind of growth which Derby was to witness, required more than just raw materials – it required imagination, innovation and enterprise. And the people who settled here through more than 2,000 years of civilisation became great industrialists, inventors, entrepreneurs, philanthropists, philosophers, heroes and artists. From the very earliest settlers the people who came here have shaped, not only the history of the city, but of the nation and the world as well.

The River Derwent

The Derwent is some 58 miles long, 12 of those flowing through Derby which is 45 miles from the source of the Derwent at Howden Moor, near Glossop, and 10 miles from the junction with the Trent at Wilne. Fish such as chub, dace, gudgeon, perch, pike, roach and barbel can be found in its depths. The banks of the Derwent are a haven for wildlife. As well as a wide variety of water birds, pied wagtails, linnets, fieldfares, kestrels and dunnocks live there. Trees such as alder, sycamore, oak, beech, crack willow, weeping willow, ash, hawthorn and elder line the bank and plants such as reed mace (bullrush), poisonous hemlock, water figwort, great hairy willow herb, goose grass, wild raspberry, Himalayan balsam, hemp agrimony, red campion, fool's watercress and garlic mustard grow there.

Markeaton Brook is home to sticklebacks and minnows as well as mallard ducks, moorhens, dabchicks, brown rats and water voles.

Chaddesden's ancient woodland

Chaddesden Wood is one of the most ancient woodlands in the country. Now a local nature reserve it has been in existence since at least 1548, at which time it covered some 100 acres (40.5 hectares) of pasture and 40 acres (16.2 hectares) of woodland. Much of the forest was felled over the centuries for use in house frames, and for boat building.

HIPPOS, HYENAS AND BEARS

FOR more than one million years, the Earth has endured repeated spells of severe cold, punctuated by milder, more temperate spells – what we know as the Ice Age. There is still evidence of the actions of vast glaciers that cut through the land which surrounds us. In the banks of Littleover Hollow today we can see huge chunks of debris brought here by those glaciers This glacial 'till' is scattered across southern Derbyshire and some has been transported from as far away as the Lake District. – caught up by the huge 'mountains' of compacted ice and deposited as the glaciers melted. The mild climate we know today is just one of many temperate periods known as 'interglacials'. The glaciers may well return once more and then recede as they did 125,000 years ago. Known as the Ipswichian Interglacial, that last temperate period saw the area we know as Derbyshire experiencing a warm climate, similar to that enjoyed today by the Mediterranean. Although this was long before recorded history, through archeological and geological studies we know a great deal about this time.

But the discovery which revealed the pre-history of Derby was an accident. In March 1895, at the Crown Hotel at Allenton, workmen were busy digging out a well in the yard when several large bones were unearthed. Soon H. H. Arnold Bemrose, a distinguished geologist, and Richard Mountford Deeley, a talented engineer and, like Bemrose, a Fellow of the Geographical Society, arrived to oversee a proper excavation of the site, their investigation financed by 'a few local gentlemen' on condition that the bones should be placed in the Borough Museum.

Over three days, more than 120 pieces of bones, many complete, were removed from the dig before the ever-rising water table got the better of the men. After careful examination the bones were identified. There was the femur of a rhinoceros, the breastbone of an elephant and a partial skeleton of a hippopotamus. The hippo was 9ft (2.7m) long and was probably an infant or adolescent at the time of its death – the hippopotamus being the largest land mammals after elephants.

Identified as *Hippopotamus amphibias* – the familiar African hippo so often on view in the world's safari parks – it most probably spent most of its days in the river, emerging at night to graze on the banks. The sediment in which the bones were found was carefully examined and found to be from 'moist meadow or swampy ground and a temperate climate'. Evidence suggested that the hippo had died where it was discovered, probably in a silt-filled channel of the Derwent.

In 1973 at Boulton Moor, just a short distance away, two of the largest hippo teeth ever to be found in Britain were discovered during work to lay a sewer. These probably came from two adult males. Elsewhere at Boulton Moor were discovered the remains of straight-tusked elephant, brown bear, red deer, hyena, oxen and an extinct form of rhinoceros. All across Derbyshire, the bones of such exotic creatures as grizzly bear, bison and even sabre-toothed tiger have been found.

Many of these remain on display at Derby Museum, providing an unexpected incarnation of life in Derby and its surrounding area.

THE FIRST DERBEIANS

N the Iron Age, the place we have come to know as Derby was heavily wooded, cold and damp, swampy and boggy. The local inhabitants – members of a Celtic tribe – shared their territory with exotic wildlife such as bears and wolves. The

The first people to live in the area which became Derby were Celts who built simple houses.

land was criss-crossed with ancient trackways, several of which came right through the area which is the modern city. The lines of these roadways are still in use today. One, from north to south, came into the city at what is now Darley Grove, continued on to Irongate and the Cornmarket and then took the line of St Peter's Street towards The Spot and beyond, later separating in two – one branch stretching to Leicestershire, the other to South Derbyshire.

Most Celtic communities were primarily small agricultural colonies. There was no trade with neighbouring tribes, so expansion was limited by

each community's ability to be self-sufficient. The Celts preferred to live on drier, higher ground and since the Derwent Valley was prone to flooding, the population of the immediate area that was to become Derby was sparse.

At Derby Museum visitors can see what few traces of Iron Age habitation have been found: a few shards of pottery, some flints and axes and a single coin. This simple way of life was to continue unchallenged until the arrival of successive invaders. Invaders who would, in turn, bring changes upon the British Isles that would form both economy and industry, and shape society.

The first of these newcomers finally established themselves upon the shores of Britain in AD43. They were the Romans.

There are few traces left of the Iron Age lifestyle in the area.

THE ROMANS BUILD A FORT

AS the Romans took control of lower Britain, they met with little resistance from the Celtic tribes who were, for the most part, 'persuaded' into submission by a combination of superior military force and by the promise of protection against rival tribes.

Remains of a Roman building in Marcus Street. Indentations in the stones would have supported wooden posts.

As the invaders moved north, to the higher ground surrounding the Pennines, local tribes were less compliant and, as a precaution against insurrection, the Romans built a series of forts around the Trent Valley. One such fort was in the area we know today as Strutt's Park, at Belper Road. In 1998, excavations at a house on Duffield Road uncovered part of the original Strutt's Park fort, dating from at least the second century. Plans to build on the land at the start of the 21st century proved controversial.

Later, by AD80, the Romans built a new, stronger fort, named Derventio on the east bank of the River Derwent, on the area today known as Little Chester, near Mansfield Road.

Initially of timber, it was repeatedly fortified and altered throughout the Roman occupation. It was rectangular in shape and stretched over an area of approximately seven acres (2.8 hectares). Some

distance outside the walls, wide defensive ditches were dug. Derventio stood alongside the Roman road of Rykneld Street, which joined the great forts of the south-west with those in the north.

Much of Derby is aligned with Rykneld Street and the agger and camber of it can still be seen in the grassed area at the front of the Forte Posthouse Hotel on the corner of Pastures Hill and Chain Lane in Littleover.

In gardens on Marcus Street in Little Chester, evidence of a Roman well remains, and several houses in the area are reputed to stand on Roman foundations.

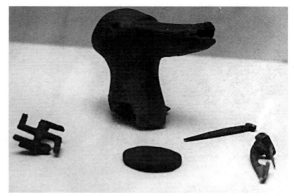

Roman pot duck's head aquamanile and brooches found on Derby Racecourse, where an industrial settlement had grown up outside the fort.

There would have been anything from 500 to 1,000 men (some foot soldiers, some cavalrymen) stationed permanently at Derventio and they would have formed a cohort – a non-Roman auxiliary force drawn from the various people of the empire. In the case of Derventio these would probably have been from Gaul (modern-day France and Germany). Legions formed from Roman soldiers were usually stationed at the larger forts, and away from the dangerous frontiers. Although primarily a military garrison, Derventio was certainly a fully-fledged settlement. Remains of a principia (Roman headquarters) have been uncovered at the junction of City Road with Old Chester Road on the site of the car-park. In a fort of its size we can also expect to have seen a praetorium (commandant's residence),

LIFE IN DERVENTIO

HAD we been able to visit Derventio in its prime, we would have seen a noisy, smelly, busy place. Many had been drawn to the Roman garrison by the lure of greater technological sophistication and by an opportunity to trade, to set up manufacturing businesses and even to settle on the periphery. Strewn along the line of Rykneld Street, to the north and south, were homes and workshops. These were simple structures and often served as both house and business. Here there were all manor of trades and crafts – skinners and tanners, leatherworkers, smiths, carpenters, weavers and even a baker's shop. There would be a constant procession of carts going back and forth with goods. Produce would be brought in from nearby farms and sold to both the military and civilian populations. Further east, at what is today known as the Racecourse, lay the industrial suburb. The prevailing wind blew any smoke or fumes well away from the residential areas.

Here iron and bronze items were made. Furnaces and ovens blazed away, and here too were pottery kilns. Among the items manufactured at Derventio were jars, bowls and dishes of all sizes. The local ware was purely functional and used for storage and cooking. It was rough, dimpled and heavy. Large quantities were made, but it was used only locally, and most of it was supplied to the military. In contrast, a more decorative and elegant ceramic ware was imported from the Continent. Known as Samian pottery, it was an attractive glossy red, often decorated with scenes depicting gods and goddesses, warriors and gladiators. It was valuable, rare and highly-treasured. Examples of both can be seen at Derby Museum.

Attached to the garrison, in addition to the administrative buildings, were the public baths. Aside from the obvious hygienic reasons for their popularity, a trip to the baths was an important social occasion. Here friends would meet up to gossip or play counter games, and businessmen would negotiate and strike deals – the baths being an excellent opportunity to make contacts. Men and women usually bathed separately.

Outside were hawkers selling drinks and snacks. Inside it was possible to indulge in a variety of spa treatments such as massage, hairdressing and even the plucking of unwanted hair.

The bathhouse was divided into several chambers, each of which would be maintained at a different temperature. The intention was to deeply cleanse the body by inducing perspiration. There were variations on the ritual, but all followed a basic pattern. First the bather might take physical exercise, running, wrestling, lifting weights for example. After changing, he or she would proceed to the tepidarium (warm room) where oils, perhaps mixed with abrasives and perfumes, would be applied to the body. Once the body had adjusted to the temperature, the bather moved into the caldarium (hot room). This was very hot indeed, perhaps even hotter than a sauna or Turkish bath. Sometimes there were separate steam and dry rooms. Here the body was rubbed and scraped with a strigil – a metal tool designed to remove oils and dirt from the skin. Then a hot bath was taken. Finally the bather would enter the frigidarium (cold room), where the body would be allowed to cool. Eventually, the bather would either take a cool bath, or have cold water poured over them to revitalise the skin and reverse the sleep-inducing effects of the heat.

Despite the common misconception that they enjoyed huge feasts and parties every night, the Romans neither ate nor drank to excess Their diet was healthy, and they consumed lots of fruit and root vegetables, as well as fish and seafood. Breakfast would be bread and fruit, lunch a salad, or cheese and eggs etc. *Cena* (dinner) was taken at around 4pm and would be a relaxed social event. Typical appetizers might be anchovies, hard-boiled eggs, and salads. This was followed by either baked or grilled fish, or perhaps one of the most popular mainstays of the diet, *pottage*. This was similar to modern-day polenta and was made from

Public baths would have been attached to the Roman military garrison at Derventio. Remains of a bath house were found at Parker's Piece.

spelt, a type of wheat. It was combined with meats, vegetables and wine sauces. Dessert would usually be fruit or occasionally a cake, sweetened with honey. Of course, the exact content and quantity would depend on the relative wealth of the family.

Derventio was not a thriving cultural centre of Roman Britain but troupes of performers – actors, musicians and even gladiators – would probably pass through from time to time. In general, though, there was little in the way of diversion from the daily ritual of battle practice.

But although Derventio was primarily a military garrison, the greatest threat to life came not from battle, but from illness. There was nothing in the way of modern medicine, only a few home 'remedies', which did little to stop the indiscriminate spread of diseases such as smallpox, tetanus, typhus and anthrax. The average life expectancy was only 40, and half the population died before the age of 20. Because the Romans had no understanding of viruses or germs, premature death was accepted as a fact of life.

Britain enjoyed a curious, yet comfortable fusion of ancient Celtic beliefs and Roman traditions, which would vary slightly from place to place. Near Derventio, at the Racecourse, several graves and a formal walled cemetery were uncovered in 1978. As was the tradition, it lay outside the walls of the fort. The dead here were either interred, or cremated. The remains of those cremated were placed in vessels (*amphora*) which were buried in the ground in chambers. Sometimes the vessels were buried with the neck protruding from the earth. On special days, wine and other offerings to the deceased would be poured in by grieving relatives. At Derventio, some of those buried were found to have been decapitated, their heads placed between their knees. This is believed to have been a funeral tradition to allow the spirit to escape the body and continue on into the afterlife. Another tradition observed at Derventio was the inclusion of two coins, with which to pay Charon, the ferryman who the Romans believed took the souls of the dead over the River Styx into the Underworld. Christianity had long been outlawed by the empire, since it opposed the Roman assertion of an all-powerful emperor. But in AD313, Constantine the Great, himself the son of a Christian woman, decreed that toleration should extend to all religions.

Roman society was very much male-dominated, although women's rights did improve in later years. Men could not marry while serving in the army, but many took common-law wives anyway, and there were encampments of women and children outside the garrisons. Many soldiers were not Roman citizens, but natives of other parts of the empire. They were required to serve for 25 years, after which they were discharged and granted Roman citizenship. Their children, although not their common-law wives, were also granted citizenship. If the troops were moved on, it was the responsibility of the women and children to follow as best they could – they would receive no assistance to do this. When the Roman army left for the Continent, many must have been left behind and many former soldiers must have remained with their families.

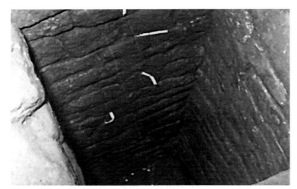

Stone-lined Roman well uncovered in Marcus Street.

granaries, armouries and a hospital. On the site of the former Manor House Farm, the remains of a large building have been found. This was possibly a base for government officials, or for imperial civil servants who from Derventio may have controlled the Derbyshire lead mining industry. There was also a bath-house on the site (at Parker's Piece). The Roman hypocaust which was found there was the Roman equivalent of under-floor central heating. It was situated beneath a suspended floor and heat would spread around the building beneath the floors and between the walls. It would have been an efficient and effective system. Remains of another high-status building were found in the grounds of a nursery by Old Chester Road.

But Derventio was more than just a military fort. It attracted all manner of tradesmen and workers and had its own residential and industrial suburbs,

as well as shops and a cemetery. Trade grew with the Celts, especially with the farmers who, through taxation, had to supply the Romans with wheat and other produce. They, in turn, learned to grow more crops and were able to sell the surplus to the people who flocked to the fort to sell their own wares. Servants and slaves were drawn from a hamlet on what is now Darley Fields.

Throughout the Roman occupation, as emperor succeeded emperor, the emphasis shifted from peace to war. The garrison at Derventio was downgraded, then re-fortified as troops were taken north to fight incursions from Caledonia (Scotland), then with increased Celtic insurrections, were returned to Derventio to help protect the Trent Valley. As time wore on, attacks upon the Romans grew more frequent and more daring. In the final third of the fourth century, Roman Britain was under attack from all corners – from the Picts and Scots from the north, and the Saxons from the south. On the Continent, the barbarians (as Rome described anyone from outside the control of the empire) grew in strength and eventually attacks on the Romans' western provinces caused Constantine the Great to withdraw his troops from Britain in AD407 to assist in the war on the Continent. The now-defenceless British were probably making desperate pleas to the Romans for protection, but the former colonies were left to their own devices. As Rome fell to the Goths, Britain was again under attack from the continent – this time by the Angles, Saxons and Jutes.

Pig of lead found at Yeaveley. Roman officials based at Derventio may have controlled the local lead mining industry.

THE ENGLISH ARRIVE

WHILE coastal areas of Britain were under attack from these new invaders, the Britons who had been left behind continued with their new way of life as best they could. But without the strength of the Roman infrastructure, and without Roman finance, the British economy would have collapsed within a couple of decades, and although trade would continue, it would have to adapt. With no money, and no coins, some kind of bartering system must have operated – the offer of one service or product in exchange for another. Serving as a very visible symbol of this general degeneration, the old fort of Derventio lay to waste and nature quickly reclaimed her.

By the sixth century, when Saxon pirates sailed up the Trent, the colonisation of the country was complete. The Saxons were a sophisticated people, who preferred to live in low-lying areas. Some settled around the ruins of Derventio, which they renamed Little Chester. This particular Saxon tribe, from Schleswig-Holstein, soon set about clearing trees along the banks of the Derwent and several Saxon graves have been found which dated from the sixth to seventh centuries.

The first areas seized by the Saxons were those already accustomed to 'foreign' rule, so the new invaders were able to seamlessly establish their control over the country. However, they are known to have been uneasy with all things Roman and they wasted little time in founding a settlement which they could call their own, one mile away from Little Chester. This new settlement grew in an area today bounded by St Alkmund's Way to the north and Derby Cathedral and St Mary's Church to the south. Further away, a separate development grew at what is now the defunct St Werburgh's Church in Cheapside, based on the water supply provided by Markeaton Brook. Meanwhile, land at Darley Fields was extensively farmed.

The Saxons valued everything they could grow or breed and used every part of the animals they killed. Apart from meat and milk, use was made of skins and wools to make clothing, and horns, bones and sinew were used to make tools, fastenings, and even drinking vessels. The Saxons drank beer and mead as well as fruit wines. Their diet was rich in fish and wild parsnips, cabbage and other root vegetables, which they made into soups and stews. In addition they ate lots of burdock root, berry and orchard fruits, nuts, eggs and dairy produce. Close to the St Werburgh's development, one particular Saxon, named Walda, established a dairy farm, known as a wick. This area became known as Walda's Wick which was soon corrupted to Wardwick.

Saxon skeleton buried outside the fort at Little Chester.

All these settlements which form part of modern-day Derby were themselves part of a very large estate, bounded by the Rivers Trent, Dove and Erewash. It was known as Northworthy (north enclosure), a name which in later years has come to be applied more to the actual city area. As Saxon Britain became divided into several kingdoms, which would eventually unite to form the basis of England, Northworthy became part of the relatively small but powerful kingdom of Mercia, whose capital was at Repton, where we can still see the stunning Saxon crypt of St Wystan's Church. The vaulted ceiling, elegantly decorated with graceful arches, is remarkably preserved.

Although some Romans had adopted Christianity, it was only when the Saxons invaded did Britain become a largely Christian country. In 597, St Augustine was sent by the Pope to convert Britain and by the seventh century Christianity was widespread. As this new religion grew in popularity, ecclesiastical buildings sprang up all across the area. An ancient church dedicated to St James certainly existed, but disappeared long before reliable records were made, so we may only guess at its location. By the time of the Domesday Book in 1086 there were six significant churches in Derby: St Peter's, St Werburgh's, St Mary's, St Michael's, All Saints' and St Alkmund's. Of those still standing today, it is St Peter's which has the oldest fabric. Much of its structure dates from the 14th century, but it does have remains that date back to the Norman invasion. St Michael's on Queen Street is now converted to offices; St Mary's no longer exists and most likely stood opposite the Cathedral at the top of what is now St Mary's Gate. (St Mary's Bridge Chapel was not built until the Middle Ages, when it served as a popular resting place for travellers as they left Derby for the open roads.) All Saints', on Irongate, was founded by King Edward in AD943 and is today Derby Cathedral. St Werburgh's in the Wardwick now lies empty, but in the Saxon period the church was the centre of a thriving community. Founded around AD700, it was dedicated to the memory of St Werburgha, granddaughter of the great Mercian King Penda. Werburgha was the first Mercian princess to be born a Christian. Son of King Alfred of Northumbria, St Alkmund was killed during a palace coup. Records suggest that his body was removed from its grave at Lilleshall in Staffordshire and left at Derby for safekeeping. There are records of pilgrims from the north-east visiting the church and St Alkmund's Well at the bottom of what is now Well Street. That particular church dedicated to his

Typically, the hall of a Saxon noble was the gathering place for everyone who lived in his house.

memory is also no more, having been demolished in 1967 to make way for the inner ring road. Sadly, also destroyed were its delightful churchyard and the lovely Georgian houses that surrounded it. During the demolition work a huge and very heavy stone coffin was discovered. St Alkmund's Sarcophagus, as it became known, was believed to be just that – the safe place in which the saint's remains had been hidden. In more recent times historians have felt it more likely that the coffin belonged to another important, although nameless, elder. Either way, the sarcophagus, which is displayed at Derby Museum, is a splendid relic of the Saxon era in Derby.

That the Saxons felt it necessary to hide St Alkmund's remains in this way, at a time when England was in constant turmoil with much fighting both between and within Saxon kingdoms, perhaps hints at the reasons why the next invaders would find it so easy to gain a strong foothold on England's shore.

VIKING DERBY

IF the Anglo-Saxon invasion of Britain had been peaceful and trouble-free, the next invasion was anything but. Throughout the ninth century, Vikings from what is now modern-day Denmark, Norway and Sweden found an English coastline poorly defended because the Saxons had concentrated their military power on invasions from within, from rival Saxon kingdoms. Initially the Vikings had come to trade, then had returned to steal property, and finally to take land and to settle. The word Viking means 'from the fjords', as well as meaning 'pirate'. Both descriptions were appropriate for such an all-conquering race. The Vikings were hostile and their raids to plunder the riches of religious coastal communities, like Lindisfarne in the north-east, soon turned inland. From their earliest attacks it was clear that they were a formidable force. By AD868 the Viking invasion had taken hold of the whole of East Anglia and reached Nottingham. It was not long before Northworthy and much of Mercia came under their control.

Although Viking rule remained virtually intact for several decades, it was punctuated by frequent skirmishes as the Saxons fought back. Finally, under the leadership of the courageous 'Lady of the Mercians', Aethelflaeda, the Mercian forces began repeated and concentrated raids on Danish strongholds. Aethelflaeda gradually gained more and more territory until, one August morning in AD 917, she and her troops marched into Normanton. There was bitter hand-to-hand fighting, but despite the loss of four of her closest commanders, she retook the town for the Saxons. The Mercians held Derby for 26 years before the Vikings took it back in 943. The Saxons briefly regained possession once more but the territory changed back and forth between Saxon and Viking for close to a century in all.

Since the Saxons were always considered a serious threat, the Vikings both occupied the existing fortifications at Little Chester and built further earthworks around the settlements, including a series at Normanton (Norseman's town). The

AETHELFLAEDA, LADY OF THE MERCIANS

AETHELFLAEDA has come to be regarded by many historians as every bit as important in Saxon history as Boudicca was to the Britons, or Joan of Arc to the French.

The daughter of Alfred the Great of Wessex, she was the wife of Aethelred of Mercia and took command of the Mercian armies upon the death of her husband. Both her father and husband had been popular figures in leading the Saxon resistance against the Vikings and Aethelflaeda continued in these traditions. She always led her armies from the front and fought with courage and determination.

Her victory at Normanton is described in the *Anglo Saxon Chronicle*:

'With the help of God, before Lammas obtained the borough which is called Derby with all that belongs to it.'

A great military leader, she died at Tamworth, where there is a statue to her memory.

In August 917, the Saxon princess Aethelflaeda led hand-to-hand fighting to regain the town.

location of the Viking headquarters is still uncertain. The most likely places for this are at Normanton, at Derventio, or somewhere in today's city centre. One common theory is that the Vikings may have built a castle at Albion Street, but there is no evidence to support this, other than a map of 1791 which shows what might have been earthworks in the area. Some later alterations were made to the old Roman fort at Derventio, but these could have been done by either Viking or Saxon. However, there is a hint in later references to rebellious Saxons entering the 'gates' of the town, and Derventio was the only area known to have had gates. Of course, this may have been no more than a romantic image conjured by the writer of the *Anglo-Saxon Chronicle*. So here, too, evidence is inconclusive. In fact, very little archeological evidence of the Vikings has been found in Derby, save for a few ecclesiastical remains and a comb made of bone, which was found at King's Mead in 1884.

Although from time to time the Saxons had managed to break the Scandinavian hold on Derby, the Vikings' influence is still felt to this day, and with good reason for the town was to become a significant centre of Viking control. The Treaty of Wedmore between King Alfred of Wessex and the Viking King Guthrum led to the foundation of Viking England, which was to be known as the Danelaw (*Danelagen*). It stretched across the country north of a line between London and the Mersey. Along with Leicester, Nottingham, Lincoln and Stamford, Derby became one of the Five Burghs of the Danelaw. Each burgh was divided into smaller political areas known as *vapnataks* (wapentakes). These were divided into many *carucates*, each of which was the amount of land a single plough team could plough in a single year (approximately 120 acres/48.6 hectares). These, in turn, were divided into *bovates* – the amount of land needed for the grazing of one ox (approximately 15 acres/6 hectares).

Derby even got its name from the Vikings. It is either derived from the Old Norse words *djur*, meaning deer, and *by* meaning place, village, town etc. Or it is simply a transformation of the old Roman name, Derventio – *deru* (oak) and *vent* (white) was the 'place of the white oaks'. Certainly the name 'place of the deer' seems significant since the deer, or more precisely the buck, has long been associated with Derby.

Under the Scandinavians the revitalised settlement of Derby grew in size and strength. And,

as part of the Danelaw, it was considered a Viking settlement which would have adopted the laws and customs of Scandinavia. In fact the word 'law' itself is of Old Norse origin. Coupled with 'by' for town, we have our English word 'by-law'. Other words brought into England by the Vikings include: reeve – king's representative (hence shire reeve or sheriff); knife; take; window; egg; ill; die; thorpe (an outlying farm); fell (mountain); dal(e) (valley); and borg/borough (fortified town). From the geographical words and other Viking terms which feature in local names, it can be seen that Viking activity was intense in and around Derby. Even the dialects of modern Derbyshire, Nottinghamshire, Lincolnshire, Leicestershire and Yorkshire have a common ground which differs from the old Anglo-Saxon area of the country, since the northern and eastern accent originates from a mix of Old Norse and Old English languages and pronunciations. The Viking and Saxon languages were similar in some ways, but in order for the people to understand one another, a melding of the two was necessary.

Although their law which decreed that a father's land must be divided between all his sons upon his death had led the Viking culture to be one of expansionism, they had become experts at integrating with the local population. Since almost all the invading Vikings had been men, intermarriage between Viking and Saxon was common. This meant that many Scandinavian traditions and ideas were fused with those of the Anglo-Saxons. Viking tradition taught that the gods lived in Asgard and that, in order to ensure health and good fortune, it was necessary to offer some sort of gift to the gods. Usually, this took the form of the sacrifice of a valuable animal. As Christianity spread beyond the Saxon kingdoms and was gradually accepted by the Vikings, such practices began to die out. Just as the Viking culture impacted upon Saxon life, the reverse was true also. In fact the Vikings in England would have been quite distinct from those in other parts of their territories.

There is plenty of evidence of the Nordic influence upon Saxon religious practices as well as on religious art. Scattered across the churchyards of the Danelaw are hundreds of gravestones and monuments bearing Viking images, many of which are the 'hogback' gravestones typical of Scandinavia.

Although battles between Saxon and Viking

Viking coin struck in Northumbria in the early 10th century, excavated from St Alkmund's and possibly left by religious pilgrims who came to pay homage to the saint's remains.

continued until King Cnut's reign, a sophisticated network of trade routes spread between and within Saxon kingdoms and Viking burghs. Although some of these were somewhat circuitous to avoid troublespots, it meant that what could not be produced locally could probably be imported. Much of the cargo went via waterways, much by road. Many of these trade routes exist today in the guise of our A-roads; the old A1 and A38, among others, have both been defined since Roman times. Although we know that coins were used, since Derby had its own mint close to All Saints', it is likely that much of the trade was still done by a system of bartering.

The Vikings were a proud people who valued personal reputation above all else. They had a strict code of laws which they enforced enthusiastically. Trials were rather different from those we practise today. The emphasis was not on factual evidence at all. Witnesses were called to testify what they *thought* had happened. Then a 'lay-sayer' would tell the court what the letter of the law said about this particular crime, and the jury of 12, 24 or 36 members (depending on the severity of the crime) would pronounce their verdict. Punishments could be severe and options included making the criminal an 'outlaw'. The outlaw would have to spend the rest of his or her life living in the wilderness where no one was allowed to help them. He or she would have to fend for themselves and it was quite acceptable for any enemies to hunt down and kill the outlaw. They were literally 'outside the law' and the law would provide no protection. Not all punishments were quite so barbaric, though. A person who was unable to pay their debts could become a slave of his or her creditors until all their debts had been repaid.

Slaves were well treated but were, of course, considered the 'lowest' section of society behind the aristocracy, the land-owners and the farmers. Under both Viking and Saxon law, men and women were considered equal. Upon marriage, a woman would keep both her money and her property, and she had the right to instigate divorce proceedings.

For all their formidable and fearsome appearance, the Vikings were a sociable people. Mealtimes were important occasions and they enjoyed fruit, fish and vegetables just like the Saxons, and also indulged in boiled meats. They were particularly fond of strong seasonings such as cinnamon, dill, ginger and coriander, as well as garlic and onions. On feast occasions the meal would usually consist of roasted meats with rich sauces. Just how ornate the dishes were depended largely on the status of the host and his guests, as well as the importance of the celebration.

Since Derby was a fortified town, close to the Saxon frontier for much of the period, it would have been home to warriors as well as to artisans and farmers. In Derby Museum is a magnificent Viking sword which was unearthed at Repton. The sight of such a robust and athletic breed of people wielding such a weapon must have been an effective caution to any Saxon with ideas of rebellion.

Viking legends were peopled with great warriors who had gained both fame and wealth by defeating terrifying enemies. The old Norse Sagas were always popular with their tales of heroism and mystery. The Vikings loved such colourful stories and would, no doubt, have passed many a dark, cold evening recounting tall tales of their own exploits. Sometimes a travelling storyteller would pass through and perform the latest epic poems in exchange for food and lodgings. Such poems might have been composed to commemorate a particular event. Perhaps this is where the fanciful modern image of the horn-helmeted warrior originated. Vikings also enjoyed physical exertion and much time was spent training for battle, since Saxon incursions could come at any time. Both wrestling and tugs of war were popular activities, along with sword fighting and spear or stone throwing. Such brutal activities would sometimes result in fatalities and so were usually 'enjoyed' by only the poorer classes. Two particularly brutal pastimes, unthinkable by today's standards, were bear-baiting and horse-fighting, for which the animals were specifically bred. The nobility reserved their strength for such sports as hunting, fishing, rowing and falconry. Vikings also played a ball game similar to hockey and enjoyed more sedate occupations such as early versions of games like nine men's morris, backgammon, counter games, and the Viking version of 'jacks' which involved tossing up pigs' knuckles from the back of the hand and catching them in the palm. Or perhaps embroidery or bone carving and wood whittling might have been enjoyed by the older or more delicate members of society.

Derby under the Vikings would probably have been quite recognisable to today's inhabitants. It stretched across what is now the Market Place, and Irongate and Sadler Gate were in existence even then. Those names themselves give us evidence of trades already present in the town, for 'gate' was an Old Norse word for street. The houses and workshops which lined those roads would have been constructed of wood or stone with thatched or shingled roofs. Several churches were in operation and most of the major roads in and out were already in place.

Irongate, pictured here in the 1850s, the street which in Viking times was home to workers in metal.

Anglo-Viking Derby, like Anglo-Viking England, was beginning to enjoy a period of stability by the time King Cnut, the son of Svein Forkbeard, took the throne in 1016. At last Saxon and Viking could live peacefully side by side. This peace brought new security and confidence to the area. Traders came from far and wide to Derby, and by 1065 the population had soared to 1,200. But just when everyday life was settling down, a new threat to the peace emerged. Tumultuous change was on its way once more.

An earthquake in Derby

The *Anglo-Saxon Chronicle* reported that in 1048, the Derby area was struck by an earthquake and fire. It said, 'This year also there was an earthquake, on the calends of May, in many places; at Worcester, at Wick, and at Derby, and elsewhere wide throughout England; with very great loss by disease of men and of cattle over all England; and the wild fire in Derbyshire and elsewhere did much harm.'

THE LAST INVASION

ALTHOUGH Cnut had successfully held the newly-united England together, within a quarter of a century of his death in 1040 there was to be a three-way battle for power.

Cnut's son, Hardicnut, died only two years after succeeding to the throne and was himself succeeded by Edward the Confessor. Edward, a devout man, had sworn an oath of celibacy, even though he had chosen to marry. When he died in January 1066, without a natural heir, there was more than one 'worthy' successor.

Harold Godwinson was one of the most powerful men in England. He was also Edward the Confessor's brother-in-law and claimed that Edward had named him as his heir. The witan (king's council) elected Harold king and he was crowned on the very day of Edward's burial. But across the English Channel waited William, Duke of Normandy. A distant cousin of Edward the Confessor, he claimed that not only had Edward named him as his successor, but that it had been Harold who had delivered the message and even sworn his allegiance to William. In Scandinavia, the King of Norway, Harald Hardrada, also claimed to be the rightful heir, claiming that his predecessors had been promised England by Edward's predecessors.

When Hardrada invaded, he was swiftly defeated by King Harold at Stamford Bridge, near York. Then William landed on the Sussex coast, near Hastings. King Harold turned his troops around and marched back to meet the new invaders. In September 1066, arguably the most famous date in English history, the fierce battle lasted only a few hours but left Harold and many of his men dead. The

Norman cross shaft, from an earlier St Alkmund's Church. It is now in Derby Museum.

Duke of Normandy was now in control of England.

Right across the country, houses and estates were taken from their English owners and granted to new Norman lords in exchange for help during the invasion. The Normans lived by a completely different system – feudalism – which they soon enforced. The king ruled overall, but each estate was ruled in turn by a nobleman or bishop. The 'ordinary' people were even less in control of their lives than they had been under the English. They were considered serfs who 'belonged' to their lords. Most had little choice but to remain, because outside of the estates they had no protection. They were heavily taxed and the women fared even worse. Under the Normans they had to relinquish almost all their rights and freedoms. Some women were allowed to continue with industrial jobs, but even noblewomen were essentially confined to the home.

Much of Derby's population fled to the countryside and by the time of the Domesday Book, and in only 20 years of Norman occupation, the town's population had dropped by half. This first census still tells us a great deal about the town. Derby is described as a self-contained, agricultural community responsible for its own food and manufacturing. There were several well-established churches and 10 cornmills, but no less than 123 dwellings were described as lying 'waste and empty'. The cost of the invasion had been felt by all and the town's annual rent to the king rose from £24 to £30 plus 18 bushels of corn. Outside the town, there were many villages and estates which have become the suburbs of today.

The Normans held almost all positions of power and

Twenty years after the Norman invasion, William ordered what was England's first census – the Domesday Book. It gave a picture of life in Derby in 1086.

importance and even wealthy local families assumed Norman names to affect some connection. The Normans also brought with them a new legal system which could be at best harsh and at worst barbaric. A man accused of murder had to be captured by his lord and handed over within five days or a large fine would be demanded. The size of the fine depended on just how long the fugitive was at large. Liability for this fine could also be passed over to the rest of the inhabitants of the district. And although William had outlawed execution as a punishment, he suggested that wrongdoers be blinded or castrated instead. If the law was not humane, neither was it even-handed. If there was a dispute between an Englishman and a Norman, whether it be for murder, theft or perjury, the onus of proof was always on the Englishman. If accused, he had to prove his innocence either by combat or by ordeal by hot iron and, if he was the accuser, he still had to prove his case using the same methods. If he refused to do this, the Norman had only to swear an oath in his own defence.

Laws were also introduced to limit the influence of certain people. The Jewish community was forced to restrict itself to an area of Derby that would become known as Jury (Jewry) Street, after a law of 1257 decreed that Jews might only inhabit certain districts. At that time, Jury Street would have been on the edge of town, on the marshy ground that bordered the Markeaton Brook. It would certainly not have been prime residential land, but here the Jews built their homes, and established their businesses. Persecution and prejudice did not stop there. Elsewhere the Jews suffered violence and vandalism,

and in 1290 Edward I expelled all Jews from England.

Norman French had become the language of government, and Latin the language of the church. Of course, the non-Norman 'underclass' continued to speak English. This trilingualism is the main reason that our modern language has such a vast vocabulary. Many of our legal words are of Norman origin (royal, judge, prison, parliament, government), while many of our religious and scientific terms have Latin roots (library, quadrant, medicine) while the basic structure remains English. Many living animal names are of English origin (sheep, ox, swine and deer), while their slaughtered or cooked counterparts (mutton, beef, pork, sausages and venison) are Norman words, because in general the English were the farmers or the butchers, while the Normans were the consumers. Where we have more than one word for a particular meaning, the larger grander words are usually of Norman or Latin origin. For example 'house' which was English and 'mansion' which was Norman. Also 'fire' which was English, 'flame' which was Norman and 'conflagration' which was Latin.

As we have already seen, historians have long debated about the possibility of a castle at Derby. Although no contemporary record has ever come to light to confirm this speculation, rumour persists and there is some circumstantial evidence. For centuries maps of the town featured favoured locations for the castle, and names such as Copecastle, Castle Mill and Castlefields have persisted. The area towards the Cockpitt Car Park was once known as Copecastle (cope = market) and this is one rumoured location for 'Derby Castle'. Copecastle later became known as the more recognisable Cockpit Hill. There is plenty of photographic evidence to show the old market standing on a pronounced mound. However, this mound was a natural feature and Copecastle was probably little more than a local nickname.

A more likely location for the castle, if it existed, is the Albion Street area. An early 19th-century map clearly shows some earthworks, which it identifies as part of a castle. Some have suggested these were part of the Viking fortifications, but others claim that they are clear evidence for a medieval castle. One possibility is that the earthworks were part of an 'emergency' fort erected by the Earl of Chester, to whom Derby had been granted in 1149. He built several such fortifications during a dispute with King

Stephen. The earl's castle would have been privately built and so would not necessarily appear on official records. It would also very likely have been destroyed once King Stephen regained control of the area. That reason, let alone the constant rebuilding and development in the area, might account for the lack of archeological evidence. But for the time being, the mystery remains unsolved. If there was a castle of any significance or grandeur, there is not yet any evidence to prove its existence.

By now the church was becoming all-powerful and it was not long before Derby became primarily a monastic settlement. The first monastery was established by a Benedictine order and dedicated to St Helen. It was near the site of the present-day St Helen's House. By the 1140s the monks had outgrown this small settlement and moved out to a large site at Darley, where the only obvious trace of the monastery surviving to the 21st century is the 13th-century building which is now the Abbey Inn and which probably served as a barn or outbuilding. Nearby, on Abbey Lane (Nos 7-9) there is evidence of 15th-century architecture which probably dates from a later extension to the monastery, although this has been extensively modernised over the centuries.

The abbey's holdings were vast and it became the largest monastery in the county, holding lands all over Derbyshire. Much of this land was divided into tofts and strips, and a small annual rent was paid by locals who farmed there. The abbey was an ideal overnight stop for kings, nobles, knights and bishops who passed this way. From its gates the monks would give food to the poor, and tend the sick. They would pray, eat and sleep, and, in their spare time, work in the gardens, or perhaps copy books by hand,

The only obvious remnant of the abbey at Darley is the Abbey Inn, probably some kind of outbuilding.

> **'Stupified by fear...' – a 13th-century UFO**
> On 14 October 1253, Nicholas of Findern and many others witnessed a bizarre sight in the skies over Alvaston. Records of Burton Abbey state that a large bright star emerged from a dark cloud. This was followed by two smaller stars which appeared beside it and began to charge against the larger one, sparks appearing to fall as it reduced in size. Eventually people fled 'stupified by fear and ignorant of what it might portend'.

the only means of reproduction in the days before the printing press. But the Darley monks were not as pure in spirit as they might have been. There were frequent rumours of high-living at the abbey at Darley and of exploitation of the locals and even the demanding of money to fish on the Derwent. In 1384 the king, tired of hearing these complaints, took control of the abbey revenue for four years.

A Benedictine priory, intended as a sister establishment of Darley, was established at King's Mead. Known as St Mary de Pratis (St Mary of the Meadows), the only remains visible today are an ancient building on Nuns Street, which now forms part of the halls of residence for the University of Derby. In 1825 a large mosaic tiled floor and a coffin containing a female skeleton were found nearby, as well as other medieval masonry.

In 1140, a Cluniac priory had been founded in connection with the church of St James. For the most part the Cluniacs remained within their priory, and concentrated on devotion and contemplation. This was in contrast to the Dominicans, who established a monastery on what was to become known as Friar Gate. They built a large friary with some 16 acres (6.5 hectares) of parkland featuring fishponds, a chapel and many other buildings. The whole of the Heritage Gate complex and the Friary Hotel are built on part of its grounds.

Throughout the Middle Ages, a succession of monarchs granted Derby important charters extending the privileges of the town. These charters had to be paid for and were an indirect, although effective, way of obtaining defence funding. The area around the Market Place, originally part of the Viking settlement, became a regular market for the first time around 1100, a purpose it served for more than

THE STREETS OF OUR TOWN

THE street names of Derby are a constant reminder of our past. They reflect history, industry and culture. Here are just a few of the most unusual, with explanations of their origins. Several date from Viking times, for example: Irongate: gate is a Viking word meaning street, so it was the street where the ironworkers lived and traded from Viking times.

Sadler Gate: where the leather workers lived and traded.

This tradition of using the word gate continued well after the time of the Vikings:

Friar Gate: location of the Dominican Friary.

St Mary's Gate: location of St Mary's Church

Bridge Gate: location of St Mary's Bridge.

Vernon Gate: a name of the 1990s for the redeveloped county gaol, although here perhaps used because the façade of the prison, with its gate, is almost all that remains.

Many street names of the early medieval period tell us much about the trades, industry and people who lived there.

Cheapside: the location of early markets.

Cornmarket: grain was sold here.

Wardwick: Walda's Wick, remembering a dairy farm belonging to a Saxon named Walda.

Abbey Street and Monk Street: reflecting connections to the Friary.

Bold Lane: from Bolt Lane where the fletchers (arrow makers) worked.

Jury Street: from Jewry Street, the location of the Jewish quarter.

Tenant Street: location of the tenth bridge over Markeaton Brook.

Deadman's Lane: the location of mass burials of plague victims.

Depot Street, off Rose Hill Street: the location of an ordnance depot

In New Normanton, Overdale, Upperdale, Lower Dale and Dale Roads were built on land owned by Dale Abbey.

Stonehill Road - once Stone-furlong - marked the boundary between St Peter's and Normanton-by-Derby parishes. The boundary stone is on Burton Road.

At Chester Green, site of the Roman fort, these names appear: Derventio Court, Caesar Street, Roman Road, Camp Street, Marcus Street and Centurion Walk.

The Lock-Up Yard between the Cornmarket and Market Hall marks the location of the small lock-up situated where the Fish Market now stands.

The roads which for decades have effectively formed the north-south spine of the city centre. All Saints' is at the top of the picture, in Irongate, and then the road passes to one side of the Market Place, then becomes Cornmarket and St Peter's Street before disappearing towards The Spot.

Throughout time many streets have born the name of noted individuals.

Queen Street: named after Queen Mary, daughter of Henry VIII and Catherine of Aragon.

King Street: named after her consort, King Philip of Spain.

Victoria and Albert Streets: named after the great queen and her consort.

Babington Lane: after Babington Hall, the townhouse of Sir Anthony Babington.

Degge Street: after the Degge family who lived at nearby Babington Hall.

Exeter Bridge and Exeter Street: named after the Earl of Exeter and his home, Exeter House.

Darwin Place: after polymath Erasmus Darwin.

Fox Street: after Sir Charles Fox, the engineer who built the Crystal Palace.

Handyside Street: after the owner of the foundry which built Friar Gate Bridge.

Ferrers Way at Allestree: after the De Ferrers family who owned the land after the Norman Conquest.

Loudon Street: after J. C. Loudon, designer of the Arboretum.

Strutt Street: after Joseph Strutt, who donated the Arboretum to the town.

Ambrose Street and Moore Street: after Ambrose Moore who had a silk mill at the corner of the two streets.

Becher Street and Leacroft Road: after Mr Becher Leacroft.

Harcourt Street: after the MP who became Chancellor of the Exchequer.

Plimsoll Street: after MP Samuel Plimsoll.

Bass Street: after the MP and member of the brewing family.

Heyworth Street: popular Liberal MP.

Mayors: Crompton, Renals, Moss, Howe, Roe, Drewry, Arthur Hinds, and Raynes (way) are also honoured in this way.

The area between Osmaston Road and Harvey Road features the names of many local notables: (John) Flamstead (*sic*) Street, (John) Whitehurst Street, (William) Duesbury Close, (William) Hutton Street.

Often the builders of streets would lend their own names.

In New Normanton alone names like Almond Street, Young Street, Scott Street and Thorn Street reflect this trend.

In more recent times, with the mass building of estates in the second half of the 20th century, estates have tended to be given themes.

At Chaddesden one development features US names like Maine Drive, Roosevelt Avenue, Oregon Way, Lansing Gardens, Chesapeake Road, Michigan Close and Cheyenne Gardens.

At Mickleover, the theme has been Australia and New Zealand, for example Brisbane Road, Cairns Close, Darwin Road, Auckland Close, Canberra Road and Murray Road.

At Alvaston there are a host of theatrical names like Garrick and Thorndyke, and poets like Browning, Dryden and Emerson are remembered off Village Street. Balaclava Road in Pear Tree recalls the Crimean War, and the old Little City off Burton Road once had names like Waterloo Street, Trafalgar Street and Cannon Street, built as they were during the Napoleonic Wars.

At Mackworth estate there has been a London theme with Finchley Avenue, Isleworth Drive, Chelsea Close, Hendon Way and Kew Gardens all appearing on the street map.

Even some of the smaller estates have themes. The Muirfield Estate between Chain Lane and Uttoxeter Road at Mickleover has roads which take on names like Carnoustie, Gleneagles, Wentworth, Birkdale and Belfry Closes, reflecting the nearby golf club.

But probably the most curious street name in the city is the one which no-one can explain. The Spot at the junction of Osmaston and London Roads with St Peter's Street has been called that since at least 1742, but there has never been a satisfactory explanation for this strange name. Perhaps it was simply a local nickname which stuck.

Examples of how medieval buildings stood at right-angles to the road. *Above:* The Old White Horse (far left) in Friar Gate, which was demolished to make way for the railway. It stood next to two cottages. *Below:* No. 19 Cornhill, Allestree, a house which stands today.

800 years. By now Derby was truly a thriving centre of trade and industry, but it still had little independence. A Prepositus, or king's representative, was charged with collecting one-third of the town's revenue for the royal coffers. But in 1204, King John granted a new charter which permitted the townspeople to elect two bailiffs to replace the Prepositus. The charter also bestowed the right to

hold twice-weekly markets and to guarantee any man living in Derby for a year and a day, freedom from slavery. A moot hall was established, which probably stood near to the Market Place, behind the buildings of Irongate

As Norman and English traditions, and people, became more integrated, so the feudal system began to evolve. New organisations came into being which would shift the balance of power in the towns away from the lords of the manor and towards the increasingly wealthy merchant class. They were the guilds.

From the end of the 11th century, those who practised the same craft or business had begun to band together in a guild, finding that this gave them greater protection and also greater power in the daily life of the town. These merchant guilds became virtually all-powerful. In Derby Market Place, a guild hall was established. The guilds regulated prices and business practices as well as standardising weights and measures. While this protected members from competition from outside the town, it effectively created a monopoly where outsiders could not trade unless they joined the guild, or paid duties and taxes on their goods, and it meant that it was quite impossible to conduct any business without official approval. The craft guilds were responsible for ensuring a fair and equal system of conditions and working hours for their members as well as a uniform price for each product. A separate guild was usually established in each town for each trade. No newcomer could even attempt to sell his wares without first becoming a member of that town's guild. The guilds were also responsible for ensuring a standardised quality and anyone entering the trade had to learn their skills from an established craftsman. Young boys were apprenticed to master craftsmen, spending up to seven years learning the appropriate skills, after which they would become journeymen, being paid for their work by the day (from the Norman *journee* = daily). Several years later, after completing their studies, they would make their 'masterpiece' and, if successful, and in possession of enough money to open their own shop, they could themselves become masters and take on apprentices of their own. There was no advertising, no undercutting of prices, no competition. Since there was no competition, the guild members usually chose to set up shop in enclaves where they could be easily located by customers. Many of these can be easily identified by looking at the street names on a modern map of Derby.

By 1326 a permanent stone bridge had been opened to cross the Derwent. It replaced the Causey – a ford across the river on the main road to Nottingham – and eventually featured the lovely St Mary's Bridge Chapel which survives to this day. Although the bridge was rebuilt in later years, an original arch can be seen beneath the foundations of the chapel. There were also a number of bridges and fords across the Markeaton Brook: St Peter's Bridge by the HSBC Bank on the corner of St Peter's Street and Albert Street; Sadler Gate Bridge at the Cheapside end of the street; and Tenant Street Bridge at the Morledge side of the Market Place. Despite culverting of the Markeaton Brook by the Victorians,

the humps of the bridges are still visible beneath the pavements. A ford also crossed the brook at what is now Ford Street.

At this time most of the buildings in Derby would have been of a cruck-framed or half-timbered construction. The frameworks were usually made from oak and were infilled with panels woven from branches and twigs and covered in mud-based 'plaster'. Sometimes the houses would sit on a brick foundation for extra security. The plots were long and narrow, having been based upon the old Saxon burgage plots, and so most of them were built gable-on at right angles to the street.

A very good example of this was the ancient Old White Horse inn which once stood on Friar Gate and was demolished by the Victorians to make way for the railway.

DERBY'S MEDIEVAL AND TUDOR REMNANTS

ALTHOUGH at first sight there are few visible remains of the Norman Conquest in Derby, there are plenty of examples of medieval architecture throughout the modern city.

St Peter's Church in Derby city centre. Parts of the church date back to Norman times, others to the 12th and 14th centuries.

The east wall of the nave of St Peter's Church in the city centre is of Norman construction and much of the rest of the church dates from the 12th and 14th centuries. The Old Grammar School on St Peter's Churchyard, now Derby Heritage Centre, was

built in the 1500s, as was the Old Dolphin public house on Queen Street. At Irongate, number 22 has a core which may well date back to at least 1540, and the Seven Stars Inn on King Street, which has held a licence since at least 1680, dates from a much earlier time. The Bridge Chapel at Bridge Gate has been in existence since the 14th century and the remains of the Priory of St Mary de Pratis has stood on Nuns Street since at least the 1500s.

At Old Chester Road both Derwent House and School Farmhouse date back to the 16th century and both are believed to contain the remains of much earlier buildings as well as Roman masonry in the cellars. Further out, at Darley Abbey, there are the 13th-century remains of the abbey.

At Church Lane, Chaddesden, stands St Mary's Church which

St Mary's Bridge, showing remnants of the piers for the medieval bridge.

dates back to at least 1357; and at Chellaston, 4 Swarkestone Road contains 16th-century material. 17 Shepherd Street, Littleover contains a very old core within its 17th-century exterior, and the nearby St

St Mary's Chapel on the Bridge, pictured some time around World War One, before it was restored. On the right is Bridge Gate, once the town ditch.

Peter's Church of 1335 still features a font dating from Norman times. At Littleover Hollow, Ye Olde Cottage is a timber-framed building from the 16th century. At Mickleover Hollow (no 4) is another pretty cottage from that century. At Church Street, Alvaston, both No 3 and Church Farmhouse have stood since the 15th century, and Elm Cottage on Elvaston Lane was built in the 16th century. The 16th-century Grange on Park Road, Spondon, stands near to the 14th-century church of St Werburgh's.

Internal staircase of the Old Mayor's Parlour.

The cottage at Mickleover Hollow which dates from the 16th century.

One spectacular remnant of Derby's medieval past met a sad fate in 1948. The five-gabled building known as the Old Mayor's Parlour dated from the late 15th century. It contained a fine oak staircase and oak panelling and stood in

The Old Mayor's Parlour in Tenant Street, pictured in 1938.

Frontage of the Old Mayor's Parlour

Tenant Street, approximately where the garden dedicated to the memory of Colonel Sir Peter Hilton, Lord-Lieutenant of Derbyshire from 1978 to 1994, is today. The garden of the Parlour reached down to the river. The name is a mystery, for it was never used in an official capacity, nor do we know who had it built. Perhaps it once belonged to a popular mayor. Whoever the first owner was, at the time of its destruction it was one of the largest urban residences of its type and date in England.

Percival Willoughby, who lived with his wife in the Old Mayor's Parlour during the 17th century, was the pioneer of modern gynaecology and midwifery. His *Observations of Midwifery* still forms the basis of modern childbirth methods. He delivered hundreds of babies throughout the Midlands and he is buried in St Peter's Churchyard.

THE BLACK DEATH IN DERBY

ALAS, the concentration of population and the busy trade routes were to provide a vehicle for the greatest natural disaster to strike these shores: Yersnias Pestis, the Plague, the Black Death.

Since Roman times the threat of disease had been ever-present. Open ditches ran down the centre of the streets, carrying sewage and industrial and household waste right through the middle of Derby. Livestock, in particular pigs, ran loose in the street and rats were everywhere. There was little in the way of formal medical care. Outside the town, at Litchurch, well away from the main settlement, there was a leper hospital dedicated to St Leonard. Although we cannot be certain of the location, it probably stood close to the site of what is now Leonard Street. Another was at Spondon on what is now Louise Greaves Lane (Lousy Graves). The insanitary conditions which prevailed and the lack of all but the most basic medical care, meant that even the most apparently minor infection could become life-threatening. But the Black Death was far from a minor threat; in fact it can still kill in the 21st century if treatment is not quickly administered.

The 14th-century medicine which was to be set to work against this terrible disease amounted to little more than a mixture of herbalism, superstition and wild experimentation. It was commonly believed that the body consisted of the four humours – choler, phlegm, black bile and blood. Each of these corresponded to an element, respectively fire, water, earth and air. Health of both the body and mind depended upon the delicate balance of all four. A change in balance might result in a change in health or even in personality. It was also believed that disease was spread through miasmas, or noxious vapours, which came from marshes and swamps, and one so-called protection was to burn incense or herbs, or to hold a small sachet of herbs or flowers close to the nose whilst outdoors. If the foul smell could be avoided, went the theory, then so could the disease. As is common in times of crisis, people sought strength from the church, touching holy relics and drinking from sacred spring water for protection. All manner of odd remedies were tried – from sleeping on the stomach to not washing the body to

prevent poisonous vapours from entering. Many such treatments were available only to the very rich, such as the eating of powdered emeralds, but the Black Death knew no such division. Rich or poor, young or old, anyone could fall into its grisly clutches.

It is uncertain precisely how the Black Death came to Britain. It was spread by the bites of fleas which lived on the black rat and other rodents. When the rats died, the fleas were forced to seek refuge on human hosts and thus spread the deadly disease. Probably the rats stowed away on merchant vessels from the Continent, where the plague was already rampant and possibly some of the bacilli were 'sleeping' in the cargo of those vessels ready to be transported right across the country. What is certain is that when it arrived, it did so with devastating force, striking hard and fast. The Italian writer Giovanni Boccaccio wrote: 'How many valiant men, how many fair ladies, breakfast with their kinfolk and the same night supped with their ancestors in the next world?'

The Black Death could afflict in any one of three ways. Septicaemic Plague was the most rare because it killed so quickly that the victim was usually dead before they could pass on the disease. It was caused when vast numbers of the Yersnias pestis bacilli entered the bloodstream, poisoning the blood - the onset of symptoms was almost immediate.

Pneumonic Plague often occurred in cooler weather when the infection passed into the respiratory system and this form spread the most easily, through sneezing or coughing.

Bubonic Plague caused ugly swellings, known as buboes, in the lymph nodes closest to the flea bites. It was the most common type seen in Britain and caused haemorrhaging beneath the skin as well as delirium. In addition to the buboes, a rash would appear, first red, then deep purple, and as the circulation failed, so the extremities would blacken.

All caused death within a week in most victims. Septicaemic sometimes killed within a few hours. Infection was almost unavoidable in those exposed, since it took only the briefest contact for it to take hold. It was a sudden, and very painful death and struck such fear into the people that families would often abandon sick relatives to escape infection. Of course, they would already be infected and would immediately pass it on to previously healthy people.

As panic spread, so accusing fingers pointed in every direction. In Europe they were particularly aimed at the Jews whose kosher rules requiring that they drank from country springs led to rumours of them poisoning town wells. In England witches were also blamed for casting spells. Of course, many of these 'witches' were simply herbalists searching for natural remedies. Many people considered 'sin' the cause of the plague and that it had either been sent by the wrath of God, or by the Devil, and that a man could not beat the disease 'if the poison be stronger than his nature'.

There are few written accounts of the Black Death in Derby, which is not surprising given the devastation it wrought. What we do know is that it arrived in the town in 1349 and that it killed more than one-third of Derbeians, the population dropping from 3,000 to 2,000. The vicar of St Peter's and St Michael's, the prioress of the nunnery and the abbot at Darley all died. Since the monks and nuns provided nursing and care for the sick, they were among the most at risk. At Osmaston-by-Derby, there were so many dead that burials had to take place in the local chapel churchyard, rather than the bodies be taken to St Peter's, which was the normal practice. At St Peter's itself, bodies were buried vertically to save space. Eventually burials had to take place outside the towns. One such mass burial site was off London Road at Deadman's Lane, its name speaking for itself.

The Headless Cross on Friar Gate, at its junction with Brick Street, plays an important role in Derby's encounters with the Black Death. It dates from as early as the 14th century and has been headless from at least the 15th. During at least one outbreak, locals left money there, soaking in antiseptic vinegar which had been poured into the depressions in the top, to protect farmers, who were supplying food to the town, from infection.

Although there were to be further outbreaks of plague in Derby – the worst in 1592 when 464 died – so many had died in 1349 that it would take centuries for population levels to recover completely. Houses stood empty, the occupants having perished or simply fled for their lives. Across the country between 35 to 45 per cent of the population were

The Headless Cross, now restored to Friar Gate. Coins were placed in vinegar here to 'disinfect' them during the time of the Black Death.

infected between 1348 and 1350, and throughout Europe in only five years, an estimated 25 million people lost their lives.

Battles and rebellions

Derby was in a state of tumult throughout the 14th century. As well as the scourge of the Black Death, there had been the Great Famine of the early 1300s and at least two destructive fires that swept through the town. Whole villages had been wiped out by disease and there were too few agricultural workers. Fields had been left untended and animals had been allowed to wander. The economy was hit hard. There were many beggars in the streets and in towns like Derby, attitudes had changed. Migration became more common as people set out on new lives and took advantage of the fact that previous class distinctions were not as important because the Black Death had created such a shortage of labour. For the first time under their new lords, labourers held the upper hand when it came to negotiating wages and they could move to wherever the best rates were paid. In 1351, Edward III introduced the Statute of Labourers to stifle this new freedom. This law stated that all people below the age of 60 were required to work for wages at levels in force before the Plague, or risk imprisonment. It also restricted the movement of labourers between estates. But it was only limited in its success. There were plenty of employers who were prepared to pay higher wages and there were plenty, too, who were prepared to take advantage of the low prices of goods and land. A new middle class of yeoman farmers began to emerge.

However, this situation did not benefit all. The shifts in power caused unrest and unease. In Kent in 1381 there had been a Peasants' Revolt in protest at the demanding Poll Tax of one shilling per man. In common with the rest of the country, the people of Derby were afraid and they were restless. Measures were introduced to combat regular riots and lawlessness, and the future was uncertain.

There were battles and rebellions within both England and in Europe. The Hundred Years' War saw Lord Grey ride into Derby at the head of his army on the way to join Henry V at Agincourt. It is likely that some Derbeians joined him. In 1454, during the Wars of the Roses, Nicholas Longford, a fervent Lancastrian, led a group of well-armed, angry supporters to the Dominican friary on Friar Gate, where they had hoped to find Walter Blount, a Yorkist sympathiser, and take him by force. The Lancastrians then marched through the Market Place, where John Gresley, the high sheriff, demanded they disperse. They ignored him and continued through the town and along London Road to Elvaston. The mob of some 40 men terrorised Blount's tenants and looted property from his estate. A sheriff's officer was seriously assaulted. Attacks were also made on his holdings at Sutton-on-the-Hill. Later, Longford and his supporters were arrested and brought before the Assizes at Derby, charged with high treason. In attendance was Richard, Duke of York, the father of the future kings Edward IV and Richard III.

The death of Richard III at Bosworth Field in Leicestershire in 1485 was to bring the war to an end and see the founding of the Tudor dynasty under Henry VII. Again trade grew with renewed vigour and many Derby families grew wealthy on this new era of prosperity. Across Europe the Renaissance was flourishing, and artists like Leonardo da Vinci brought new ideas, concepts and inventions to the fore. Explorers like Columbus, Cabot and Cortes set out for the New World. And Caxton's printing press, invented in 1476, meant that the written word would become more widely available.

Life for the average Derbeian was beginning to settle once more, but new unrest was just around the corner.

REFORMATION AND DISSOLUTION

THE magnificent Gothic tower of All Saints' Church (now Derby Cathedral) had been completed in 1530, after 20 years' work. Visible for miles around, it must surely have served as a great advertisement, not only for the town of Derby, but for its many religious houses. Yet when King Henry VIII broke with the Roman Catholic Church and founded the Church of England in 1531, after a dispute over his divorce from Catherine of Aragon, the nunnery and monasteries within Derby were closed and the religious infrastructure of the town was dismantled.

The Dissolution of the Monasteries, which began in 1536, saw the vast holdings of the church redistributed among the gentry, who built great houses on their new estates. The former Dominican friary on Friar Gate, where a prior and 30 monks had lived, was acquired by William Bainbrigge, who built a timber-framed house there in the 1560s. When the present hotel building was erected in the middle of the 18th century, human remains were found during construction of the cellars. These were assumed to be the bodies of the Blackfriars.

By this time, Darley Abbey was a vast estate consisting of a church, cloister, chapter house, vestry and abbot's residence of some 14 rooms. The abbot's residence became a family home for Sir Thomas West and later the Allestreys, before William Woolley demolished it and replaced it with a new house in 1727. The large parish of All Saints', with several farms and a good income, was sold to Thomas Smith and Henry Newsum. Two of the farmhouses in All Saints' parish stand today, both on Old Chester Road. Stone House Prebend is the oldest surviving domestic building in the centre of the city. The exterior chimney breast is medieval, the rest of the structure dates from the late 16th century. Opposite, Derwent House is a red brick building of the 17th century, but it was built over a medieval vaulted cellar and traces of a great hall were also found. The College, which stands next to All Saints' on College Place, was built in 1808 on the site of a medieval house once belonging to the sub-dean and canons. Around the time of the Dissolution the holy relics of St Alkmund were lost, either destroyed or

taken to a place of safety. When Queen Mary, Henry VIII's daughter by Catherine of Aragon, took the throne, she re-established St Alkmund's and All Saints' as churches.

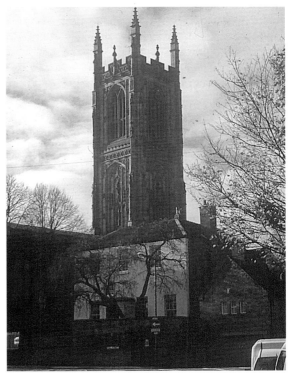

The Gothic tower of All Saints' Church, which has dominated the Irongate area of Derby for almost 500 years.

The Dissolution also meant the dismantling of the only formal education available to the children of Derby. Local boys had been taught Latin and arithmetic by the monks, many being trained for the priesthood. Girls attended lessons at the nunnery, where they learned to read and to sew. It wasn't until 1554 that the need was filled when Queen Mary founded the Free Grammar School for boys. She granted an annual gift of £13 16s 8d. The school was housed in the stone structure on St Peter's Churchyard which is now occupied by Derby Heritage Centre. Derby School enjoyed a fine reputation and the wealthy of the area paid to have their sons educated there, although for the sons of freemen and burgesses, education was provided free of charge. In 1863, Derby School moved to St Helen's House and in 1972 to Moorway Lane. It became a comprehensive school when Labour abolished the grammar schools, and more recently was renamed Derby Moor Community School. In 1995 grammar school education returned to Derby with the founding of the Derby Independent Grammar School for Boys at Littleover. Although having no direct historic link with the old Derby School, this establishment assumed a connection with the original school's long and distinguished history.

By the time of Henry VIII's death in 1547, and after 16 years of Anglican rule, the Church of England was generally accepted as the Established Church. However, many ordinary people had remained covertly Catholic. And when the whole process was forcibly reversed by the Catholic Queen Mary, who inherited the throne from her brother Edward, the majority of the population simply reverted to Roman Catholic practices. For many it mattered little, for some it was a matter of safety over personal preference. Encouraged by their queen, who had earned the nickname 'Bloody Mary' with good reason, many Catholics up and down the country were only too keen to report anyone found practising Protestant beliefs. It was not safe to openly reveal one's religious leanings for fear of reprisals. And there was almost as much fear of being seen not to report dissenters, as there was of being arrested for dissent itself. Although Derby was not especially noted for its religious fervour, under these conditions of suspicion and fear, it was not long before someone was reported to the authorities – someone like the young blind girl, Joan Waste.

Before Mary's death, some 300 Protestants were

Derby's royal doctors

Thomas Linacre, born in Derby in 1460 and a pupil of Derby School, was the most eminent physician of 15th-century Europe. He established the first college of physicians and was personal doctor to Henry VII, Henry VIII, Edward VI and Mary I. Upon his death, his body was interred at St Paul's Cathedral.

Sir John Shore, MD, another former pupil of Derby School, became medical advisor to King Charles II and his lover Nell Gwyn.

tried and executed in England. But it was not just Protestants who suffered in this way. When Elizabeth I became queen in 1558, it was the Catholics who were in fear for their lives.

In 1558, Nicholas Garlick, Robert Ludlam and Richard Sympson were executed in Derby. All three were Catholic priests – and therefore guilty of high treason. Garlick had previously been arrested and exiled to France, but had returned almost immediately. He was discovered, along with Ludlam, at the Padley estate of the resolutely Catholic Fitzherbert family where they were hiding in a chimney. The Earl of Shrewsbury had come to arrest the Fitzherberts, but the discovery of the priests was an even greater coup. The two men were taken to Derby gaol where they met the disillusioned Richard Sympson. Sympson had been born and raised a Protestant, but had converted to Catholicism and, like Ludlam and Garlick, had been ordained in France. Knowing that he must keep his faith a secret to all but a few trusted people of like mind, he had been travelling in the Peak District when he met a man who claimed himself to be a Catholic. Sympson

JOAN WASTE - PROTESTANT MARTYR

THE story of the martyr Joan Waste has become a familiar one to many Derbeians, due in large part to the spectacular and unexpected collapse of a stretch of Mill Hill Lane in the mid-1970s. It fell into Windmill Pit, allegedly the location of the burning of a witch. There soon

circulated rumours of her ghostly presence causing the landslide. But Joan Waste was no witch. She was not even tried as a witch, but as a heretic. She was a Protestant martyr and her story is one of the most poignant tales of religious persecution in the Tudor period.

Although blind from birth, orphaned and with almost no formal education, Joan Waste was a knowledgeable and devout Christian. She could recite long passages from the Bible and debate theological issues. She was sweet-natured and every day attended church services at

Joan Waste is led to her death at the Windmill Pit.

All Saints'. *Foxe's Book of Martyrs*, one of the most important texts in the early Protestant faith, described her as 'a poor honest godly woman'.

She earned a little money as a stocking-maker and saved enough to purchase a copy of the New Testament, which she carried around the town persuading people to read passages to her. She would visit the borough gaol beneath the Guildhall and engage in conversation about the Scriptures. At the debtors' prison she befriended John Hurt, who read to her one chapter of the Bible each day. She also met with John Pemberton, clerk to the parish church, who discussed with her matters of theology. Either through naivete or determination, Joan made no attempt to hide her Protestantism, widely proclaiming her views, many of which clashed starkly with Catholic doctrine. Her behaviour was not born from hatred; she had been raised a Protestant and felt it wrong to deny this simply because her queen decreed it. She was brought to trial at All Saints'

Church and asked to explain her heresy. As the clerics listened, Joan explained her position and her convictions, at one point declaring calmly and confidently that the Sacrament (the bread and wine taken at Communion) was merely a representation of the body and blood of Christ. This was the common belief among Protestants, whereas Roman Catholic doctrine stated that the bread and wine actually became the body and blood of Christ during the service (a process known as Transubstantiation).

Asked to renounce this belief, she said she would do this only if the bishop would agree to answer for her at the Day of Judgement. At first, Bishop Ralph Baine agreed, before being reminded by his Chancellor, Dr Anthony Draycott, that he may not defend a heretic. The bishop was reluctant to condemn her, arguing that her lack of formal education meant she did not truly understand what she was saying, but Dr Draycott requested a second interrogation. This time, in the presence of Sir John Port and Lord Vernon, Joan reiterated her beliefs and stated firmly that they were founded on the Holy Scriptures and that many learned men had died for those beliefs, asking the bishop if he would be prepared to do the same. Joan refused to defend herself any further and remained silent, even when she was threatened with imprisonment, torture and

eventually death. She was found guilty of heresy and imprisoned for several weeks. On 1 August 1556, 23-year-old Joan Waste was summoned to All Saints' once more where, this time, Dr Draycott preached to the congregation, declaring that as a heretic she was beyond redemption and should not be prayed for. He said she was 'blind not only in her bodily eyes, but also in the eyes of her soul' and demanded that 'her body should be presently consumed with material fire, so her soul should be burnt in hell with everlasting fire'.

Upon finishing this tirade, he returned to his bed to rest, while Joan was led to her death. As she walked the mile-long journey through the town from All Saints', her twin brother Roger held her by the hand. At Windmill Pit, the procession halted and Joan was prepared for her execution. Thankfully, it is quite impossible for us to imagine the unspeakable agonies Joan Waste must have suffered there. It was customary to strangle a heretic by hanging from a rope before burning, but in most cases the victim was merely unconscious or subdued. As the rope burned through, the victim fell into the tar-fuelled fire, often having been first covered in tar themselves.

This tragic case became notorious throughout the land and was cited by the reformer John Knox as a particularly cruel example of religious persecution. It is also referred to in Charles Kingsley's *Westward Ho!*

told him that he was a priest and the two continued on together until they reached the next town. Here his companion was revealed as a spy and Sympson was arrested. In prison at Derby, his spirits had fallen and he was said to be close to renouncing his beliefs in order to save his life. Ludlam and Garlick comforted him and he became as resolute as they. The three stood trial accused of 'trying to seduce Her Majesty's people'. Garlick denied this, saying that he had returned to England 'not to seduce but to induce' the people back to Catholicism. He added that he would continue to attempt this until the day he died. All three were found guilty and on the night before their own executions they gave comfort to a fellow prisoner, a woman condemned to death for murder.

On 24 July 1558, the three were taken to St Mary's Bridge, along with the murderess. Each had been tied to a frame and dragged, upside down and backwards, by horses through the street. When they arrived, the execution site was not ready and Garlick grasped the opportunity to preach the word of God to the last, just as he had vowed at his trial. As heretics they were sentenced to a vile punishment. They were to be hanged, drawn and quartered. As a means of execution it was meant to be symbolic, but in fact it was simply sadistic and was one of the most brutal of all execution methods. The men were hanged until unconscious, then their bodies were cut open and their entrails and organs removed and boiled or burned. There are reports that one (Garlick) at least, was still conscious at this point. Finally, they were beheaded. Their bodies were cut up and pieces 'exhibited' around the town. Their severed heads were placed on St Mary's Bridge as a warning, to anyone entering or leaving the town, that Derby did not tolerate heretics. In the nights that followed, some of their sympathisers removed the remains and prepared them for burial.

These executions were of particular significance, coming as they did only two years after an attempted Catholic coup which had been co-ordinated by a resident of Derby, and which bears his name – the Babington Plot.

Since Elizabeth I was the last of Henry VIII's children, and since none of them had produced an heir, there was a great deal of intrigue concerning who should be the next monarch. In fact there had long been plots to remove Elizabeth and her siblings and replace them with other 'worthy' claimants.

Queen Mary had been forced to arrest Lady Jane Grey, a great niece of Henry VIII, before she was able to take the throne. Mary, Queen of Scots was herself a great niece of Henry, and her late husband, Lord Darnley, was himself the grandson of Henry's sister, Margaret. Mary had been effectively imprisoned by Elizabeth I since 1568. The Earl of Shrewsbury, an important figure in Derbyshire, was appointed to be her 'guardian'. Mary passed through Derby on at least two occasions as she travelled between one prison and another, although few Derbeians would have seen her because townspeople were ordered to stay indoors as she passed by. On one occasion, in 1585, she stayed at Babington Hall which stood on the corner of St Peter's Street and what is now Babington Lane. It was the owner of that house, Sir Anthony Babington, who was to be one of the ringleaders in the plot formulated, a year later, to assassinate Queen Elizabeth and replace her with Mary. The plot had the full approval of King Philip II of Spain, who had promised to send his navy to assist after the assassination. Babington's main residence was at Dethick Manor, near Matlock, and he had served as a page to the Earl of Shrewsbury and, in turn, to Mary during her captivity and had become devoted to her. He was a Catholic and had met with some of Mary's followers in Paris. He returned to England and gathered together a group of trusted co-conspirators who included Father John Ballard. Babington began writing to Mary and the correspondence went back and forth, detailing the planned coup. Elizabeth, aware that such a plan was almost inevitable sooner or later, had her spies everywhere. Anthony Babington, meanwhile, was hardly discreet and when there was enough evidence to incriminate Babington, his collaborators and Mary, too, arrests were made. At his trial, Babington tried to play down his own involvement and heaped the blame upon Father Ballard. But Babington and seven of his fellow plotters were found guilty of treason and sentenced to death, being hanged and quartered. Their nobility spared them the humiliation of being 'drawn' as well.

In 1587, two years after Mary, Queen of Scots was executed, King Philip II of Spain's Armada set sail for England. Derby sent two archers and three billmen as their contribution to the superior force that, along with bad tactics on the part of the Spanish and a series of awful storms, defeated the Armada.

THE WEALTHIEST WOMAN IN ENGLAND

BESS of Hardwick was one of the most colourful characters of the Elizabethan era and had connections to both the Padley Martyrs and to Mary, Queen of Scots through her fourth husband, the Earl of Shrewsbury.

Bess married four times and each time accrued wealth, eventually owning vast lands and a wide range of business and industrial interests. She became the wealthiest woman in England after the queen. Her personal income in 1600 alone amounted to £10,000.

She was born around 1527 and, upon her father's death, she and her sisters were left just £26 as a dowry. Ambitious from the outset, when she went into service with Sir John and Lady Zouche of Codnor Castle, Bess met her first husband, who she married when both were just children. When her sickly husband died just a year after their wedding, she inherited a small amount of £60. Her second marriage, at the age of 27, was to Sir William Cavendish of Suffolk. Cavendish was a wealthy man and Bess soon persuaded him to sell his lands in East Anglia and found a new estate at Chatsworth. They had eight children and together founded the great Cavendish dynasty. Her second son, William, had a house in the Cornmarket which he called Devonshire House. In 1750, his descendants commissioned Joseph Pickford to rebuild the

house and much of it remains to this day at 36 Cornmarket. In 1967, five of the original nine bays were demolished for redevelopment. The remaining half has a modern shop front and for a time housed the Knotted Snake pub. This exotic name came from the Cavendish family crest.

Bess was appointed lady-in-waiting to Elizabeth I and, after Cavendish died, she used her involvement with the court to look for another husband. Two years after her husband's death in 1557, she remarried once more, this time to Sir William St Loe. Bess's new spouse was a close ally of Elizabeth I, having helped protect her when her life had been at risk. Fiercely protective of both her children and her status, she had insisted that, if her husband were to die before they had any children of their own, then his lands and fortune would pass to Bess and her children. When this did happen, St Loe's own children were disinherited.

Bess's fourth husband was George Talbot, Earl of Shrewsbury. Talbot was even wealthier and more influential than Cavendish and St Loe. He owned South Wingfield Manor, Buxton Hall and Tutbury Castle as well as Sheffield Manor, Sheffield Castle, Rufford Abbey, Welbeck Abbey, Worksop Manor and two properties in London. Yet again, Bess looked after her whole family's interest before making any vows. The entire

union relied upon Talbot's second son, Gilbert, marrying Bess's youngest daughter, Mary Cavendish, who was 12 years old, and Talbot's daughter Grace, aged just eight, marrying her eldest son, Henry Cavendish, who was 18. Bess also arranged a secret marriage between her daughter Elizabeth Cavendish and Charles Stuart, Earl of Lennox - a member of the Royal Family, who was required to obtain the permission of the monarch before marrying. That Charles was the younger brother of Mary, Queen of Scots' husband Lord Darnley, and the great nephew of Henry VIII with a strong claim to the throne, was concern enough for the Virgin Queen. That Mary had encouraged the marriage only convinced her of conspiracies afoot.

The incensed Elizabeth I summoned Bess and the Countess of Lennox to the Tower of London to explain their actions. Bess was released after a short time, but the countess was forced to remain. Bess was also sent to the Tower when she kept from the queen knowledge of the marriage and subsequent pregnancy of Lady Catherine Grey, sister of the 'queen for nine days', Lady Jane Grey, and herself a claimant to the throne. Feeling humiliated by this rather public rebuke, Bess spread rumours about the queen, which could hardly have eased the tension. Charles and Elizabeth had a daughter, Arabella Lennox, who became second in line to the throne behind James IV of Scotland. Bess raised the girl herself after both parents had died. Her husband had been appointed guardian of Mary, Queen of Scots. The office carried with it a great deal of prestige and, at first, Bess had been delighted. But she loved her home at Chatsworth and hated to be away. Effectively serving as gaolers, the Shrewsburys had to move each time Mary was moved and, since there were constant plots to free her or to harm her, these moves were frequent and sudden. Bess spent more time with Mary and they enjoyed many hours sewing and chatting. This cannot have pleased her monarch. Neither did her actions when her husband was taken ill. Bess returned with him to a more pleasant environment, leaving Mary behind. Again, the queen rebuked Bess, but forgave her.

Rumours circulated that Shrewsbury was conducting an affair with a servant named Elenor Britton. When Bess discovered that this was true, she took immediate action to discredit her errant husband. Soon more rumours circulated, this time that the relationship between Mary and her gaoler was less than 'professional'. This time, though, the architect was believed to be Bess herself. Claims were even made that Mary had given birth to two children by Shrewsbury. In 1583, Bess was again called before Elizabeth to explain her actions. She and her sons, accused beside her, begged for mercy and

swore that they had not spread malicious rumours. They even signed a statement declaring that Mary had not given birth whilst in England. Soon Bess and her husband had embarked upon separate lives, she at Hardwick and he at Sheffield with Elenor Britton. Mary, Queen of Scots remained in the Earl of Shrewsbury's custody until her death in 1584, when he attended her execution.

For many years Bess had been aware that her granddaughter, Arabella, could have a serious claim to the throne, and so tried several times to secure a suitable and advantageous marriage for her granddaughter. But all failed. Eventually Arabella grew tired of waiting for her grandmother to find her a husband and decided to act on her own behalf, but this served only to aggravate Queen Elizabeth who demanded that Bess keep a closer eye on her granddaughter. Elizabeth, concerned that the Catholics would try to manipulate the girl in order to regain control of the country, did everything possible to prevent her marriage. After the death of Elizabeth and the ascension of James I there was a plot to replace him with his cousin Arabella, although this failed almost before it began. Arabella was sent away from Hardwick, out of harm's way. In 1609, James had her imprisoned to prevent her marriage to a foreigner. Eventually, Arabella married William Seymour, Marquess of Hertford, himself a distant claimant to the throne.

The memorial to Bess of Hardwick in Derby Cathedral. She personally oversaw the design of her last resting place.

Both were arrested, although Seymour escaped to the Continent. Arabella was not so lucky and was sent to the Tower of London where she died in 1615.

Bess continued to manoeuvre and negotiate for the welfare of herself and her family throughout her life. Even her funeral was delayed so that her son William could be married. But she was also a generous woman, bequeathing to the town the Devonshire Almshouses in All Saints' parish in 1599.

Bess of Hardwick was buried at All Saints' in Derby, three months after her death in 1608. She designed her elaborate and expensive tomb herself.

The Cavendish family vault, which lies behind her effigy, contains remains and memorials to a great many of her descendants.

THE CIVIL WAR

EVENTUALLY, in 1603, the English throne had fallen to the son of Mary, Queen of Scots – James VI of Scotland – who was now also known as James I of England. For now, the countries of Scotland and England would be united and in 1606 the Union Flag would be adopted for the first time. But religious conflict would continue. Mistrust between Protestants and Catholics led to the latter being banned from living near London or from holding public office, and, because they were loyal first and foremost to the Pope, Catholics were required to swear an oath of allegiance to the Crown. This virtual disenfranchisement had led, ultimately, to the Gunpowder Plot of 1605. At the same time, all across Europe men such as Martin Luther were beginning to question the accepted doctrines of the established churches. The same was true in the British Isles. In Scotland, there were the new Presbyterian and Calvinist churches, and in England the Congregationalist church was gathering momentum. There were Puritans, too, who sought to simplify their lives and their worship, stripping away the ritualistic trappings of the High Church. In a bid to bring the Scots into line, King James had established the Church of Scotland, a companion to the Anglican church. And the new King James Bible was created in 1611, as a replacement for the official Bishop's Bible of the 1500s, and as a preferred alternative to the increasingly popular Geneva Bible, which was disliked by both Anglicans and Catholics, but treasured by other Nonconformists. The Geneva Bible contained controversial marginal notes which declared that man need only be answerable to God, not to a pope, or to a king. James made possession of the Geneva Bible an illegal an act which, of course, simply antagonised the Presbyterians and Puritans who championed it. There was much concern at the perceived interference of government in everyday life. Many Puritans were of high social standing and eventually they had a majority in Parliament. The explosion of new ideas in art, science and philosophy that had heralded the start of the Renaissance would continue well into the 17th century and just as the newly popular realistic, fleshy portraits had offended the Church, so many of the new scientific discoveries and theologies would appear to oppose established Christian doctrine. Art, science and politics were moving away from religious controls. So by 1625, when James died to be succeeded by his son Charles I, in Britain in particular, State was beginning to pull away from Church. There was a battle for power developing which would soon see a country torn in two.

Like his father James, Charles I believed in the divine right of kings. This asserted that kings received their authority directly from God and so no ordinary mortal might question their will. It quickly brought Charles into conflict with his mainly Puritan parliament. Puritans across the country, and in particular those who were MPs, had long grown wary of a monarch who was adamantly High Church. There were even suspicions that he was secretly a practising Catholic. His queen, Henrietta Maria, sister of the King of France, certainly was. In 1629 Parliament issued the Petition of Rights, a list of guaranteed civil liberties that the MPs required from the king. They demanded that no taxes be levied without the consent of Parliament, that no subject could be imprisoned without just cause, that no soldiers could be forcibly quartered with private citizens and that there could be no martial law in times of peace. On paper Charles accepted these demands, but in reality he had no intention of sharing power. John Pym, the moderate Leader of the House of Commons, complained that 'to have printed liberties, and not to have liberties in truth and realities, is but to mock the kingdom'. When Parliament refused to sanction any more taxes without further guarantees, Charles dissolved his Parliament and ruled alone for the next 11 years.

During this time Charles set about a series of wars across Europe, continually requesting money from his subjects to cover the costs. One such attempt at gathering money was the re-introduction of the ancient ship tax, in which all ports had to provide money for a ship, her crew, its food and ammunition in times of war. But Charles sought to extend this to inland towns as well and this meant that Derby, which is about as far distant from the coast as it is possible to get in England, was required

Sir John Gell, a former high sheriff of Derbyshire and Parliamentary governor of Derby from 1642-46.

to supply a ship of some 350 tons together with wages, food and arms for a crew of 140 men. The man responsible for collecting this money was Sir John Gell, the high sheriff. When Gell attempted to gather the tax, the wealthy defiantly withheld the money. Gell complained to the king of the 'ill example which Derby is setting other towns'. He also stated that the 'very many rich men' could afford to pay, not just the £140 demanded, but as much as £300. Charles did not take him at his word and raised the tax only to £175. But the king soon found that the dissatisfaction of his Derbeian subjects was being mirrored in towns the length and breadth of the land. The more money the king tried to take, the greater the resistance he encountered. Eventually, Charles was forced to admit that even he still needed his Parliament for some services. When he tried to impose the Anglican Book of Common Prayer on the Scots, they invaded northern England and Charles was forced to recall Parliament to deal with the matter.

After 'Eleven Years' Tyranny', the MPs returned to Westminster with a long list of questions, challenges and demands for their king. They refused to sanction any of his requests until their own grievances had been addressed. Charles refused and dissolved this 'Short Parliament' after only three weeks. But later in the year, with the Scottish invasion continuing, Charles was forced to rethink. Once more Parliament was recalled, this time it would sit for 13 years and was known as the Long Parliament. Resentful that they had been effectively disenfranchised for more than a decade, not only did MPs have religious concerns, they were also the very people who had been bearing much of the burden of increased taxation. With the Scots making ground in the north and a full-scale revolt under way in Ireland, Charles had little choice but to negotiate. The king did have considerable support from many fiercely loyal MPs who were determined to maintain the status quo, but elsewhere in Parliament there was also dissent from the Presbyterians who wanted to reform the Church of England, and the Independents who wanted to abolish the Church of England altogether.

There were also a number of minority groups who would eventually call for more radical reform. There were the Levellers who wanted to remove the monarch, the House of Lords and the House of Commons, and form a new parliament to be elected annually by all men including the working classes (although not servants or the poor). And there were the Diggers who demanded an end to all private ownership and to organised government of any kind. Most of the more moderate political reforms were accommodated, but the same was not true of the religious disputes.

Matters came to a head when the House of Commons angered Charles by producing the Grand Remonstrance which listed all Parliament's concerns over the king's actions and behaviour.

It complained of 'grievous fines, imprisonments… mutilations, whippings' to which the people had been subjected and it stated: 'The root of all this mischief we find to be a malignant and pernicious design of subverting the fundamental laws and principles of government.'

Outraged, Charles I entered the Commons and demanded that Pym and his immediate followers be handed over for trial, but the men had escaped. It was the first and only time a reigning monarch has entered the chamber of the House of Commons and his action lost Charles the support of many moderates. In June 1642, Parliament presented the king with 19 Propositions which were something of a 'last chance' to allow Parliamentary control over both Church and State. Among the requirements was the power to appoint the king's officials and even the tutors of his children. But the key requirement, and the one which was to precipitate full-scale war, was the handing over to Parliament of control of the army. Charles had no intention of relinquishing control of his troops. The country had reached breaking point. The army and the nation were divided and the increasing probability of civil war caused the burgesses of Derby to petition both the king and Parliament to quickly resolve their differences.

But there was to be no way back. In August 1642, Charles I raised his royal standard at Nottingham, effectively declaring war. He had passed through Derby on his way and was to pass through once more on his return. After three days in Derby, the king took with him £300 and some firearms and marched for the Welsh border with the 20 extra men who joined his cause. He must have been disappointed with his meagre haul of recruits for the county of Derbyshire had immediately embraced the cause of the monarchy and Derby itself had been more than happy to court the favour of their king in 1635 when Charles had stayed at the house of William Cavendish, the Duke of Newcastle.

The house once stood on the site of the current Assembly Rooms in the Market Place. At that time the burgesses of Derby had been anxious to impress their king. They were looking to acquire a new charter which would, among other benefits, allow the town to replace its two bailiffs with one mayor. In the first-floor 'Great Room' the king and his subjects ate a great feast at the expense of the town's burgesses. The central oval from the ceiling of that room was preserved when the building was demolished in 1971 and it is now set into the new Assembly Rooms. The feast laid before the king must have been sufficiently sumptuous since, one year later, in exchange for a fee, the charter was duly granted.

In some ways the town joined the Parliamentary cause almost by default. Fearful of what might follow and reluctant to declare their support for one side over the other, many of the town's gentry had retreated to their country homes. Those that were left were more than content to allow the Parliamentary 'invasion' that occurred six weeks later. On 31 October 1642, at the head of a detachment of Lord Essex's troops, Sir John Gell rode into Derby from Wirksworth and set up his

headquarters. It was somewhat ironic, that the very man who had actively encouraged the king to increase the taxes demanded from the people of Derby, should now be in command of the town as part of a revolution against that king. But Gell probably had good reason to turn against the Royalist cause. He, too, would have been a victim of the new taxes. Gell owned a number of lead mines and since these mines were on property owned by the Crown, they were liable for taxation. In fact Charles had doubled the tax on all lead mined on his lands. Lead was a valuable resource in high demand, particularly in times of war.

Gell was appointed Governor of Derby at the head of several thousand men, 860 of whom were from the town itself. Some of these troops would have been lead miners employed by Gell and many more were from outside the county. This sudden increase in population was not likely to have been welcomed, since Gell's men were described as 'the most licentious, ungovernable wretches that belonged to Parliament'.

In 1643 John Pym died, leaving the way clear for a more militant Parliamentary leadership. Pym had been a model politician. He had unified and controlled a disparate Parliamentary party for several years, had formed a Parliamentary army, established an effective system of taxation and introduced duties on English goods. He was a popular, articulate and intelligent man, who had continued to negotiate for a peaceful settlement. Had he not died, perhaps the years and centuries that followed might have been very different.

Back in Derby, the war was beginning to gain momentum and Gell's men fought against a Royalist force at Hopton Heath near Stafford. When their leader, the Earl of Northampton, was killed, the Royalists fled. Although victorious, Gell's exhausted men, many of them wounded, were forced to rest at Uttoxeter for three days on the return march to Derby. On their arrival in the town, the naked corpse of the earl was paraded through the streets before being interred at the Cavendish vault at All Saints'. When the dead earl's son requested the return of the body, Gell demanded embalming charges and the return of all weapons captured in the battle, and the matter was dropped.

Gell's men also took part in several battles around Burton upon Trent and at the siege of Tutbury Castle

Gell's house in Friar Gate, headquarters of the Parliamentary forces in the town. Today it houses a restaurant.

as well as a battle at Gainsborough, from where many Royalist prisoners were brought. Throughout the Civil War, Derby would have been home to hundreds of prisoners-of-war.

As a town without a castle, Derby was of limited defensive value, but its vital role as a strategic command centre meant that it was targeted for recapture by the Royalists. Under their leader Prince Rupert, nephew of the king, they marched towards the town, having taken control of Lichfield, where they had used the first bomb in the history of warfare.

The prince's troops got as far as Burton before being recalled, and Derby was spared. Had the Royalists arrived at Derby, they would have faced a well-protected community. Deep earthworks had been built around the town. Each road into Derby was secured by iron gates and there were around 30 ordnance stations around the town. St Mary's Bridge was fortified and a drawbridge erected. A 24-hour watch was posted on the tower of All Saints' and local villagers were conscripted. Records of 1691

suggest that there was even a gunpowder mill beside the Derwent near St Michael's Church.

Although Derby saw no invading forces, no siege and no battle, there was disorder and conflict, and there were casualties. During one skirmish, on 2 April 1644, an innocent woman, Catherine Gower, was caught in the crossfire and was 'killed with a pistoll bullett, shot through the head by accident'.

Gell's Parliamentary headquarters was his house on Friar Gate. This beautiful three-storey, four-gabled house (no 16) dates from around 1630. It remains to this day, largely unaltered, and must be one of the country's best-preserved properties of that era. From his headquarters the new governor took total control of town life. Immediately removing the local burgesses from power, Gell formed his own local government from family, friends and allies from outside the town. This proved so unpopular with Derbeians that Parliament instructed Gell to involve at least three prominent locals in his government. One of them, Thomas Sanders, was to become a fierce rival and a vocal critic. Gell and Sanders neither liked nor trusted one another and made no secret of the fact. When a new MP was needed to replace William Allestrey, who had chosen to join the king's own parliament at Oxford, Gell nominated his brother Thomas. Sanders, on the other hand, had chosen Robert Mellor – the son of the town's first mayor. After a very sour election, which was riddled with confusion and manipulation, Thomas Gell was elected to Parliament.

Gell's behaviour was to attract severe criticism, even from his own supporters. As each Royalist estate was seized by Parliament, Gell was granted control of the income. His poor record-keeping and maladministration attracted the unwanted attention of Parliament. His procrastination had caused his troops to miss important battles and his men had responded too slowly to capture King Charles as he fled from Naseby to Leicester in 1645.

After another year of fierce fighting, Charles surrendered to the Scots who handed him over to Parliament. But there were to be more convulsions yet. Although the Westminster Parliament had been able to push through numerous reforms since Charles had fled to Oxford, the more radical members of the army were less than satisfied with Parliament's failure to make the dramatic changes they had demanded. Parliament had even reached a negotiated compromise with the king which might have paved the way for a constitutional monarchy, but Charles delayed and when it became clear that part of this agreement called for the disbanding of the army, that army rebelled under its leader Oliver Cromwell and took the captive king from Parliament's control, then marched on London.

Now in complete control of any negotiations, Cromwell turned his attention to the provinces. In Derby, Sir John Gell's army had not been paid for two years and were close to mutiny. Cromwell acted swiftly, disbanding the regiment and merging it into his New Model Army. Gell was removed from office and ordered to London to explain his mismanagement of the town.

By 1647 the Scots had realised their co-operation with the English Parliament was not going to deliver the reforms they required, such as the establishment of Presbyterianism in England, and came to an agreement with King Charles. The Scots lent military support to the Royalists, but even this combined force was soon defeated by the New Model Army.

Although he shied away from the radical reforms demanded by some, which in more than one case amounted to anarchy, it was Cromwell who oversaw the arrest, trial and eventual execution of the king. At 1pm on Tuesday, 30 January 1649, as snow fell on Whitehall, King Charles I was beheaded for what the death warrant called 'many treasons, murders and other heinous offences.'

Parliament declared that 'all people… are discharged of all fealty, homage and allegiance'.

As one of the men who signed Charles I's death warrant, and who had witnessed his execution, Oliver Cromwell should have paid heed to a warning given by the king. As he prepared for his death, Charles spoke his last recorded words: 'I pray God you do take those courses that are best for the good of the kingdom and your own salvation.'

It would have been a valuable warning had Oliver Cromwell, soon to be dictator of England, chosen to heed it.

Derby under the Republic
The new republic was known as the Commonwealth and, for the time being at least, everyday life in Derby returned to normal. The responsibility of local government lay once more in the hands of the burgesses, and eventually trade began to recover.

Immediately, the monarchy, the House of Lords and the Anglican Church were all abolished. Scotland and England were integrated and a Council of State ran the country. Although he refused the title of king when offered it, Oliver Cromwell became the Supreme Ruler of the State and was king in all but name. Eventually, though, Cromwell would prove even more unpopular than the king he had deposed. He was ruthless, removing from Parliament all those who opposed him, and even executing many Levellers. He was to adopt the deposed king's policy of absolute power and England swiftly became a military dictatorship.

The laws enforced by the Commonwealth were harsh and punishments were severe. Crimes such as adultery and blasphemy could result in the death penalty, and vulgar behaviour was punished severely. Civil weddings replaced religious ceremonies and many churches were stripped of their finery. At Darley, in particular, everything of value was removed. Cromwell did everything in his power to limit the influence of the Roman Catholic Church and, although he had appeared to advocate religious toleration, Catholics were not permitted to travel more than five miles from their homes unless in possession of an appropriate license.

Another group to suffer at the hands of Oliver Cromwell was the Society of Friends. Their founder, George Fox, had long been disillusioned by the established church. He believed that in every human soul was a part of Christ's goodness and that, therefore, every person was able to understand fully the word of God for him or herself, and so permitted to express their own spiritual opinions. He also believed in total equality – man or woman, slave or freeman, all were of equal worth. He and his followers would not show any special signs of respect to those of 'higher' position or those in power, such as doffing their hats, bowing or curtsying, not to the monarch and not to Oliver Cromwell. They believed it was not necessary to perform elaborate services or wear special costumes or perform certain rites in order to worship God. The

George Fox, founder of the Society of Friends, who in his journal described his imprisonment in Derby.

Friends also believed that each person had direct access to God and so there was no need for church buildings, which Fox called 'steeple houses' since he considered the community of worshippers in itself was enough to form 'a church'. Nor did he see any need for ministers. It was enough that Fox spoke out against the ministers, but his followers also refused to pay taxes to the Church or to swear an oath in court, since they held the only person they need be answerable to was God. They even campaigned for an end to slavery, for improvements in prison conditions, and for better care for the poor, the sick and the mentally ill. Fox travelled the country and met with mixed reactions, one of the most discouraging of which was at Derby in 1650. According to Fox's own account in his auto-biographical journal published in 1690:

'I lay at the house of a doctor whose wife was convinced; and so were several more in the town. As I was walking in my chamber, the bell rang, and it struck at my life at the very hearing of it; so I asked the woman of the house… She said there was to be a great lecture there that day and many of the officers of the army and priests and preachers were to be there, and a colonel that was a preacher.'

Fox entered the church, probably All Saints', where he spoke out.

'But there came an officer and took me by the hand and said that I and the other two that were with me must go before the magistrates… They asked me why I came thither. I said God moved us so to do, and I told them, "God dwells not in temples made with hands." The power of God thundered among them and they did fly like chaff before it. They put me in and out of the room often, hurrying me backward and forward.'

Fox would have good reason to remember this visit to Derby, for it was here that he and his followers were to be given the name by which they are so often known today – the Quakers. The justice at Fox's trial, Gervase Bennet, 'was the first that called us "Quakers" because I bade him tremble at the word of the Lord.'

Fox was found guilty, having effectively pleaded that way. He was sentenced to six months' imprisonment. A letter sent from the court read:

'To the master of the house of correction in Derby, greeting.

'We have sent you herewithal the bodies of George

Fox… and John Fretwell … brought here before us this present day, and charged with the avowed utterings and broaching of diverse blasphemous opinions, contrary to the late Act of Parliament… and them therein safely to keep during the space of six months, without bail or mainprize. Hereof you are not to fail.'

During his time in prison, there had been much debate over the fate of Fox. He had been fortunate enough to have avoided the death penalty, but he was certainly unwelcome in the town.

Fox noted: '…because of the wickedness that was in this town; for though some were convinced, yet the generality were a hardened people. I saw the visitation of God's love pass away from them. I mourned over them. There was a great judgement upon the town and the magistrates were uneasy about me; but they could not agree what to do with me. One while they would have me sent to the Parliament, another while they would have me banished to Ireland… they called me a deceiver, a seducer and a blasphemer.'

As he came to the end of his sentence he was requested to take charge of a military force against the Royalists, but repeatedly refused, and for this he was sentenced to another six months in prison, this time in the gaol.

The draconian rule of Cromwell and his Commonwealth did not go otherwise unopposed. There was plenty of dissent in Parliament and elsewhere as groups as disparate as the Levellers, the Puritans, the Episcopalians and the Royalists engaged in political and religious debate. The Commonwealth era saw the development of early forms of communism, of women's rights and vegetarianism. There were even those who promoted polygamy and the Ranters who encouraged casual sex and the free recreational use of alcohol and tobacco. It was little wonder, then, that Cromwell, under such immense pressure from dissenting voices, found it necessary to dissolve Parliament just as his late monarch had done. Ultimately, only Cromwell and his New Model Army had any real power.

This absolute rule, this dictatorship caused even those who had readily supported Parliament at the outset, to join with those calling for the restoration of the monarchy. Even Sir John Gell, who had been quick to support the revolution, campaigned for this.

Cromwell had him arrested and he was sentenced to three years' imprisonment. Government and army were completely opposed. The country was on the verge of chaos. And back in Derby there was rebellion too. On 25 August 1659, inspired by the arrival of Colonel Charles White, Captain Nathaniel Doughty persuaded many dissatisfied locals to revolt against their Parliamentary rulers. On Nuns Green (part of Friar Gate) the rebels gathered, asking Gell's old rival Thomas Sanders to lead their cause. Sanders refused and instead reported the situation to the authorities. Troops were immediately dispatched the quell the revolt but by the time they arrived, the situation was resolved and only the arrest of Colonel White was deemed necessary.

On 3 September 1658 the register of All Saints' in Derby had recorded: 'Oliver Cromwell, the terror of England, died.' Not long after the death of the 'Lord Protector' the republic too was dead. Cromwell had been succeeded by his son Richard, nicknamed 'Tumbledown Dick', a more gentle and moderate man than his father. And he had been overthrown only a year later. Initially the army had taken control, but the country had little confidence in the ability of the army to rule evenly and before long Charles II was asked to accept the throne in succession to his father. It was with much relief and joy and ringing of church bells that the people of Derby proclaimed the Restoration of the Monarchy in May 1660.

Europe had been at war for many years and European powers had been engaged in the adventures of exploration and colonisation of the New World. But seafaring was fraught with risks. There was no way to accurately navigate whilst at sea and this had resulted in the loss of dozens of ships, both naval and merchant, either in battle, or in shipwrecks.

The new king was more than aware of this problem and that it was commonly believed that the key to safe marine navigation was to accurately fix the position of longitude. France had already established a Royal Observatory to address this question and Charles was keen that England should resolve it first. To this end he established the Royal Observatory at Greenwich and turned to the leading astronomer of the day, the 29-year-old John Flamsteed of Derby, to be his first Astronomer Royal.

JOHN FLAMSTEED –
FIRST ASTRONOMER ROYAL

JOHN Flamsteed was born in 1646. His father was a successful maltster in Derby, although Flamsteed was born at nearby Denby to where his family had fled to avoid the dangers and disruptions of the Civil War and later an outbreak of the Plague in their hometown. Flamsteed attended Derby School in St Peter's Churchyard where he was taught the Classics and Mathematics. Later in life he would write several autobiographies, the first he completed before the age of 21 'to keep myself from idleness and to recreate myself'.

He was already resigned to a lifetime of illness which would see him suffer from severe pain and tire easily. 'A day's short reading caused so violent a headache.' He had contracted a rheumatic condition after swimming with friends, and his health would never fully recover. In one of his autobiographies he recalls:

'At fourteen years of age, when I was nearly arrived to be the head of the Free School, I was visited with a fit of sickness, that was followed with a consumption and other distempers, which yet did not so much hinder me in my learning, but that I still kept my station till the form broke up and some of my fellows went to the Universities for which – though I was designed, my father thought it not advisable to send me, by reason of my distemper.'

Confined to his bed for much of the time, John Flamsteed would gaze out into the night sky, fascinated by the stars. A visitor to his home was Immanuel Halton, the local agent of the Duke of Norfolk. Halton had become one of the pioneers of astronomy and he fired in Flamsteed a passion for which he was perhaps destined – his father having recorded the exact time of his birth so that a horoscope could be drawn. Encouraged by Halton, Flamsteed constructed a quadrant 'of which I was not meanly joyful' to measure the Sun's approximate distance from the Earth. He was a bright student and stated that 'by the time I was fifteen years old, I had read Plutarch's Lives, Appian's and Tacitus' Roman Histories'.

He draw up a catalogue of some 70 major stars, computing their ascendance, declination and position. In 1670 he sent some of his calculations to the Royal Society, although he was reluctant to give his own name, instead using a pseudonym 'In Mathesi a Sole findes' which meant 'the Sun pours out in mathematics'.

His words of introduction to the Society betray a certain, yet modest confidence. 'Excuse, I pray you, this juvenile heat for the concerns of science and want of better language, from one who, from the sixteenth year of his age to this instant, hath only served one bare apprenticeship in these arts, under the encouragement of friends, the want of health and all other instructors, except his better genius.'

It was not long before Flamsteed's genius came to the attention of the king. Although there had long been an abundance of theories of how to fix longitude, Flamsteed argued that, since the star charts were so inaccurate, it mattered little what method was used to calculate the meridians. Charles II, impressed with Flamsteed's ideas and with his previous work, decreed: 'We have appointed our trusted and well-beloved John Flamsteed, Master of Arts, our Astronomical Observator that he should apply himself with the most exact care and diligence to the rectifying tables of the motions of the heavens, and the places of the fixed stars, so as to find the so-much-desired longitude of places for the perfecting of the art of navigation.'

Flamsteed moved to London to oversee the building of the Observatory. He stayed for a while at the Tower of London, where the huge resident ravens caused endless problems by fouling his telescopes. Flamsteed complained to the king and Charles was about to have the ravens killed when he was reminded of the legend that if the ravens ever leave the Tower of London, then the Tower will soon fall, and with it the monarchy. No doubt mindful of his father's fate, Charles insisted that the ravens remain, although somewhat reduced in number, and Flamsteed moved to Queen's House at Greenwich.

The Observatory was built by Sir Christopher Wren, at a cost of £520; wood from a demolished gatehouse at the Tower of London and iron, lead and bricks from Tilbury Fort were some of the materials used. The famous Octagon Room had large windows on all sides and was ideal for viewing the stars, but not so for positional observations since none of the windows lined up with established meridians. Many of the vital discoveries made by Flamsteed were, in fact, made from an outbuilding in the grounds, although the king was never to find out.

Flamsteed was soon to discover, though, that his appointment to so important and seemingly valued a position would not attract as much financial support as he might have hoped. His salary was fixed at £100 a year, which was to be paid at three-monthly instalments, although there is some evidence to suggest that it was often late or even never paid at all. What payments he did get were certainly not sufficient to cover the costs of running the Observatory. He was forced to take a post as a vicar and also to give private tuition to some 140 pupils over the years. When the Observatory opened, he found he had no equipment and was forced to borrow, initially, and then to construct his own. He also had to complete his work alone, for no assistant would be provided for some years. He was paid so little for what was considered work of prime importance, it is of little surprise that he began to suspect his work was not being taken seriously and so he guarded his findings jealously.

Much of Isaac Newton's ground-breaking work was dependent on Flamsteed's data and pioneering discoveries. Newton was to say, 'If I have seen farther than others, it is because I was standing on the shoulders of giants.' Flamsteed was surely one of those giants, yet in a remarkable turn of events he and Newton would become nothing less than enemies. What became one of the biggest controversies in scientific history would create shockwaves throughout the scientific community and through society itself. It would also help to ensure that Flamsteed would be little known outside his contemporaries and peers.

To appreciate fully the ugly dispute that erupted between Flamsteed and Newton, it is necessary to understand the viewpoints, personalities and perhaps weaknesses of the two men. Newton was a bombastic, and rather affected man and had proved himself as somewhat manipulative in the past. He was known to have been jealous of others' abilities,

even deliberately obscuring their work in favour of his own. His *Principia Mathematica*, which had relied heavily on Flamsteed's data, has since become perhaps the most influential physics book ever published. Flamsteed, on the other hand, was stubborn and meticulous in his research. This had been one of the traits that had made Flamsteed such a good astronomer but he was unwilling to give anyone access to his work until it had been checked and re-checked. Whilst this ensured absolute accuracy, it often meant delays in the general release of new data. Anxious to complete his own studies, Newton became impatient with Flamsteed's reluctance to release his data. But Flamsteed had no intention of publishing his work piecemeal to anyone, least of all to Newton, whom he neither respected nor trusted. He was still struggling to make ends meet at the Observatory, relying heavily on his extra-curricular earnings to subsidise his research, and concerned that his studies were receiving so little in the way of official support. And whilst Newton had been lauded publicly, elected President of the Royal Society, appointed to the lucrative position of Warden of the Mint, and had even been knighted – the first scientist to achieve this honour – Flamsteed's vital contributions, had gone virtually unnoticed. The great American writer and philosopher Ralph Waldo Emerson would later write: 'I have several times forgotten the name of Flamsteed, never that of Newton.'

Flamsteed must have resented the contrast. He must also have been more than a little frustrated at not being able to publish his whole work, but to have it dissected and used by others. Flamsteed's dislike of Newton is made clear in his own history of the Greenwich Observatory.

'Whilst Mr Flamsteed was busied in the laborious work of the catalogue of the fixed stars, and forced often to watch and labour by night, to fetch the material for it from the heavens, that were to be employed by day, he often on Sir Isaac Newton's instances furnished him with observations of the Moon's places in order to carry out his correction of lunar theory.' He continued, 'Mr Flamsteed could not but take notice that as Sir Isaac was advanced in place, so he raised himself of his conversation and became more magisterial.'

Over many years Newton tried repeatedly to prise Flamsteed's work from him, but Flamsteed had become increasingly suspicious of Newton's motives. When persuasion and then bullying proved ineffective, Newton did not hesitate to use his presidency of the Royal Society to place himself on the committee which was directly responsible for the Observatory. Eventually Flamsteed agreed to release the first 97 pages of his work and to allow Newton to read another 175 pages, but was adamant that this not be published until completed. In November 1705 a copy of Flamsteed's first thousand or so pages fell into the hands of the Royal Society, either by accident or by subterfuge, and were passed to Newton. Presumably Newton seized this opportunity enthusiastically and showed them to Prince George of Denmark, Queen Anne's Consort, and a contract for printing was signed.

Soon Flamsteed discovered that, not only was his life's work to be published against his wishes, but that the editor was to be Edmund Halley, a former protégé of his who Flamsteed had long ago come to loathe.

His fury was only increased when it emerged that the newly-published volume was full of technical, factual and editorial errors which had not appeared on Flamsteed's original manuscript, and the Astronomer Royal began to suspect not so much carelessness on the parts of Halley and Newton, but malice. In addition, Halley had provided a preface for the work in which he implied that Flamsteed had been lazy in his work and that it had included many errors that he had been forced to correct. Flamsteed referred to Halley as 'a malicious thief'.

From that moment, rivalry and mistrust was matched equally with hatred and anger. Flamsteed refused to release a single word more of his research and was called before the Royal Society. The Society decided that since Flamsteed's work was official and since he held official office, that any work he did was public property. There was no official record of the hearing, but there were many accounts written by the participants. Perhaps the most revealing is a letter written by Flamsteed to his assistant Abraham Sharp.

'I have had another contest with the President of the Royal Society, who had formed a plot to make my instruments theirs and sent me to a Committee where only himself and two physicians (Dr Sloane and another as little skilful as himself) were present. The President ran himself into a great heat and very

John Flamsteed, the first Astronomer Royal, who was educated at Derby School.

indecent passion… I complained then of my catalogue being printed by Raymer [his nickname for Halley, after the man who had been a jealous detractor of Flamsteed's own hero, Tycho] without my knowledge, and that I was robbed of the fruit of my labours. At this, he fired and called me all the ill names, puppy etc that he could think of… He told me how much money I had received from the Government in 36 years I had served. I asked him what he had done for the £500 per annum that he had received.'

Eventually, upon the death of Queen Anne, Flamsteed was permitted to seize the remaining unsold copies of the illicit publication. He burned them at Greenwich 'as a sacrifice to heavenly truth' and devoted the remaining years of his life to correcting these errors and to completing his work.

Newton was so furious with Flamsteed that he had all references to the Astronomer Royal removed from all subsequent editions of the *Principia*.

By the time of his death on 31 December 1719, Flamsteed had granted official approval for publication, and the first volume, and much of the second had been printed. His devoted assistants Abraham Sharp and Joseph Crosthwaite translated, checked and completed the remaining work – Flamsteed's *Atlas Coelestis* (Celestial Atlas).

During his time as Astronomer Royal, Flamsteed made more than 30,000 stellar observations. In recognition of his efforts and achievements, there is a Crater Flamsteed on the surface of the Moon.

Here are some of the other achievements of his life:

- In summer of 1666 predicted a partial solar eclipse and calculated its path over Derby.
- He calculated the ebb and flow of the tide for King Charles II and presented the king with a thermometer and a barometer of his own invention, along with details of his weather forecasting techniques.
- He calculated the distance from the Earth to the Moon and established that the distance varied due to the irregular path of the Moon.
- He proved that the Earth revolved at a constant rate, so that it would be possible for astronomical observations to be used for navigation.
- He measured the sidereal day of 23 hours, 56 minutes and 4 seconds.
- He observed that the Sun's revolution is 27 days, four hours as seen from Earth.
- He observed sunspots.
- He identified both Uranus and Neptune, although at the time he thought they were fixed stars, rather than planets.
- He formulated the *Equation of Natural Days* a series of tables which showed the relationship and difference between noon as shown on an accurate clock and noon according to the position of the Sun. The tables showed how the difference changed according to the time of year and the Earth's position in relationship to the Sun. These tables helped astronomers and clock makers to establish an accurate, meaningful system of time measurement.

- The Greenwich Meridian was initially fixed at the middle point of Flamsteed's telescope.
- He invented conical projection, an important technique where a sphere could be projected on to a plane surface, which revolutionised cartography.
- He invented a system of numbering for the fainter stars. These numbers are still known as Flamsteed Numbers. Each star is given a number based upon the name of the constellation and the order in which it appears going from east to west.

Flamsteed's Comet?

As one last example of John Flamsteed's essential role in laying the foundations for all modern astronomy is the story of what might have been Flamsteed's Comet. In 1677 Flamsteed released his findings on comets, confirming for the first time that they had continuous, repetitive paths and that they 'make their returns as in stated times and move about the fixed stars at a vast distance'. In the early 1680s, Edmund Halley observed what everyone supposed to be two comets – one which approached the Sun, and later one which appeared to leave the Sun. Halley wrote to Flamsteed on the subject and Flamsteed replied that it was clearly one comet with a curved path around the Sun. He was not sure exactly why this happened, but suggested that it was something to do with a reversal of magnetic field as it reached the Sun.

Halley continued to study the comet, which he found had visited the Earth every 70 or so years. In 1705 Halley published a book using Flamsteed's data. The book was a breakthrough in cometary study and that comet was forever known as Halley's Comet.

THE GLORIOUS REVOLUTION

DURING his time as Astronomer Royal, John Flamsteed had served no less than six monarchs – seeing the end of the Stuart era and the beginning of the House of Brunswick/Hanover. He had also seen a shift in power from monarch to Parliament, the formation of new political parties, yet another revolution and the official foundation of Great Britain.

Charles II was more tolerant than most who had gone before. Nevertheless, in 1673 measures were introduced to prevent Catholics and Dissenting Protestants from holding public office. In 1678 a meeting of some 500 Catholics, or 'papists' as they became known, was scheduled to take place on Nuns Green in Derby. In 1681 George Busby, a Jesuit priest, was tried for treason at Shire Hall on St Mary's Gate. He was found guilty, but was reprieved.

In 1685, Charles II was succeeded by his brother James II. At first the new king had been greeted enthusiastically, but his reckless nature and his intention to return the nation to the Roman Catholic faith resulted in fierce opposition. He placed Catholics in high positions, and there had been a small rebellion led by James's nephew the Duke of Monmouth. This had soon been crushed and James appointed Judge Jeffries to deal with the rebels, many of whom were tortured, sent into slavery or executed. By now James had lost the support of both sides of the political spectrum and of the nobility and merchant classes too. There was even fiercer debate when James's second wife, the Catholic Mary of Modena, gave birth to a son, also named James. Parliament had long had plans for James's Protestant daughter Mary, by his first wife Ann Hyde, to succeed him. Mary had been married to her first cousin, William of Orange, and Parliament, no longer feeling able to trust James II, invited William and Mary to jointly rule the country.

On 21 November 1688 the Earl of Devonshire, High Steward of Derby, rode into town at the head of 500 men. He held a dinner at his home in the Cornmarket where he threw his support behind William of Orange. The people of Derby seemed less enthusiastic, but later in the year welcomed William's officers when they requested billets in the town. James II left for a life of exile in France and the new monarchs took his place. The shift in power became known as the Glorious Revolution but however smoothly this bloodless revolution had been executed, it was not without opposition. At All Saints', the Revd Dr Henry Sacheverell used his regular sermon to attack the rule of William and Mary and the removal of the Stuarts from power; his views drew popular support within the town. Thus encouraged, Sacheverell repeated his sermon at St Paul's Cathedral. Here, however, his message was not welcomed. He was arrested and sent to trial. When news of his light sentence reached Derby, the bells of all the town's churches were rung and bonfires were lit on Nuns Green and in the Market Place.

Since William and Mary left no heirs, Mary's sister Anne succeeded to the throne in 1702. She, too, died with no surviving heir and was to be the last Stuart monarch. Under her rule the Act of Union became law in 1707, uniting England and Scotland and thus creating Great Britain. Her death in 1714 left Britain in a constitutional crisis. Her half-brother, James Stuart, as son of James II, should have succeeded her. But Parliament, reluctant to allow power to be returned to a Roman Catholic, promoted the case of George, Elector of Hanover. The great-grandson of James I, his claim to the British throne was more tenuous. but he became the first Hanoverian ruler of Britain. The news was greeted with riots in Derby and by protests from the local clergy.

George I was never a popular king. He did not adapt to British ways and made no attempt even to learn English, spending much of his time in Germany. He had brought with him two mistresses, leaving his wife in prison in Hanover accused of adultery. His entourage was unpopular too, stories abounding of their uncouth manners, lying, cheating and stealing. A movement grew towards replacing George with James Stuart. Calling themselves Jacobites and gaining the support of the French king, they were unable to make significant progress until 1745, by which time the king had been succeeded by his son George II and the Old Pretender's cause had been taken up by his son, Charles Stuart – Bonnie Prince Charlie.

THE CENTRE OF THE UNIVERSE?

IT seems barely credible today, walking through the centre of Derby, weaving in and out of crowds of shoppers, that just over 250 years ago the town was the location for one of the defining moments in British – and arguably world – history. That, for three days at least, it was the centre of the universe.

In Derby, in the December of 1745, events unfurled which shape the lives of the British people even to this day. It was here that Bonnie Prince Charlie made the fateful decision to abandon his attempted coup and which led him, ultimately, to a life of exile. Had he pressed on and been successful, then British and world history would have altered course dramatically.

Although the promised military and financial help of the French failed to materialise, the Young Pretender decided to sail for Britain regardless. On 19 August 1745, Bonnie Prince Charlie raised his father's standard at Glenfinnan and set out for London to claim the British throne in his father's name.

Although now regarded as a symbol of Scottish national pride, Charles Stuart did not represent the majority of Scots, nor was he a Scot himself. He was born in Italy in 1720 to a half-British, half-Italian father, James Stuart, and the Polish princess, Maria Casimire Clementina Sobieska. He had lived in France for much of his life but apparently spoke English with a heavy Italian accent. Rather than being welcomed here warmly, he had been forced to land in Scotland and had gained widespread support only from the Scottish Highlands. Indeed, when his campaign came to an end at Culloden, there were as many Scots fighting for the British Government, as there were for the Jacobites.

News of his invasion soon reached Derby and in late September the Duke of Devonshire called a meeting of local gentry and clergy to formulate a plan of action to repel the approaching invaders. A tax was levied and a force of some 720 men, to be known as the Derbyshire Regiment, was formed.

On 22 November the king's troops came through Derby and, as each day passed, word arrived of the Jacobite advance which crept ever closer. By the time messengers confirmed that the Highlanders were at Ashbourne, the gentry in Derby had fled, taking with them their valuables and weapons. The mayor, Robert Hague, and most of the town's aldermen soon followed suit. The Derbyshire Regiment, who had been practising on the Holmes, were sent home to prepare for action, but since the Jacobites had been expected to march to London via a more westerly route, the bulk of the army was waiting in Wales. It was decided, then, that it would be better for the local militia to retreat to Nottingham, leaving Derby utterly defenceless. British propaganda had long circulated stories of atrocities committed by the Jacobites, even that they ate English babies, and many Derbeians must have feared for their lives. Even so, there had been enormous support in Derby for the Stuart cause during and after the Glorious Revolution. Some citizens would have welcomed the Young Pretender. Regardless, the atmosphere in Derby on the night of 3 December 1745 must have been one of unprecedented unease.

What actually happened in

Statue of Bonnie Prince Charlie between Derby Cathedral and the River Derwent.

Derby over the next three days is open to debate. Some things are certain, some are not. There are plenty of first-hand reports but all of these were naturally subject to personal and political bias. It is only by considering both sides, all standpoints and each account, that we may begin to fully understand the events.

The most complete account comes from the *Derby Mercury*. Published just a few days after the events, the newspaper gives full details of the arrival of the prince and his men and of their activities and behaviour throughout their stay, but it should be remembered that the *Derby Mercury* was most definitely a Whig journal and strongly anti-Jacobite.

We know that the Jacobites came into Derby down Ashbourne Road, Markeaton Lane, Friar Gate, across Sadler Gate Bridge, up Sadler Gate and into the Market Place. The first outriders arrived in Derby at about 11am and went to the George public house (now Lafferty's and Fould's) on the Market Place, demanding to be directed to the magistrates. The magistrates had, of course, long gone and so the invaders requested billeting for some 9,000 people.

According to the *Mercury*, the Jacobites had already proved the British propaganda true and 'gave a Specimin of what we were to expect from such villains by seizing a very good Horse belonging to young Mr Stamford'.

Soon more soldiers arrived 'cloth'd in Blue, faced with Red, most of 'em had on Scarlet Waistcoats with Gold Lace… They were drawn up in the Market Place and sat on Horseback two or three hours; at the same Time the Bells were rung and several Bonfires made, to prevent any Resentment from 'em that might ensue on our shewing a Dislike of their coming among us.'

Far from showing a dislike, many Derbeians welcomed the Highlanders with open arms. According to one soldier's account, the bonfire-lighting and bell-ringing was quite spontaneous and accompanied by much rejoicing.

Another soldier, Peter Auchterlony, in a letter to his wife, posted on 5 December from Derby said: 'Wee arrived here last night amidst the acclamations of the people, and publick rejoicing, which we have had in severall places.'

In the middle of the afternoon the rest of the army arrived. The *Derby Mercury* reported: 'In tolerable Order, six or eight abreast with about eight Standards most of them White Flags and a Red Cross. They had several bagpipers who play'd as they march'd along; and appeared in general to answer the description we have all along had of 'em viz. most of their main Body a Parcel of shabby, lousy, pitiful look'd Fellows, mix'd up with old Men and Boys; dressed in dirty Plaids, and as dirty Shirts, without Breeches, and wore their Stockings made of Plaid not much above half Way up their Legs, and some without Shoes… and Numbers of 'em so fatigu'd with their long March, that they really commanded our Pity more than Fear.'

Before the prince himself arrived in Derby, the town crier was required to proclaim the Old Pretender as the true monarch.

A tall and striking man, 'The Prince (as they call'd him) did not arrive till the Dusk of the Evening; he walked on foot being attended to by a great Body of his Men, who conducted him to his Lodgings… Every House by this time was pretty well fill'd… and we tho't we should never have seen the last of 'em.'

Exeter House in Full Street, on the site of the later police station and magistrates court. The Young Pretender stayed here.

There are many houses still standing in Derby today that played host to some of Bonnie Prince Charlie's men. The commanders, of course, were billeted in the grander houses, and the prince stayed at Exeter House, which stood on Full Street, on the site of the 1930s police HQ. Although the *Mercury* implies that the Jacobites forced themselves on their hosts, it seems likely that many were happy to billet the soldiers. However, the town would certainly have been overcrowded. The 9,000 soldiers, officers, wives, families and servants that suddenly descended on Derby almost doubled the population in an instant. Although some soldiers would have been lucky enough to have slept on beds and with a roof over their heads, on those December nights many would have had to settle for a ceiling of stars and a bed of stone and straw.

The conduct of the Jacobites during their stay is also open to question. According to the *Mercury*, 'They were very alert the next Day, running about from one Shop to another, to buy, or rather steal, Tradesmen's Goods... The town being filled 'em looked like some Fair on the Highlands. Nothing was too common for 'em if they liked a Person's Shoes better than their own to demand them off their Feet... The longer they stay'd the more insolent and outrageous they grew, demanding every Thing by Threats, drawn Swords, and Pistols clapp'd to the Breasts of many Persons, not only by the common Men, but their officers; so that several Persons were oblig'd to abscond to preserve their lives.'

Many other accounts, though, state clearly that all the items supposedly 'stolen' were in fact paid for. And while some sources accuse the Jacobites of demanding items and money by force, even by pointing their heavy artillery at public buildings, there is no substantiating evidence for this. What is a fact is that the Jacobite artillery was kept on Nuns Green, too far from any public building to present much of an immediate threat. There are other accounts of Jacobite soldiers queuing up at the cutlers to get their swords sharpened. It should also be remembered that many of the Jacobite soldiers did not speak good English, so it is not unreasonable to assume that many misunderstandings must have taken place.

The prince surely had some fond memories of his welcome in Derby. In Derby Museum is a diamond ring that once belonged to the prince and was given either to a local boy, chosen as his food taster, or to Alderman Samuel Heathcote as a gift of thanks. He also bestowed a number of miniature portraits of himself upon several ladies of the town.

As they prepared for the final march to London, the Jacobites collected money. All those who owed tax to the Crown were required to give that money to the prince, and each of those who had contributed to the militia fund were required to contribute an equal sum to the prince's cause. In addition £100 was acquired from the posting office. There were also more accusations of stealing. According to the *Derby Mercury*, 'they broke open Closets, Chests, Boxes etc at several Gentlemen's Houses, took away all the guns, pistols, swords, and all other arms they could find in every house... they committed almost all manner of outrages which, were they to be particulariz'd, would more than fill our Paper.'

The rebels also tried to recruit local men but only a handful joined up. In total in the 25 or so days he had been in England, the prince had only managed to recruit around 400 men.

The *Mercury* published one particular anonymous gentleman's complaints:

'The delightful Compliment of 'em quarter'd with me look'd like so many Fiends turn'd out of Hell, to ravage the Kingdom and cut throats... my Hall stunk of their Itch and other Nastiness about them, as if they had been so many Persons in a condemn'd hole and twill be very happy if they've left no Contagion behind them.'

Several sources state that the prince rode to outlying villages to canvass support for his cause, but to no avail. Other sources claim that he attended a service held at All Saints'.

The householder again: 'The religion of these common Creatures (if they had any at all) seem'd to be a Medley of Heathenism and Popery with a little Tincture of Scotch Kirk, but after all this Complication of odd Matter there did not appear the least Stricture of Humanity amongst them.'

As word spread that the rebels were regrouping at Derby, a number of government spies came into the town, more than one bringing bad news for the prince. Dudley Bradstreet delivered news that the army was blocking the London road at Northampton. Another spy reported that the king's troops were approaching much quicker than expected and that they numbered at least 30,000 men, Charles wanted to push ahead but his advisors, in particular Lord Murray, did not.

The prince's council of war met in the drawing room at Exeter House. Murray pleaded with the prince to return to Scotland to raise reinforcements. They were vastly outnumbered, he said, and would not get any substantial help from within England. Retreat was the only option. One by one the prince's commanders concurred with Murray. Only the Duke of Perth remained on his side. Reluctantly, the prince drew up the orders for the retreat. At Derby Museum in the Bonnie Prince Charlie Room, oak panelling from the drawing room at Exeter House has been used, together with other mementoes of the prince's

This was once the George Hotel in Irongate, where Bonnie Prince Charlie's outriders demanded billets. The building to the left of the public house, now Lloyds Bank, was originally 18th-century and is Grade II listed. Colonel Gordon of Glenbucket stayed here in December 1745.

stay and contemporary furniture, to show visitors what the room in which the fateful decision was taken would have looked like on that December night over 250 years ago.

That night the prince attended a grand dinner at the Assembly Rooms, attended by his men and by a large number of locals. The excitement was so great that a crush developed, then there was panic and the prince's standard was toppled, the staff breaking in two – a bad omen said many who witnessed it.

At that moment only a few knew of the planned retreat but soon it would become apparent to everyone. The rebellion was over.

The *Derby Mercury* again: 'Early on Friday morning their Drums beat to Arms and their bag-pipers play'd about the Town, no one then knowing their Route, but most people imagin'd they would march to Loughborough for London. However we were soon undeceiv'd by their precipitate Retreat the same Road they came, marching off at 7 o'clock in the Morning.'

The Jacobites wound their way back to Scotland, only to be pursued by the Duke of Cumberland and to eventual defeat at Culloden. The embittered prince said later: 'In future I shall summon no councils, since I am accountable to nobody for my actions but to God and to my father, and therefore I shall no longer either ask or accept advice.'

Perhaps he was right to adopt this attitude, for just as the prince and his advisors were making the decision to retreat, the people of London were in panic. Many had fled the capital and King George II had prepared an escape. His barge, loaded with money and treasure, waited for him on the Thames. Many historians now think that had the Jacobites continued they may have met with little resistance and might well have secured the throne for the Stuarts once more. Had that happened then Britain would have taken a different course …and with it many world events would have been altered too.

INDUSTRY, ENDEAVOUR, ENLIGHTENMENT

THE continued political machinations that had so divided Britain in the 17th and 18th centuries might well have caused a stagnation of growth and enterprise. Instead, all this upheaval was to coincide with the beginning of a period of unprecedented innovation and unrivalled accomplishments in science and industry. And Derby was part of its genesis.

As early as 1691, the 23-year-old George Sorocold, himself something of a protégé of John Flamsteed, proposed a pioneering scheme which would pump water around the town centre. Sorocold, an expert in hydraulics, devised a system whereby water from the River Derwent was pumped by a water wheel-powered engine into a tank on top of St Michael's Church. It was the first town centre water supply system in the British Isles. From the tank, water was piped along King's Street, Irongate, the Market Place, Rotton Row and the Cornmarket. Prior to this, citizens had to walk to the nearest well to obtain fresh water. The system was so efficient that not only did it provide power to a drill which bored the pipes from elm wood, it also powered a malt mill and remained in operation until 1841. Sorocold was later asked to provide a similar system for Leeds town centre, and in 1702 he was the first civilian to be called an 'engineer' – a title previously reserved only for those on military service. That same year Thomas Cotchett, a barrister from Mickleover, asked Sorocold to build him a timber-framed mill on the

George Sorocold's water engine house at Derby in 1765.

banks of the Derwent. Here, Cotchett and his assistant, the skilled mechanic John Lombe, attempted to perfect a fine silk which would rival that which was imported from Italy. Stocking making had long been a major industry in Derby, but it was something which was done almost informally, as a cottage industry, and it became Cotchett and Lombe's plan to change all that.

Although employing the very latest technology available in Britain, Cotchett's 'Old Shop' was unable to achieve anything like the fine quality needed to produce fashionable dress silk. In particular, Piedmontese silk had long been regarded as the best in the world, and the technique in which such fine thread was spun from the raw silk was a closely-guarded secret. Disappointed at his failure and on the point of bankruptcy, Cotchett bowed out of the business. Now unemployed and convinced that it was still possible to reproduce fine silk, Lombe travelled to Piedmont to study the skills and technology for himself. Whilst employed there he secretly drew diagrams of the machinery and smuggled them back to England inside bales of silk fabric. Using investment from John Lombe's stepbrother Thomas, machines based on the schematics were installed around the town, in particular in the old disused guildhall, and work began on perfecting the technique. Returning to Derby, Lombe, who must surely have been one of the very first international industrial spies, took out a lease on an island in the Derwent and arranged for George Sorocold to erect a brick mill there. It took three years to build Lombe's Silk Mill at a cost of £30,000. It stood five storeys high, was powered by a large water-wheel and featured eight apartments and no less than 468 windows. Although it was largely rebuilt on a slightly smaller scale following a serious fire in 1910, it is still a magnificent and imposing structure and today serves as the home of Derby's Industrial Museum, It was the first true factory in England – with all the processes under one roof and all powered from a single energy source.

In 1718, Thomas Lombe applied for a patent on a

'new invention of three sorts of engines never before made or used in Great Britain'.

William Hutton, who was later to become a renowned historian of the town, worked at the Silk Mill for many years. Although conditions there were probably typical of the industry, Hutton seems to have found them quite intolerable at times.

Above: On 5 December 1910, Derby Silk Mill – England's first true factory– caught fire and was severely damaged.
Below: The Silk Mill was largely rebuilt, although reduced to three tiers, and today houses Derby Industrial Museum.

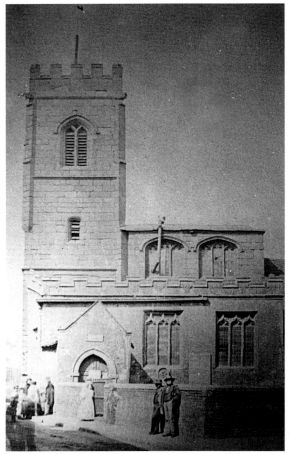

St Michael's Church pictured in the 1850s. The tower was used as a reservoir for the first town-centre water supply in Great Britain.

'There were 300 persons employed in the mill, I was the youngest. I had now to rise at five every morning; submit to the cane whenever convenient to the master; and be the constant companion of the most rude and vulgar of the human race.'

Another writer observed, '...some of the Silk Mill machinery was worked not by water but by children who walked on a treadmill. I observed an ass and two small boys walking upon it.'

However, it does seem that the mill workers and other Derbeians held John Lombe, in particular, in high regard. According to Hutton, Lombe's funeral was 'the most superb ever known in Derby.' He also described Lombe as 'a man of peaceable deportment, who had brought a beneficial manufacturing into the place, employed the poor, and at advanced wages, could not fail to meet with respect'.

The exact cause of John Lombe's death is the subject of conjecture. Many believe that he was poisoned by an agent sent over by the Piedmontese determined to exact revenge for the loss of their fine silk monopoly.

The business now fell to Thomas Lombe, who for 14 years had held the patent for fine silk throwing, the factory at Derby being the only one permitted to use that type of machine to produce silk. But in 1732 the patent ran out. Lombe petitioned to have it extended, citing the length of time it had taken to have the factory built after the patent had been obtained, as well as the time lost when the Piedmontese had withheld the supply of raw silk in retaliation. He claimed that by the time these issues had been resolved and his workers had been trained and the machinery fine-tuned, the patent had almost run out. Parliament suggested the patent be extended for another 10 years but the king's advisors disagreed and Lombe had to settle for a compensation settlement of just £14,000 while the process was thrown open to all. Already, though, Derby, with the first true factory in the country, had established itself as the first industrial town and the cradle of the Industrial Revolution.

This was not merely the dawn of a new industrial age, though. These huge technological strides were also to alter the agrarian world. Since medieval times the British landscape had been divided into small strips, each farmed by a single family. New Acts of Parliament (c.1770-90) were introduced to form fields or 'enclosures' from dozens of small strips, each field becoming just a small part of a larger farm. Some of the oldest streets in many of Derby's suburbs, which were once independent villages, are 'closes' – a shortened form of the word enclosure and are a reminder of the sudden changes wrought upon the local countryside. The Normanton Enclosure Act of 1768, for instance, saw many poorer farmers forced to sell their plots to the few who were rich and who were now able to establish very large farms around the village. New methods of ploughing etc were also introduced, making it possible for just a few workers to complete the work of many. Less labour-intensive farming meant more men and women with no work and no income. Those who had been displaced departed for the towns.

By the middle of the 18th century a new middle class was emerging. They were more wealthy than ever before and began to crave a more opulent lifestyle and to dress in fine clothing, and surround themselves with fine furnishings and ornaments. Several towns became known for their luxury goods, none more so than Derby. Especially when, in 1756, a new factory was opened – the Derby Porcelain Factory.

ROYAL CROWN DERBY

ALTHOUGH there had been ceramic production in Derby since Roman times, it was not until 1756 that the town became known for such high-quality porcelain as we have come to expect from Royal Crown Derby.

In that year William Duesbury, originally a native of Longton in Stoke-on-Trent, founded his porcelain factory on Nottingham Road. From the very beginning the factory began to produce the kind of elegant, elaborate china recognised and treasured the world over. A wide range of figurines and practical wares were produced. Designs of the day featured delicate florals, exotic birds, classic blue and white and fashionable rich oriental styles.

The factory proved so successful that, in 1770, Duesbury was able to buy the famous Chelsea factory, eventually moving all production to Derby. In 1773 Duesbury opened a London showroom and both King George III and Queen Charlotte became enthusiastic customers. In 1773 George III gave permission to mark Derby china with a crown, and Crown Derby was born. Not everyone was satisfied, though. On a visit to the factory in 1777, Dr Samuel Johnson declared: 'It was too dear! For that he could have vessels of silver as cheap as here were made of porcelain!'

The company remained in the Duesbury family until the early 1800s when William Duesbury's grandson, also called William, decided to try several new ventures. All of these proved

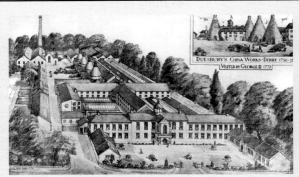

Illustration showing the Royal Porcelain works and (inset) Duesbury's china works. In 1944 the US ambassador to Great Britain said that Derby China was 'a household word for loveliness the world over.'

unsuccessful and Duesbury emigrated to Lowell, Massachusetts to join several Derby expatriates (*see American Connections: Kirk Boott*).

In 1811 Robert Bloor bought what remained of the company and re-established it in premises on King Street. By 1890 it had so recovered, that larger premises were required and the whole factory moved to the former workhouse on Osmaston Road. It was officially opened by Queen Victoria and she granted the royal warrant, allowing Crown Derby to become the more familiar Royal Crown Derby.

Duesbury had called his factory 'the second Dresden'. This bold claim was not far from the truth because it was certainly the finest porcelain concern in Britain. Duesbury had amassed the most gifted ceramics painters in the country and it was a tradition that was to continue. In the mid-19th century William Coffee was one of the factory's most noted employees. He also emigrated to the United States

A pair of Derby figures modelled as Turks in a dancing position, made in 1760.

where he became a leading sculptor and worked for such prominent figures as Thomas Jefferson, James Madison and President Monroe. And in 1878 the great Dresden porcelain artist Georg, 6th Count von Holzendorff, was lured to Derby to work at the factory. Throughout its history, Royal Crown Derby has been synonymous with opulence and beauty. It has been used and treasured by royalty, by millionaires, and by 'ordinary' people from all over the world.

When the ill-fated *Titanic* left Southampton in 1912, she was the most luxurious ship of her era. Naturally passengers in her first-class dining areas were served meals upon specially-commissioned Royal Crown Derby services.

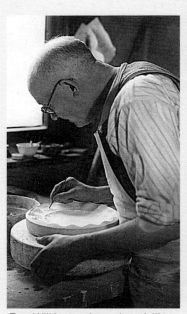

Tom Wilkinson pictured modelling at the Crown Derby works in the mid-1940s.

The Royal Crown Derby works on Osmaston Road, situated in the former Union Workhouse which was built in 1838 and was known locally as 'the Bastille' after the notorious French prison.

Dr Johnson and 'Tetty' Porter
On 9 July 1735 the lexicographer Dr Samuel Johnson married Elizabeth 'Tetty' Porter at St Werburgh's Church in Derby. The reason for their choice of Derby remains a mystery.

At the beginning of the 18th century Derby was blessed with a group of enterprising and inventive entrepreneurs.

Essentially, this has continued right until the present day. But there was a period in the town's history, from the middle of the 18th century to the middle of the 19th, when some of the greatest minds in Europe would make their homes in Derby.

By fate, or perhaps by mutual influence, many of the leading figures of what was now becoming the Industrial Revolution were living in the Midlands. There was Wedgwood at Burslem, Watt and Boulton at Birmingham and, of course, a more than plentiful supply in Derby.

In addition to these men were scientists, philosophers and inventors. These leading lights corresponded constantly, swapping ideas and inventions. Many of them were Nonconformists, barred from some of the more traditional occupations for men of their ilk. And although they were the driving force behind the new industrial and scientific age, they brought with them a new liberalism and a sense of social responsibility. The era was to become known as the Age of Reason or the Enlightenment.

THE MOST ORIGINAL MAN – ERASMUS DARWIN

ALTHOUGH largely overlooked by modern historians and scientists, Erasmus Darwin was the most remarkable of men, in the most remarkable of eras. A physician by training, he excelled in a wide range of scientific and humanitarian areas. He not only reflected the Age of Enlightenment, he also he directed it.

Although born in Nottinghamshire in 1731, Erasmus Darwin will be forever linked with Derby. He attended medical school in Edinburgh and established a practice in Lichfield, where he began his long association with the greatest luminaries of the day. He was a founder of the famous Lunar Society which met once a month in Birmingham at the time of the full moon, to allow sufficient light for its members to travel home safely. Fellow members included Josiah Wedgwood, Matthew Boulton and Benjamin Franklin.

He made a determined effort to enjoy life and was a man of strong passions, for medicine, for science and equality. His first wife Mary Howard – with whom he had five children, three of whom survived infancy – died in 1770. Darwin then embarked upon a long-term relationship with one Mrs Mary Parker. The couple had two daughters – Susanna and Mary Parker. Finally, in 1781 he married the widowed Mrs Elizabeth Pole of Radbourne Hall – a former patient of his. The couple had seven more children. Shortly after this marriage he moved into a house on Full Street in Derby. Such was his reputation that, as well as establishing a practice in Derby, he continued to be invited to the wealthiest homes in the country. But Darwin did not restrict his ministrations to the upper classes. He treated any person, rich or poor, and charged according to their ability to pay. In Derby, Darwin established a clinic and dispensary which was funded by subscribers. Its aim was to eradicate smallpox, a disease of which Darwin himself reportedly bore the scars. Darwin and other local physicians provided free advice to the poor and needy, and local pharmacists made up prescriptions in rotation. The clinic became the immediate inspiration for what is now the Derbyshire Royal

Erasmus Darwin, one of the most remarkable of men, who directed the Age of Enlightenment.

Infirmary. These humanitarian actions earned Darwin great respect from all corners of the town. One story provides a perfect example: Darwin was accosted by a robber who, upon realising the identity of his intended victim, fled with no money. When the would-be robber was caught, Erasmus visited him in gaol to ask why he had let him go. The man replied that he could not steal from Dr Darwin since he had once treated his poor mother without charge.

Many of Darwin's treatments and cures were innovative, but by today's standards might be considered quirky to say the least. For the disease known as ' palor et tremor a timore', Darwin prescribed, 'Opium, Wine, Food, Joy'.

But Darwin was also keen to promote temperance as a cure. According to a letter written by the artist Joseph Wright, 'Dr Darwin, a very eminent physician of this Town, is very much disposed to gout and he told me while he continued in the use of wine he was afflicted with it… He has for some time past drank nothing but water and now he has no gout at all.' His enthusiasm for temperance even led to him dare instruct the Duke of Devonshire to give up alcohol.

Although he repeatedly turned down the offer, Erasmus Darwin's knowledge in the fledgling field of psychiatry led the royal household to request his services as personal physician to the ailing George III. Some of Darwin's practices, however, would cause outrage today. Believing that all disease was a result of 'disordered motion', he invented a gruesome device known as the 'Darwin Chair'. Patients, particularly those with mental health problems, were strapped into the chair which was rotated at great speed until they bled from the nose, mouth and ears. Amazingly there were a number of reports of successful treatment.

In 1791 he suggested that all nerve impulses were in essence electrical in nature. Darwin also pioneered the use of electrotherapy treatments to renew the mobility of paralysed limbs. It was these 'experiments of Dr Darwin' which author Mary Shelley claimed had inspired her to write *Frankenstein's Monster*. A friend of Mary's father, Erasmus had been a frequent visitor to her childhood home.

Whilst part of the Lunar Society, Darwin had introduced Alexander Watt to Matthew Boulton and together the two would design more than 500 steam engines. Although Darwin did not move into Derby until 1781, he had long been in contact with several prominent local men, including John Whitehurst who was a fellow member of the Lunar Society. In Derby, Darwin had encountered some of the most fertile minds of his generation. Bringing with him his knowledge and contacts with the great scientists of his Lunar Society, he had decided to re-establish another remarkable organisation where the greatest and most creative minds in the country could meet to exchange ideas, theories and inventions. It was known as the Derby Philosophical Society and had been in existence since at least the 1760s, although it had apparently fallen away somewhat in recent years. It was essentially a creative cradle that would nurture the most remarkable advances in science and engineering, in culture and philosophy, in humanitarianism and in philanthropy. The Derby Philosophical Society met at the King's Head Inn in the Cornmarket on the first Saturday of every month at 6 o'clock in the evening.

Darwin was renowned as a man of great wit. He had long suffered from a severe stutter and was once asked whether this impediment ever bothered him. He replied that it did not since 'it gives me time for reflection before I speak, and saves me from asking impertinent questions'.

Erasmus Darwin was a resourceful man; he invented a more stable type of carriage after a fall from one left him with a shattered kneecap and a pronounced limp.

Darwin was a skilled poet and among his many publications were poems which speculated upon future innovations such as turbines, rockets, oil drilling, submarines and even air travel.

From his work, *The Botanic Garden*
'Soon shall they arm, unconquer'd steam!
afar Drag the slow barge or drive the rapid car,
Or on the wide-waving wings expanded bear
The flying chariot through fields of air.'

In addition he invented a number of futuristic devices including a primitive copying machine. And he invented an artificial speaking machine.

'I contriv'd a wooden mouth with lips of soft leather… which could be quickly opened or closed by the pressure of the fingers, the vocality was given by a silk ribbon… stretched between two bits of smooth wood, a little hollowed; so that when a gentle current of air… was blown on the edge of the ribbon, it gave an agreeable tone, much like the human voice.'

Matthew Boulton had offered him £1,000 if he could invent a machine 'capable of pronouncing the Lord's Prayer, the Creed and the Ten Commandments in the vulgar tongue'. Whilst Darwin's machine may not have lived up to this challenge, it did accurately pronounce a number of vowel sounds.

Darwin had successes in a number of fields – he was the first to discover how clouds formed, and helped in the development of water closets and ventilation systems. In his house at 3 Full Street, he successfully sank an artesian well. He invented a horizontal windmill which was erected by Wedgwood at his Etruria factory. He tried to design a system of shorthand, a huge canal lift capable of moving barges, a miniature artificial bird, an electrostatic doubler, and weather vanes and meteorological equipment. He also constructed a manually-operated private ferry across the Derwent.

Although he invented many things, he did not take out a single patent, allowing friends to take his initial ideas and make improvements. He always felt his position as a physician came first and did not want to jeopardise that.

Particular interests of Darwin's were chemistry and physics. His great-grandson George Darwin established the fission hypothesis of the formation of the Moon – that the Earth had been spinning so fast that a bulge had appeared at the equator, the huge bulge had broken away and formed the Moon, leaving behind the Pacific Ocean in its place. But it seems to have been Erasmus who first suggested this theory when he discusses the origins of the Earth.

Here he uses a poetic device in which gnomes are used to represent the spirit of the Earth.

'Gnomes! how you shriek'd! when through the troubled air
Roar'd the fierce din of elemental war;
When rose the continents, and sunk the main,
And Earth's huge sphere exploding burst in twain.
Gnomes! how you gazed! when from her wounded side
Where now the South-Sea heaves its waste of tide,
Rose on swift wheels the Moon's refulgent car,
Circling the solar orb, a sister star,
Dimpled with vales, with shining hills emboss'd,
And roll'd round Earth her airless realms of frost.'

Darwin was also one of the first Britons to promote a new and controversial form of chemistry that was being pioneered in France. It was commonly believed in Europe that air and water were both elements. Darwin stated that, in fact, they were compounds consisting of a combination of other elements. In one of his poems he alludes to the marriage of such 'acqueous' gases (oxygen and hydrogen) to produce water. He was the first man to promote the terms 'oxygene' (*sic*), 'hydrogen' and 'azote' (now called nitrogen) in any English language publication. Another common belief of the time was that all combustible materials contained a substance known as phlogiston, which was released upon burning. Again Darwin disagreed and told his friends at the Derby Philosophical Society and Lunar Society that all organic structures were composed of a combination of water and charcoal, what he termed 'hydrocarbonnuex', a mixture of hydrogen, carbon and oxygen, which today we term carbohydrate.

Darwin was also a very liberal humanitarian. He felt strongly about civil rights. He and other members of the Derby Philosophical Society and Lunar Society were vocal in their opposition to slavery. Many members of both groups – Darwin and his friend John Whitehurst in particular – were friends and correspondents of Benjamin Franklin. But their beliefs were opposed by many. When the Lunar Society had supported both the American and French Revolutions, the Birmingham chemist Joseph Priestley found his house under attack from an angry mob for three days and Darwin's scientific work was cruelly parodied by George Canning in an attempt to discredit him.

Darwin also had strong views on hygiene and child rearing and promoted a number of radical ideas. He felt passionately about education and determined that girls as well as boys should be taught science. He wrote a paper entitled *Conduct for the Education of Females* and to this end established a school in Ashbourne. His daughters, the Misses Parker, were schoolmistresses there. Seven of his children studied at the school of Matthew Spencer whose school followed the lines laid out by Darwin and provided a strong scientific basis.

In his later years he wrote many papers, poems and books. In a letter to Watt in 1795 he said,

'Now I grow old, and not so well amused in common society, I think writing books an amusement.'

Darwin's poetry influenced Romantics such as Wordsworth and Shelley and he was himself regarded as one of the leading English poets. Coleridge called him 'the first literary character in Europe, and the most original man'.

Although his poems were in a romantic, pastoral form, the subject matter was usually scientific. He often chose to discuss industry in his poems, such as this passage on the steel industry:

'Strokes follow strokes, the sparkling ingot shines
Flows the red slag the lengthening bar refines
Cold waves, immersed, the glowing mass congeal
And him to adamant the hissing steel.'

Between 1789 and 1792 *The Botanic Garden* was published in two parts – *The Economy of Vegetation* and *The Loves of the Plants*. The work consisted of science-themed poetry accompanied by scientific explanations, and helped to popularise science across Britain.

The house in Full Street where Erasmus Darwin lived.

His *Phytologia* (1800) suggest that plants have sensations and are capable of free will 'though in a much inferior degree than even the cold-blooded animals'. He discusses the 'muscles, nerves and brains of vegetables' and was the first person to accurately describe the process of photosynthesis.

He wrote the book *Zoönomia, or the Laws of Organic Life* (1794), which was both a medical journal, with disease classification based upon the nervous system with a record of treatments and their effectiveness, and an attempt to explain evolution.

Much of his work was concerned with whether all living species descended from a single common ancestor. 'When we observe the essential unity of plan in all warm-blooded animals – we are led to conclude that they have been alike produced from a similar living filament… It is not impossible but the great variety of species of animals, which now tenant the Earth, may have had their origin from the mixture of a few natural orders.'

He discusses the processes of evolution and wonders if it might not be 'directed by imitations, sensations, volitions and associations, and thus possessing inherent activity of delivering down those improvements to by generation to its posterity world without end?'

He spoke on the changes to birds' beaks 'which seem to have been gradually produced during many generations by the perpetual endeavour of the creatures to supply the want of food'. Essentially he believed that evolution was a deliberate process.

He suggested that man and ape were related, and talked about adaptive colouration and plant movement. He also believed that competition and sexual selections could cause changes in a species. 'The final course in this contest among males seems to be that the strongest and most active animal should propagate the species, which should thus be improved.'

These ideas in particular caused great controversy since they appeared to conflict wildly with religious doctrine.

In *Zoönomia*, he suggested that 'the world itself might have been generated rather than created' – perhaps an early suggestion of the 'Big Bang Theory'.

And in his posthumously-published *Temple of Nature* (1803) he considers the origins of life itself.

'Then Nurs'd by warm sun beams in primeval caves,
Organic Life began beneath the waves
Was born and nurs'd in Ocean's pearly caves
Hence without parent by spontaneous birth,
Rise the first specks of animated earth
First forms minute, unseen by spheric glass
Move on the mud, or pierce the watery mass
These as successive generations bloom
New Powers acquire and large limbs assume
Whence countless groups of vegetations spring
And breathing realms of feet and fin and wings…
Cold gills aquatic form resplendent lungs
And sounds aerial flow from slimy tongues.'

Remarkably, in the late 18th century Erasmus Darwin discussed almost all the important theories of evolution developed by his world-famous grandson Charles, well over a century later. Although

Erasmus died seven years before his grandson's birth, his work was certainly an important influence on him.

In reflection of his deep belief in Life's origin being in the oceans, he adopted a family motto of 'E conchis omnia' – everything from the shells. He even had the motto painted on his carriage before complaints from the clergy that it was heretical forced him to remove it.

Charles Darwin said of his grandfather: 'Throughout his letters I have been struck with his indifference to fame and the complete absence of all signs of any over-estimation of his own abilities, or the success of his works.'

In all Erasmus Darwin had 41 grandchildren. The most famous of these was, of course, Charles Darwin, but another grandson played an important, if notorious role in social history. Francis Galton, a grandson from Darwin's second marriage, was a talented, inventive man in many fields. He pioneered the use of fingerprints for identification purposes, proposed the idea of blood transfusions, invented the modern weather map, described cyclonic and anti-cyclonic weather systems and invented the word association psychology test. But there is another 'invention' for which Galton will be more readily remembered – eugenics. He believed that all attributes, both physical and mental, were inherited and that it was not only possible, but desirable to manipulate the occurrence of these attributes so to 'improve' the human race and so to engineer human evolution. He took the principles of his grandfather's and his cousin's work and applied them to his idea of artificial rather than natural selection. In Galton's own words: 'Eugenics is the science which deals with all influences that improve the inborn qualities of a race; also with those that develop them to the utmost advantage.'

His intention was 'to give the more suitable races or strains of blood a better chance of prevailing over the less suitable than they otherwise would have had'. Galton believed that Christianity was flawed because it stated that the meek, rather than the strong and intelligent, shall inherit the Earth. He said: 'The feeble nations of the world are necessarily giving way before the nobler varieties of mankind.' To decide precisely who constituted the 'nobler varieties' Galton invented a form of 'intelligence testing' and then set out a system of classification to establish 'The Comparative Worth of Different Races'.

At the top were the Athenians, then the British; at the bottom stood those of African descent and the indigenous peoples of Australasia. Galton imagined a time at which the less 'gifted class' might be 'considered as enemies to the State, and to forfeit all claims to kindness' should they continue 'to procreate children inferior in moral, intellectual and physical qualities'. He suggested that not only should more 'worthy' people be encouraged to procreate, but that others should be discouraged and even, if necessary, prevented from so doing. Perhaps Galton believed eugenics would serve humankind well, but in the 20th century it was the basis for the type of hate, prejudice, racism, persecution, genocide and ethnic cleansing seen during the Nazi era and which has continued to blight humanity into the 21st century.

Had the liberal Erasmus Darwin been alive to read his grandson's theories, he would surely have been the first to speak out against their immorality. As it was, Erasmus died at Breadsall Priory in 1802, just two months after moving there from Full Street. He left behind him a remarkable legacy of discoveries and inventions, a legacy shared by the other members of the Derby Philosophical Society.

AN ELEGANT MIND –
JOHN WHITEHURST

JOHN Whitehurst was born in Congleton, Cheshire, in 1713 and by the time he moved to Derby in 1736 he was already an accomplished clock maker. He was granted permission to establish a business in the town when he produced a turret clock for use in the old Guildhall.

Whitehurst became both a member of the Lunar Society and a founding member of the Derby Philosophical Society. He was also elected to the American Philosophical Society in 1786, an honour bestowed upon him by his friend Benjamin Franklin. Both men, of course, had connections with the Lunar Society.

Whitehurst lived in a house in Irongate (now occupied by GA Property Services) until 1764 when he moved to a house at the top of Queen Street (number 27), an address which had previously belonged to John Flamsteed and would later be occupied by Joseph Wright.

Whitehurst invented and produced a huge number of innovative clocks, including the first round-dial long-case clock. He also produced astronomical and sidereal clocks (to measure the movement of the Earth in relation to other planetary bodies) amongst others. In addition, Whitehurst collaborated with men such as James Ferguson, Matthew Boulton and Benjamin Franklin to produce other timepieces. He sold one of his clocks to Franklin for £12 12s (£12.60). In 1765 he wrote to Franklin about the new 'Timekeepers' of Thomas Harrison, which had finally solved the longitude problem that had so absorbed scientists, among them John Flamsteed.

'I have been considering what further improvements are wanting to render… and flatter myself with some hope of contributing towards that need,' he told Franklin.

Whitehurst sought to improve accuracy certainly, and to produce a more economic timepiece, but also to reduce the number of parts and so the chance of malfunction. It was a principle that he and Franklin would adhere to when designing a four-hour clock suitable for use in the North American colonies, which were so far from replacement parts.

Those colonies were a particularly contentious issue at the time and, as we have seen with Darwin, members of the Lunar Society were noted for their support of their colonial cousins. Unlike many of his closest friends, Whitehurst was not by nature a radical, but does seem to have had sympathy with the American cause. In January 1770, when controversy over the Stamp Act and the heavy duties levied upon the American colonies was reaching its height, Whitehurst asked of Franklin,

'Pray sir, what will be done about the duties imposed upon the North Americans? I should so deem it a singular favour to know your sentiments on that.'

Franklin was soon to become one of America's founding fathers and a key figure in the War of Independence, and subsequent peace. As hostilities

John Whitehurst, one of the most innovative men of his time. He lived in Irongate and later Queen Street.

increased, Franklin left England and correspondence between the two was suspended. It was revived as soon as was practicable – once the British had surrendered in 1781, and peace had been fully restored two years later.

Writing for the first time to the new United States citizen, Whitehurst congratulated Franklin and wished that 'all the provinces be governed by laws... for the mutual benefit of every individual'.

Franklin and Whitehurst were to remain lifelong friends despite their respective homelands' conflict. They were held together by what Whitehurst would describe to Franklin as 'the natural tendency of philosophers minds to promote useful knowledge'.

Whitehurst, like Franklin and Erasmus Darwin, had a voracious appetite for discovery. In addition to his clocks he constructed all manner of precision instruments including barometers, compasses, timers for pottery kilns, hygrometers (to measure humidity) and pyrometers (to measure very high temperatures in furnaces). He also designed stoves, boilers, roasters, central heating systems, water supplies, steam engines, spinning machines, wc facilities and even water features for country parks. One invention of his, the hydraulic ram pump, is still in wide use today because it is capable of pumping stream water great distances, using only the water's inertia. It is efficient, cost-effective to run, and environmentally-friendly.

Whitehurst is also regarded by many as the 'grandfather' of modern geology. In 1778 he published a work he had tested out on Franklin and other members of the American Philosophical Society. It was entitled *An Inquiry into the Original State and Formation of the Earth; deduced from facts about the laws of nature.*

Its purpose, according to Whitehurst was 'to inquire after those laws by which the Creator chose to form the World'.

His work on geology did precisely that. He described volcanoes and noted for the first time the immense influence of the Moon and tides on the planet, and that molten rock could be intruded (forced) into existing layers of rock. But perhaps his most significant achievement – above all else because of the dramatic impact it would have on the economy – was his accurate descriptions of the various strata of the Earth. This enabled himself and others to accurately predict the location of rich seams of minerals such as coal, copper and iron and so lay the way clear for the mining of such minerals. In turn this would both feed and power the burgeoning Industrial Revolution.

His work also helped to popularise the use of Derbyshire's Blue John in decorative items and jewellery. He advised Josiah Wedgwood on the best minerals to use in his porcelain glazes and invented a system of measurement which pre-dates and closely resembles the metric system.

In 1774 Whitehurst's friend, the Duke of Newcastle, granted him the position of Stamper of the Money Weights at the Royal Mint. Initially, although this position provided a salary, it did not require any actual duties. By 1780, though, Whitehurst was forced to move to London to be nearer his responsibilities.

John Whitehurst died in London in 1788.

BENJAMIN FRANKLIN

AT least twice during his life, John Whitehurst played host in Derby to Benjamin Franklin. This founding father of America spent many years living in London, where he made the acquaintance of the leading intellectuals in the land. Franklin was impressed by the knowledge and invention of his scientific friends, whom he referred to as 'sensible, virtuous and elegant minds'. Among these were Erasmus Darwin and John Whitehurst. The men corresponded regularly and contact was suspended only during the American Revolutionary War.

The dates of his visits to Derby are uncertain, although from their letters we know they had met prior to 1763. Certainly Franklin had visited Birmingham as early as 1754. Whether the noted philosopher, scientist and diplomat, one of the most important figures in American history, resided at 24 Irongate, or 27 Queen Street, we may never know, but he would surely have mingled with Derbeians of all walks of life as he meandered down Irongate.

KEY INDUSTRIALISTS –
STRUTT AND EVANS

NOW that men such as John Whitehurst had provided the science and knowledge with which to accurately locate plentiful supplies of ore and coal, science and industry, invention and economics had conspired to nudge industry forward. But now there came such a sudden expansion in mechanised industry that rural areas were beginning to feel the effects too. Labourers were being replaced by machines that could do the work of 10 or more of them. Hundreds of thousands of workers came to the towns looking for work.

In Derby the textile industry was by far the largest employer. Silk manufacture continued and there were tape mills and cotton mills too. And here the Derby Philosophical Society and its circle played another important role. For two of Derby's – and indeed England's – key industrialists were part of that group. They were Thomas Evans and Jedidiah Strutt.

Jedidiah Strutt was to found a dynasty that would be remembered with affection and gratitude by the people of Derby. He and his descendants were to epitomise the philanthropic age.

Jedidiah Strutt, the key industrialist whose family were to give so much to Derby.

Born in 1726, Strutt was apprenticed to a wheelwright at Findern when only 14 years old. Even at such an young age he was fascinated with all things mechanical and it would be this fascination that would lead him to make his most significant discovery. Together with his brother-in-law William Woollatt, Strutt invented a machine that revolutionised the textile industry. The Derby Rib, as it became known, adapted conventional technology by fitting an attachment which reversed the loops to make a rib stitch. This deceptively simple innovation meant that, for the first time, a close-fitting ribbed silk hose could be produced. This new technology also enabled the production of mittens, shirts and other fine goods. Initially Strutt and Woollatt had difficulty in attracting investment for their new idea, but eventually they were successful and a patent was obtained.

The *Derby Mercury* declared that it was 'received here with joy, particularly by the workmen and others employed therein'.

Strutt and Woollatt opened a silk factory and rented out further machines to workers to use at home.

In 1769 Strutt formed a partnership with Richard Arkwright and built a mill at Cromford. They were extremely successful but eventually Strutt dissolved the partnership, fearing that Arkwright's rapid expansion plans would lead to financial disaster.

In 1792 Strutt opened a new mill in Derby, between Albert and Tenant Streets, roughly where Osnabruck Square stands today. It was the first fire-proof mill in England and stood six storeys high. It was constructed of hollow bricks in the floor and cast-iron columns and timber beams which had been plated in metal for protection. It was the first time iron-framing had been used in the construction of a multi-storey building, and in many ways it laid the foundations for the development of the steel-framed skyscraper.

The Derby mill was also the first factory to produce a pure cotton cloth known as calico.

Strutt's calico mill was even more successful than his silk factory. It became the largest cotton producer in England and at one time Derby was in direct competition with Manchester as the cotton capital of Britain.

Jedidiah Strutt's interests, however, were not centred solely on profit. He was liberal-minded, a member of the Derby Philosophical Society and very much aware of the needs and rights of his workers and of his responsibilities towards them. Although, like all mill owners, Strutt employed children, the experiences of the Derby mill worker were certainly more pleasant than many others.

It was remarked by an observer of the time that it was a pity that other mill owners did not exhibit such an 'enlarged benevolence and active philanthropy'.

Shortly before his death Strutt wrote his own epitaph, and it is one which effectively, although modestly given his achievements, sums up his life.

'Here rests in peace Jedidiah Strutt who, without fortune, family or friends, raised to himself a fortune, family, and name in the world; without having wit, had a good share of plain common sense; without much genius, employed the more substantial blessing of a sound understanding; with but little personal pride, despised a mean or base action; with no ostentation for religious tenants and ceremonies He led a life of honesty and virtue not knowing what would befall him after death, he died resigned in full confidence that if there be a future state of retribution it will be to reward the virtuous and the good, This I think is my true character.'

This epitaph could just as easily have applied to Strutt's great friend, Thomas Evans, who was born in 1723.

After the spectacular failure of a local bank run by John Heath, a former mayor of the town, Evans had acquired assets which included a mill at Darley Abbey. He built and expanded the mill complex and opened a cotton mill, a brickworks, paper mill, red lead (lead tetroxide – used in glass and paint manufacture) factory and a cornmill. The Evans family remained the sole employers in the village for more than 150 years and created what is now a delightful Regency suburb. Evans built an entire workers' village on the other side of the Derwent.

He was just as aware as Strutt of his workforce's dependence upon him and established a system of welfare well in advance of its day.

To attract workers to Darley, the Evans family placed the following advertisement in the *Derby Mercury*:

'Darley Abbey, Cotton Mill, WANTED, Families

The weir at Darley Abbey, built to help maintain the height of the Derwent which served the mills there.

Particularly women and children to work at said mill. They may be provided with comfortable houses and every convenience at Darley or Allestrey; particularly a milking cow to each family.'

Villagers were provided with a home which was kept in good condition by the Evanses, rent was subsidised, and there was a coal allowance and shawls and blankets in cold weather. The elderly and sick were entitled to hot meals and all villagers were inoculated against smallpox and allowed use of a private convalescent home in Llandudno. In addition, all burials and gravestones were provided at the expense of the Evans family.

In return villagers were expected to work up to 70 hours a week and to observe a set of strict rules. These included a 10pm curfew and a ban on swearing and drunkenness. So determined were the Evanses to prevent this that until the 1970s Darley Abbey remained one of the few villages without a public house. Anyone found guilty of contravening these rules was subject to a night in the lock-up and a morning appearance before one of the Evans family. Children were employed from the age of nine.

The Evans family continued to watch over the village until 1929 when, following the death of Mrs Ada Evans, residents were permitted to purchase their own homes.

As remarkable men such as Strutt and Evans, their friends and associates continued to invent, to innovate and to create, a talented local artist was recording them for posterity.

JOSEPH WRIGHT OF DERBY

JOSEPH Wright – Wright of Derby – was one of the most important painters of the Georgian era. He became famous for his studies of light, be the source the Moon, a candle, a fire, a furnace or even phosphorus. His work appears in galleries across the country: at Derby, of course, where there is a special Wright Gallery; in the National Gallery, the Tate and the National Portrait Gallery in London; in the Fitzwilliam Museum in Cambridge; and in the Walker Art Gallery in Liverpool.

Abroad, his work is displayed at the J. Paul Getty Museum in Los Angeles, the National Gallery of Art in Washington DC, the National Gallery of Victoria in Australia, and in the Hermitage Museum in St Petersburg, Russia.

Joseph Wright was born in Irongate on 3 September 1734. The house has long been demolished, but a memorial to him stands at its site. Wright's father was an attorney and Joseph attended Derby School before moving to London to study under the painter Thomas Hudson.

In 1775 Wright had his first exhibition in London and it was here that his trademark style was first seen. Although several European artists, such as Rembrandt, had already been producing work that made particular use of the contrast of light and darkness, it was the subject matter chosen by Wright that was so unique. He was fascinated by science and industry and his work very much epitomises the age. Both in its subject and its treatment, Wright gave an almost magical quality to the work of the scientists he portrayed.

His most famous work is *A Philosopher Lecturing on the Orrery*, which can be seen in the Joseph Wright Gallery at Derby Museum. The orrery was a popular instrument of the time – a mechanical representation of the solar system and the Earth and planets and their movement around the Sun. A fine example of a working machine can also be seen in the gallery. The philosopher depicted is probably demonstrating an eclipse, or the change in seasons. Although we do not know the identity of the model for the philosopher, Wright's two friends John Whitehurst and James Ferguson were both known to conduct this demonstration.

Joseph Wright – Wright of Derby – the painter who catalogued the great and good of the town.

Another of his works, *An Experiment on a Bird in an Air Pump* shows a disparate group observing another scientific demonstration. In this picture the group epitomise the conflicting reactions to such experiments that abounded at the time – fascination, uncertainty and even horror at the poor bird's fate.

Two more, very typical, paintings are *The Alchemist Discovering Phosphorus* and *The Blacksmith's Shop*, both of which are on display at Derby.

First aquatint
The first aquatint (a revolutionary engraving which resembles a water colour painting) was produced by Peter Perez Burdett, a Derby land surveyor and cartographer, who sold the formula to an artist, Paul Sandby.

Wright was also fascinated by geology, painting a number of interesting rock formations and travelling to Italy in 1773, where he painted dramatic interpretations of Vesuvius in eruption.

One of Spondon's most lovely buildings – the Homestead, once the property of the Cade family, descendants of Joseph Wright. For many years some of Wright's best works adorned the walls. Set back from Sitwell Street behind a high wall, the Homestead, built in the early to mid-18th century, remains one of the prettiest Georgian properties in the county. Its lovely garden is all that remains of the once-vast pleasure grounds, much of it purchased for development. The cast-iron balustrades on the entrance steps are by Robert Bakewell (and may have been removed from Darley Hall) and the original staircase and much of the original panelling remain in excellent condition. The original gatepiers and the coach house also remain. The Homestead now serves as a restaurant.

The Gresleys
In addition to Joseph Wright, Derby has produced a number of talented and successful painters. The Gresley family of Chellaston were among the most productive. J. S. Gresley was a noted landscape artist, his son Frank specialised in water colour and oil landscapes of the Trent Valley, and his grandson Cuthbert worked for Royal Crown Derby as a porcelain painter. JS's son, Harold, attended the Royal College of Art and exhibited his work at the Royal Academy. Several of his landscapes of the Derby area are held in Derby Museum.

In 1775 he decided to try to expand his business. He moved to Bath in an attempt to inherit the wealthy clientele of portraitist Gainsborough, who had himself moved to London. But Wright's honest style proved unpopular with the Bath gentry who were used to Gainsborough brushing out all their perceived imperfections. Wright returned to Derby where he completed a vast number of portraits of local men and women, which would turn out to be a virtual 'who's who' of the Derby Philosophical Society, the Lunar Society and the beginnings of the Industrial Revolution itself. Numbering among his portraits are those of Darwin, Whitehurst, Strutt and Arkwright.

Catherine the Great added some of his work to her collection and the poet William Hayley wrote an ode to him. Wright's work brought him to national and international attention but he would probably have been an even bigger name had he not declined election to the Royal Academy, because he did not want to live in London.

Joseph Wright died on 29 August 1797 at his house at 27 Queen Street. His daughter, Anna Romana, married Dr James Cade of the Homestead at Spondon. One of Wright's descendants through her was Rowena Cade, founder of the world-famous open-air Minack Theatre at Portcurno, Cornwall.

PICKFORD'S DERBY

MANY of the men painted by Joseph Wright had established businesses across the town. The landscape was quickly changing and suitable mill space was running out. The Derwent provided water and power for most of the factories, but it was at Markeaton Brook, behind Friar Gate, that much of the development would concentrate. The Second Nuns Green Act of 1792 allowed the sale of land remaining from a previous such Act of 1768. By the 1820s the area around Bridge Street, Brook Street and Agard Street was filled with mills and workers' housing, most of which was of a very poor standard. It became known as the West End and, despite the romantic accounts of life there which have abounded in recent years, conditions were truly appalling by modern standards. Large families were squeezed into very small houses, which often shared only one outside 'privvy', and diseases like tuberculosis were common. Steady improvements were made over the next 130 years, but whilst it could no longer be regarded as squalid, it was not until the 1960s, when the bulldozers swept much of it away, that the area was completely upgraded. The whole development had proved controversial from the start. Residents of the other half of Nuns Green, along Friar Gate, feared the industrialisation of their neighbourhood. After the First Nuns Green Act, plots had been snapped up and elegant, high-grade housing had been erected, much of which

The 1765 Assembly Rooms, designed by Joseph Pickford. The building was severely damaged by fire in 1963 and the façade was re-erected at the National Tramway Museum at Crich.

The attractive thoroughfare of Friar Gate, built as part of the Nuns Green Acts which swallowed up previously open public land.

survives to this day. There had been strict rules of purchasing the plots. Within five years the new owner had to build 'one or more dwelling houses handsome in front towards the publick street not less than three storeys high decently sasht.'

This was adhered to in principal but there had been some bending of the rules. Development had taken longer than five years in many cases and, although industrial development had been forbidden, a silk mill had been established behind what is now 45 Friar Gate. The frontage, though, is every bit as elegant as its neighbours' and this is due to the fine work of its architect, Joseph Pickford.

Joseph Pickford was born in Warwickshire in 1734. He was orphaned and sent to live with an uncle in London. He came to Derby as clerk of works and it was here that so much of his finest work was done. He also established his business in the town, and built his own home.

Pickford had studied under some of the most talented architects of the time. He had worked at Kedleston under the supervision of Robert Adam and

specialised in the Palladian style of architecture, so popular at the time.

But it was in Derby that much of his work was done, including his own home on Friar Gate. Elsewhere on Friar Gate his work can be seen at numbers 27, 42 and 44, which all formed part of the Nuns Green development. He designed the rebuilt 26-27 Queen Street (another architect later replaced Pickford's façade) and The Cedars (no 35) Ashbourne Road, as well as the Orangery at Markeaton Hall and the old Assembly Rooms which stood in the Market Place, the frontage of which was moved to the National Tramway Museum at Crich after the building was badly damaged by fire in 1963. In the Cornmarket he rebuilt Devonshire House for the Cavendish family. His most famous project in Derby, however, is most probably St Helen's House in King Street, once described as one of the finest Palladian townhouses in the country. It was built in 1767 for John Gisborne of Yoxall, Staffordshire.

Outside of the town he worked on projects such as Ogston Hall, Longford Hall, Calke Abbey, St Mary's

No 44 Friar Gate, designed by Joseph Pickford.

St Helen's House in King Street, pictured just after World War One.

Church in Birmingham (which features an unusual octagonal shape), Long Eaton Hall, several properties at Ashbourne, County Hall on High Pavement in Nottingham and Etruria Hall for Josiah Wedgwood, as well as the Etruria Works. This factory featured a huge windmill which had been designed by Erasmus Darwin.

Pickford built his own house as part of the Nuns Green development, at 41 Friar Gate. It served as both residence and business premises. Any prospective client visiting the architect would surely have been impressed by the range of smart housing he had created here. Since the remaining Nuns Green Pickford houses are out of bounds to the general visitor, having been converted to offices, it is well worth visiting the Pickford's House Museum in the architect's own home. For some years it has been a fascinating museum of Georgian life and features authentically furnished sitting rooms, bedrooms, kitchens and even bathrooms. As the other Pickford houses in Derby have been repeatedly adapted to provide modern facilities, No 41 is the most intact example of his work. Joseph Pickford died suddenly, in July 1782.

AMERICAN CONNECTIONS

IN the 18th century, Derby was fast becoming known around the world for its innovative technological advances and people from the town were pioneering industry and science across the globe, nowhere more so than North America. Yet Derbeians have made the arduous transatlantic crossing since the very earliest colonial days and have contributed immeasurably to the establishment of communities across the North American continent.

Derby's Pilgrims

When the Pilgrim Fathers landed at Cape Cod in 1620, they did so in great hope that they would be able to establish a community which would not suffer interference from authority, in particular a community that would enjoy freedom from religious intolerance.

They had come to Massachusetts to found an independent settlement based upon Puritan principles. In the three years that followed, a steady stream of new arrivals boosted the population of this fledgling village, which had been finally established on the mainland, at a place they would name Plimoth (*sic*) after their port of origin.

In 1623 John Oldham, his wife and his sister Lucretia, arrived at Plimouth on the *Anne*. Both John and Lucretia had been born in Derby and, although not Puritans, threw themselves enthusiastically into their new lives, although Lucretia would find the transition much easier than her brother. In 1624 she married Jonathan Brewster, son of the colony's leader, William. John Oldham, however, found it difficult to adapt to the strict rules imposed by the Puritans.

He constantly rebelled and was eventually banished from Plimoth when he and an associate were found to be in communication with a group in England who wanted to overthrow the Puritan colony and replace it with a British-controlled settlement. Oldham went to Nantucket and to Cape Ann and was eventually granted control of a stretch of land between the Saugus and Charles Rivers, on the outskirts of what is now the modern city of Boston. Here he became an important member of the community and helped establish a thriving settlement. In July 1636 he disappeared while on a trading mission at Block Island. Feeling sure he had been the victim of an Indian attack, fellow settlers retaliated and murdered many of the local native population. This and several similar incidents led to the Pequot War – the first of the American-Indian wars. The fate of Oldham remains a mystery.

The founder of Boston

One of the focal points for the Pilgrims while they were in England was the church of St Botolph's in Boston, Lincolnshire, the famous 'Boston Stump'. The minister here, John Cotton, was another native of Derby and he would become the founder of one of the New World's most important cities.

John Cotton, son of a local lawyer, was born in Derby in 1585. He was educated at Derby School and Cambridge University. For 29 years he served as minister at St Botolph's where his increasingly puritanical sympathies led him into conflict with his bishop who described him as being 'infected with Puritanism'.

In 1633 he was all but forced to sail for America and from Massachusetts he became the major civil and religious leader in New England and the founder of the city of Boston. He wrote many books and papers which helped to shape life in the colonies, and the way in which new settlements were established.

He wrote: 'When He makes a country, though not altogether void of inhabitants, yet void in the place where they reside. Where there be a vacant place, there is liberty for the sons of Adam or Noah to come and inhabit, though they neither buy it, nor ask their leaves… no nation is to drive out another without speciall commission from Heaven.'

John Cotton was minister of the first church in Boston and when he died in 1652 he was buried in the King's Chapel Burying Ground.

The scourge of 'witchcraft'

John Cotton's grandson, Cotton Mather, was also a Puritan preacher and he played a vital role in the Salem Witch Trials of 1692. Mather believed strongly in witchcraft, publishing a book in 1689 outlining a particular case of bewitchment that had occurred in Boston. In 1692 a circle of girls in Salem began to exhibit exactly the same symptoms he had described in his book. Almost immediately Mather declared: 'An Army of Devils is horribly broke in upon the place which is our centre.' Although Mather did not serve as a judge at any of the hearings, nor is there definitive evidence to prove he attended the trials, all the judges were familiar to him, and three of them were members of his congregation in Boston where he would frequently lecture them on the dangers of 'bewitchment'.

The judges did not have the benefit of modern opinion which suggests that the people of Salem may have been the victims of fakery, of a prank gone wrong, of drug abuse intentional or otherwise, of psychological disturbance or even a form of food poisoning which brought about hallucinations. Whatever the cause, it was Mather who eventually drew a halt to the proceedings, presumably by now concerned that the growing number of witches and victims threatened to account for the whole colony. However Mather continued to fear witchcraft. In 1693 he wrote an account of the trials from court records, which effectively excused the horrors.

The town that almost became 'Derby'

No doubt there were many more Derbeians who would begin new lives in North America, many in New England. One father and son from Derby were able to transport the essence of the Derby Philosophical Society and the Industrial Revolution across the Atlantic.

Kirk Boott was the son of a Derby greengrocer and market gardener. In the spring of 1783 he left his home on King Street and set sail for Boston, taking with him 25 packages of seeds and hardware which he intended to sell to the burgeoning population. When he arrived in June, he found it nearly impossible to sell his wares, since it seemed the entire population was trying to do the same. Eventually, he managed to sell enough goods to send for more supplies, this time tailoring them to the needs of his customers. It was not long before his business of selling clothing and household goods began to make a good profit and by November he was able to open a shop. Among his early customers was the Revolutionary hero Paul Revere. Boott married Mary Lowe, an Englishwoman who had

Above: Kirk Boott junior, who oversaw the development of the US town of Lowell after being inspired on visits to his father's birthplace of Derby. *Below:* Memorial tablet to Derby-born American merchant Kirk Boott senior, in the King's Chapel, Boston, Massachusetts.

travelled on the same ship as he and who owned her own millinery business. Kirk and Mary had nine children and they built a grand mansion in an affluent part of Boston.

Two of their sons, John and Kirk junior, were taken to England to obtain a formal education at Rugby School. Both boys travelled around England and frequently visited their aunt in Derby. Kirk, in particular, formed a lifelong affection for the town. In 1806, the young Kirk attended Harvard but did not graduate. He fought in the British Army in the Napoleonic Wars and in 1817, Kirk senior died in Boston. One year later Kirk junior married Ann Haden at St Michael's Church in Derby. Ann came from a well-to-do family and as a young girl had been painted by Joseph Wright. Kirk returned to Boston to join the family business.

Back in Massachusetts, Boott sought to branch out. Whilst in Derby he had been inspired by the work of the Strutts and he could see endless possibilities for his American home state. He set out a proposal to establish a cotton manufacturing business on the banks of the Merrimack River. With the assistance of William Strutt, who helped Boott design the mill and machinery, Boott oversaw the entire project, which was to be the first large-scale industrial planning project on the North American continent. The mills were very like those in Derby and the workers' cottages were neat and tidy. There was even a boarding house for single women workers. In the 1840s, Charles Dickens toured the town and was most impressed with the facilities provided.

There had been a number of investors in the project and it was one of them, Francis Cabot Lowell, after whom the rest of the investors elected to name their settlement. Boott had wanted to name the new town Derby, but he was able to design the town's first church, St Anne's, as a copy of St Michael's. Boott had a great deal of influence in Lowell, being a director of almost every corporation that was established from the Boston and Lowell Railroad, and the Lowell Bank to the Lowell Brewery and the Lowell Fire Department. Some felt that Boott was in control of too many organisations, but he was generally regarded as fair-minded and well-mannered.

Kirk Boott junior died in 1837 when a carriage tipped over on a street corner. He was greatly missed.

Many Derbeians travelled to Lowell to work for Boott, including William Duesbury III who bigamously married a Lowell widow and eventually committed suicide. Another resident was William Coffee, the former Crown Derby painter and sculptor. By 1844 the population of Lowell had grown to 28,000. It now stands at over 100,000 and the Boott mills are open to the public and are a popular tourist destination. Boott's former home is a hospital.

Among the more famous sons of Lowell are the artist James Abbott MacNeill Whistler and the author Jack Kerouac.

As American as the hotdog?

Over the centuries there have been many Derbeians who have moved to North America and made their own impact upon that land, but few have contributed something which, whilst it did not change the world, nor did it save lives, has had an impact on American popular culture itself.

The hotdog, that most American of American fast-

Derby around the world

In 1642 Derby gave its name to a small settlement in North America – Derby, Connecticut, is the smallest city in the state with 12,000 residents. Originally an important trading post, the area had been inhabited by Paugassett and Pootatuck Indians for several centuries, but the first permanent European settler was Edward Wooster. During World War Two, Derby, CT donated a fire truck to be used by Derby, England. German naval forces in the Atlantic sank the transport carrying the vehicle and it was lost at sea. In 1779, several citizens of Derby, CT founded a new settlement close to the Canadian border. Today Derby, Vermont has a population of around 4,500 people. Another Derby, this time a larger settlement of some 18,000 people, was founded in 1869 in Kansas as a stage and freight stop serving the local agricultural community. Originally known as El Paso, it bears the nickname 'The Tree City'.

Derby, Western Australia, was an important centre during the first Australian gold rush, and was founded in 1880 as a cattle station and port for the export of cattle from the area. To this day, it remains known for its pastoral and mining industries. It lies surrounded by spectacularly pretty coastal scenery and is becoming an important tourist destination. A few miles away stands the famed Boab Prison Tree, which was used as an overnight cell for prisoners on their way to Derby, WA.

Elsewhere across the globe there are at least 20 other settlements bearing the name Derby, as well as ridges, gullies and canyons. Quite a legacy.

food snacks, has conquered the world. Be it the steamy streets of New York City, the local cineplex, the hullaballoo of the fairground, or the cold, damp Saturday afternoon on the way to Pride Park, the hotdog is the perfect comfort food. And as American as 'Mom's Apple Pie'? Well no, not really. The modern hotdog was created and marketed by a man from Derby. His name was Harry Stevens, a Derbeian through and through, and his story, and the story of the world-famous snack, are inextricably entwined.

Harry Stevens was born in Litchurch in 1856, the eldest son of James Stevens, a foreman at the Midland Railway. He emigrated to the United States in 1890, settling in New York City and, as one of literally thousands of immigrants seeking employment, at first struggled to make his way. But Stevens was a resourceful, imaginative man and saw the booming sport of baseball as a way of making money. He set up a business printing and selling baseball scorecards and bought a concession in New York's famous Polo Grounds – then home of the New York Giants – where he sold vast quantities of his scorecards, quickly making a small fortune.

Stevens reinvested his money, setting up a number of concession stands inside the ballpark from which he sold snacks to spectators. It was Harry Stevens who was credited with inventing the idea of drinking carbonated drinks from a bottle using a straw, so as not to miss any vital action on the field. His business boomed and fans queued eagerly for the staple fare of hard-boiled eggs, ice-creams and sodas.

But while this type of food was popular throughout the hot and humid New York summers, springtime in the city can be very cold, and one particularly chill day, around the turn of the century, the fans were refusing their usual game-time snacks. Although unable to sell any of his own food, Harry knew just what to do. He was well-acquainted with the popular German 'dachshund' and 'frankfurter' sausages sold locally from shops and stands in the streets. Out went his vendors into the neighbourhood to buy as many of the long, thin sausages as they could. He cooked them up in hot water tanks, served them wrapped in bread as sandwiches and watched as his invention took off. He sent his hawkers around the ballpark calling: 'Get your red-hot dachshund sandwiches!'– and the crowds had found a new favourite.

Harry built up his business, setting up dachshund carts and stands on street corners across the city. Word spread and in just a few years, local versions of Harry Stevens' hotdogs were being sold at ballparks and on street corners right across the United States.

At this time, though, they were not known as 'hotdogs'. In Chicago they were 'red hots', on Coney Island 'frankfurters', elsewhere anything from 'wieners' to 'wurst'. For 'hotdogs' we have to return to the Polo Grounds, New York. One day Tad Dorgan, a cartoonist from the *New York Sun*, was at the game seeking inspiration – his task to report back with a topical baseball-related illustration. As he sat there, one of Stevens' hawkers walked past, shouting the familiar cry: 'Get your red hot dachshund sandwiches here!' An idea struck Dorgan and the next edition of the *New York Sun* carried a cartoon of a real dachshund dog, smeared in mustard and served up in a bread roll.

The legend goes that Dorgan either couldn't spell 'dachshund' or that the word was too long to fit his cartoon. In any event, Dorgan's caption read: 'Get your hot dogs here.' The idea captured the public imagination and the little sandwiches became universally known as 'hotdogs'.

Harry Stevens died a wealthy man in 1934, leaving his two sons to continue the thriving family business and the world was left with an 'American' legacy from a Derbeian born-and-bred.

RIOTS AND STRIKES

ONE of the side effects of the Enlightenment movement had been a greater awareness of the inequalities which were embedded in society, not least in the electoral system. Mass migration from the countryside to the towns had not been mirrored by any change in political boundaries. Populations in rural wards had decreased dramatically, while those in urban wards had done the reverse, leaving small pockets of wealthy landowners having a disproportionately strong influence on Parliament; many others in the towns were without representation at all.

Needless to say there was widespread discontent and in 1831 a Reform Bill had been passed through the House of Commons to even-out the anomalies. However, at 7pm on 8 October that year news reached Derby by mail coach that the Tory-controlled House of Lords had refused to pass the bill. Almost immediately sporadic unrest broke out. An angry crowd formed in the Market Place demanding the keys to the town's churches and a constant slow and steady peal of bells rang out through the night. Homes and businesses of those thought to have spoken against the bill were attacked. Windows in the

Market Place were broken and property damaged. The mob then moved on to the Friary where even the entreaties of William Baker, the Reformist banker of 44 Friar Gate, was unable to calm them. The scene was repeated right across the area as Tory properties as far apart as Markeaton and Chaddesden Halls were damaged. At the borough gaol a lamp post was uprooted and used as a battering ram to break open the door and set all 23 prisoners free. Prison guards at Vernon Street warned the rioters to keep away. But the mob moved onward and shots were fired into the crowd. Several people were injured, including a man named Garner who later died from his wounds. The disturbances continued for four days until word arrived that the bill had been passed, and by the time it was all over, two more had lost their lives – Henry Haden, son of a former mayor who had been attacked by a group of rioters, and an innocent who had died whilst sheltering in the doorway of the Greyhound Inn. Protesters had also torn up the empty stalls in the Market Place. The restoration of peace was only temporary however. Two years later Derby was in the midst of one of the world's first industrial disputes.

Markeaton Hall, damaged during the Reform Bill Riots of 1831. Over a century later the hall was demolished after years of neglect had left it unsafe.

The Silk Mill Lock Out

A minor economic recession hit the textile industry in the early 1830s and owners had been searching for cheaper methods of production. Some had reduced their workers' pay and others had taken advantage of new developments in technology and laid off many of their employees. As a means of protection, workers began to form small trades unions. Such unions had been banned by an Act of Parliament of 1799, during the war against Revolutionary France. In 1825 this was repealed and union membership was, in theory at least, lawful. In practice it was difficult because employers could still place workers under pressure not to join.

Now, however, conditions had changed and workers felt that, with so many of them joining together, the owners would surely listen to their voices, grant them some measure of security, improve their working conditions and perhaps even increase their pay. But the owners were suspicious of the unions, fearing they would at best interfere with the smooth running of the factories and mills and at worst seriously challenge their authority.

In November 1833, this came to a head in Derby when Ralph Frost, a silk mill owner, dismissed a worker who had refused a fine imposed for shoddy workmanship. Immediately, his colleagues walked out in protest. The unions soon rallied to the cause and workers all across Derby joined the strike. As seemingly minor an incident as it had been, this one dismissal was only the first encounter in a test of strength that would see employer and employee pitted against one another for several months. Derby, meanwhile, became the centre of attention for union leaders and factory owners across Britain.

Concerned that the dispute was spiralling out of control, the mill and factory owners met at the King's Head in the Cornmarket where they resolved to prevent any escalation. Naively they believed that if they refused to employ any worker who was part of a union, then the workforce would back down and the conflict would be avoided. The scene was set for the Derby 'Turn Out' or 'Lock Out' as it became known.

The unions became even more determined and as many as 1,800 workers may have joined the strike. Desperate to restore production, many owners brought in workers from outside the area, which served only to anger the unions still further. They called these incomers 'Black Sheep' and they and their families were subjected to verbal and some-times physical abuse as they went to and from the mills. Seemingly every day an argument between the strikers and the Black Sheep resulted in an appearance before the magistrates. Usually the defendant was a striker who might have been arrested simply for mocking his rival. Two women union members were arrested for allegedly insulting 'scab' women workers, and Thomas Mead was imprisoned for three months for trying to persuade another mill worker to join the strike.

Sometimes these disputes erupted into serious violence such as the events of 8 February 1834 when one of the Black Sheep met up with some of his colleagues who were just leaving the Seven Stars on King Street. He complained of some minor trouble he had had with strikers and his fellow workers decided to seek out the strikers and mete out some trouble of their own. A scuffle developed when the rival groups confronted one another and one of the Black Sheep, a man named Ingram, stabbed a man he believed to be one of the strikers, seriously wounding him. Ironically the victim, Joshua Brown, was not a member of the union and was standing in his own doorway simply observing the scene when he had been attacked. Ingram was sentenced to death, but this was commuted to transportation for life. Dragoons and special constables were deployed around the town to keep order.

One of the workers tempted to Derby by the promise of work in a brand-new factory said later: 'When we arrived at Derby, Lord, how ashamed I was! We were hooted and hissed by the women and children at the entrance to the factory in a dreadful manner… We were locked in night and day like prisoners on board a hulk…' Eventually he and a colleague climbed over a wall and escaped back to London.

By March 1834 the strike pay of 7s (35p) per week had run out and in April most of the strikers asked to be reinstated, although 600 found there was now no job for them. Trouble rumbled on, however, and as late as June, a strike-breaker who had been in Derby for only a week was brutally assaulted near Kedleston Street. Soon, however, a bill was passed through Parliament confirming the rights of workers to form trades unions and the 'Derby Silk Mill Lock Out' entered the annals of trades union folklore.

TRANSPORT BY CANAL

ONE of the key elements in the Industrial Revolution had been the easy transportation of materials and goods brought about by the completion of the canals, and later the railways. For literally hundreds of years the rivers of Britain had been used to transport goods around the country. But while this had been an efficient system for much of that time, by the middle of the 18th century many rivers were beginning to silt up, and although enormous efforts were made to redefine the banks and ensure that rivers were deep enough for safe passage, this was proving both ineffective and expensive. The River Derwent, in particular, had never been particularly easy to navigate. Like many ancient rivers it meanders and loops around on itself, becoming shallow in many places. There did exist a canalised stretch of the river from the Trent at Sawley to the centre of Derby which was known as the Derwent Navigation.

Water colour painting by George Vauser junior, looking towards Derby from the canal at Nottingham Road about 1858.

The building of artificial canals, which would not silt up and could take the most direct routes right into the centre of urban areas, was becoming popular across the country. A huge network was being built, linking all corners of England, and it was essential for Derby to join that network or risk losing its competitive edge. Where canals had been built, local industries had been revolutionised. One horse could pull a cart carrying two tons, but the same horse could pull a canal barge carrying 100 tons. Materials and goods could be transported quickly and cheaply, so costs were being reduced and profits increased; canals were of benefit to both manufacturer and consumer.

The White Bear Lock on Derby Canal around 1900. It took its name from the pub which until 1969 stood on the corner of Exeter Street.

To ensure that Derby could compete with other industrial settlements, Benjamin Outram and his partner, William Jessop, were assigned to survey for an appropriate route. Two proposals were put forward. The first was for Derby to be connected to the proposed Nottingham and Derbyshire Canal via a specially-constructed branch. The second was to build a Derby Canal which at one end would link with the Erewash Canal at Sandiacre and at the other with the River Trent, crossing the newly-opened Trent and Mersey Canal in the process. The second option was selected since it had the added advantage of linking the town with the surrounding coalfields. Investors were found immediately but an Act of Parliament ruled that they could receive dividends of no more than eight per cent. All other profit was to be held in reserve to subsidise tolls and keep prices down. Another condition was the toll-free delivery of at least 5,000 tons of coal to the poor of Derby.

The Derby Canal was completed in 1796 and was 20 miles in length with nine locks and a three-mile branch to Little Eaton. One spur flowed past the Nottingham Road porcelain factory and, towards Darley Abbey, part of the river was canalised. Much of the cargo was coal, of course, but the Derby Canal also transported grains, stone and a variety of other goods.

The Long Bridge near Derby River Gardens. It carried the towpath of the canal over the River Derwent.

The Grand Junction Canal Company ran daily boats to and from London, Leicester, Leamington and Warwick and had offices on Cockpit Hill. In the centre of Derby, at the Morledge where the canal crossed the river, several busy cargo wharves were established. From here twice-weekly boats left for Hull and Wolverhampton and there were regular services to Liverpool, Manchester and the Staffordshire Potteries. Each Friday a boat would travel from Swarkestone to Derby for market day, the ride costing 6d (2½p).

A legacy of Derby's canal days. The Canal Tavern on Cockpit Hill.

One particularly interesting feature which remained intact, although obscured, until 1971 was the 44ft-long Holmes Aqueduct (1796), built to take the canal over the Derwent and Markeaton Brook. It was the world's first cast-iron aqueduct, beating Thomas Telford's more famous one at Longden Wharf by several weeks. In addition, it was only the third cast-iron bridge of any kind in the world – after Abraham Darby's Ironbridge at Coalbrookdale (1781) and the old Wearmouth Bridge (1796) at Sunderland.

Because the Derby Canal joined the River Trent directly, it was now possible for boats to reach the Derby area without having to travel along the Trent and Mersey Canal, but merely by crossing it. Not surprisingly the operators soon became unhappy with this arrangement and enforced a sizeable toll on anyone trying to cross at this junction. This section of the Derby Canal eventually lost so much money that the only feasible option was to close it and terminate the canal at the Trent and Mersey.

For a number of reasons the Derbyshire coalfields were losing out to those in Staffordshire and the Derby Canal was asked to lower coal carriage charges. The board reluctantly agreed, but soon discovered that this had no positive effect on the Derbyshire coalfields' business, so they restored the prices, increasing the mining companies' losses in the process. Soon, mining companies were investigating the possibility of a new, more exciting mode of transport – the railways – and the days of the canals were numbered.

The new railways had several advantages over the canals, not least that they were exempt from the restrictions which had handicapped the waterways. They were not expected to subsidise industry or passengers. The railways quickly became dominant and, in most cases, the canal companies were able to sell their concerns to the local railway company, but the railways showed no interest in the Derby Canal. It literally wasted away. Although it was not until the second half of the 20th century that the last vestiges of the Derby Canal were removed, it had been little more than a strip of stagnant water for decades.

A RAILWAY TOWN

FOR many years there had been a widespread horse-drawn freight service from Derby to destinations such as Alfreton, Burton upon Trent, Chesterfield, Heanor, Matlock and Ilkeston. The main form of passenger transportation, meanwhile, had been the stage coaches. Regular services ran from the Tiger and King's Head in the Cornmarket to London, Birmingham, Manchester and Nottingham; from the Bell in Sadler Gate to London, Manchester and Nottingham; from the King Street offices of the Royal Mail to London, Manchester, Birmingham and Sheffield. However, the high cost of these services had prohibited all but the wealthiest citizens.

Regular stage coach services ran from the King's Head in the Cornmarket.

At 1.18 pm on Thursday, 30 May 1839, the first steam locomotive drew up at Derby station and 500 passengers stepped on to a temporary platform. That first journey, from Nottingham, had taken just 48 minutes and it would instantly and irrevocably change the lives of every Derbeian. Five days later the first public passenger service between the two towns began, operated by the Midland Counties Railway Company. There were four trains each day on Mondays to Saturdays and two on Sundays. The second-class fare cost 2s 6d (12½p) and, although this was more than the average daily wage, it was much cheaper than the stage coach service.

In August of that year the Birmingham & Derby Junction Railway introduced three trains every weekday with two on Sundays. A regular Birmingham to London service had recently been introduced and for the first time it was possible to travel from Derby to London by train. In June the following year, the North Midland Railway established a route between Derby and Leeds.

In the early days, plans had been made for a centrally-located railway station near to the Market Place, but these had been rejected; mercifully, the rail lines had been kept away from the centre of town and the mass demolition and redevelopment of the area was thus avoided. Now the new station, situated on Castlefields, was far enough away that special horse-drawn carriages had to be laid on to ferry passengers to the town centre and back.

By 1840 work had begun on a 30-acre (12-hectare) complex to replace the temporary wooden platform that had welcomed those first trains to Derby. As well as the station itself, workshops, offices, a locomotive works, a hotel and railway workers' cottages were planned. The Midland Hotel – still in operation today – opened in 1843 and is claimed to be the first purpose-built railway hotel in the world. The delightful Railway Cottages were a world-first too and have recently benefited from a programme of conservation and restoration to make them much sought-after properties. The station was used by all three companies which amalgamated in 1844 to form the Midland Railway. The Derby Locomotive Works had opened in 1840 and by 1851 were designing and building complete locomotives.

Derby's railway cottages, the first such purpose-built homes in the world.

In 1876 the new Great Northern Railway opened, utilising a purpose-built station to the west of the town at Friar Gate. The construction of the line had caused considerable controversy since its route took it through many of the prettiest parts of the town, most notably Friar Gate itself. Construction of the line and the station meant the demolition of a number of houses, both working and middle-class dwellings, and Parliament had assigned local photographer Richard Keene to record the condition of the buildings which were at risk. However, it seems that only the more run-down and industrial premises were presented and so permission was granted to proceed. One particular casualty was the lovely and ancient timber-framed Old White Horse inn, which stood approximately where the cobblestoned yard next to Friar Gate Bridge is today. Despite protestations the licensee, Ann Taylor, was not permitted to transfer the licence to other premises and a traditional drinking venue of several hundred years was lost forever.

The ornate iron Friar Gate bridge which carried the railway is itself now legally protected and does present an elegant, if dominating, sight. Alongside the station a huge goods yard was established, including an unusual trapezium-shaped warehouse which survives to this day, although it has been horribly neglected over recent years. It served as a huge store for all manner of goods over three levels. In the basement, 12ft (3.6m) below ground, bonded goods were stored; on the ground floor was more

storage with several hydraulic lifts and winches. The storage loft above featured two grain chutes and 10 hydraulic cranes. There was also a large office complex within the warehouse.

Another railway station was opened on Nottingham Road, not far from the Racecourse and the County Ground, but like the station at Friar Gate its day has long gone. On Osmaston Park Road, Pear Tree station survives as a halt for workers.

Although the industry has been largely decimated by modern developments and changes of ownership, Derby's railway heritage continues, a proud tradition, to this day.

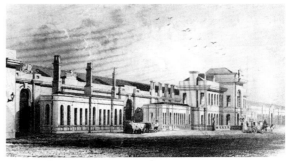

Derby's Midland station in the 1870s.

The positive impact which the coming of the railways had on Derby as a whole cannot be underestimated. Manufacturing grew and shops and other businesses flourished. But its side-effects, coupled with those of the Industrial Revolution itself, had serious repercussions. We have already seen what had happened in the West End when many workers were packed into a small area, and the same pattern was in danger of being repeated right across

Passengers wait at Derby Midland station in the early years of the 20th century.

Friar Gate in 1872, showing the house built for William Fallowes about 1760. The photograph was one of several taken by the eminent Derby photographer Richard Keene, who was commissioned by those wishing to demolish the properties to make way for the railway. The London plane trees are newly-planted.

the town. There was an urgent need for improved facilities to serve the burgeoning population which grew from 13,000 in 1811 to 23,000 in 1831; 37,000 in 1841; and 81,000 in 1881. By the census of 1851, only 12 years after the arrival of the railway, more than 40 per cent of the adult population had been born outside the county borders. Huge areas of land, much of which was taken from the estates of the wealthier families, were given over to housing for the new workers, much of it concentrated in the area surrounding the new railway complex. In addition to the Railway Cottages, there was the development of Castlefields, Litchurch, Normanton, New Normanton, Pear Tree, Rose Hill, Strutt's Park and the Rowditch.

However, in all urban areas which were growing apace, crime was on the increase too, and in Derby, as elsewhere, new measures had to be introduced.

Friar Gate, showing Handyside's bridge in 1931 with an LNER train passing over it.

CRIME AND PUNISHMENT

THE Nuns Green Acts had established a commission to oversee the vital task of town improvements and were so-called because much of the money used to benefit the town was raised from the sale of plots on that part of the town. The commissioners were active until the Public Health Act of 1848 and they steered through a radical programme of development. Once more at the helm was the Strutt family – in particular William and Joseph, who served as mayor in the 1830s.

The sudden increase in population and, in particular, population density had led to elevated crime levels. Although Derby was a relatively peaceful town when compared with somewhere like Nottingham, there was plenty to keep the Assize Courts busy. Concerns were growing for the safety of the townsfolk and in 1836 a small borough police force was formed. Consisting of eight constables and 10 watchmen who served night duties, it preceded the Derbyshire Constabulary by 20 years although an informal system of local constables were put in place there by 1838. The Derbyshire force was responsible for policing some of modern Derby's more outlying suburbs which then lay outside the borough.

Officers were issued with cutlasses to defend themselves against troublemakers and drunks and regular cutlass drills, as well as inspections, were held in the Arboretum. Each officer had a large area to patrol but had to do so on foot. Only senior officers were permitted the use of pony and dog carts. Some local businesses in the county employed their own police officers, who served a similar role to modern-day security guards. After World War One, motor vehicles were introduced for senior officers and regular motor patrols began in 1931; during World War Two the first policewomen were employed as drivers. Two-way radios were introduced into motor vehicles in 1951 but well into the 1960s foot patrolling policemen had no personal radios. In case of emergency, they would have to attract attention using a whistle, or perhaps by using one of the police boxes. They made their 'points' with their sergeant. Otherwise, contact with other officers was minimal. There were few patrol cars and officers would often have to walk arrested suspects through the town to

their station. As the borough grew to absorb surrounding suburbs, so the force grew in numbers. In 1967, Derby Borough Police merged with Derbyshire Constabulary. The police station for the old borough force was in Full Street, where an extension was added in the 1960s, and the Derby HQ for the county force was in St Mary's Gate. The Derbyshire force's HQ is now at Ripley but in March 2001 a state-of-the-art police headquarters for Derby and South Derbyshire was officially opened by the Princess Royal at St Mary's Wharf.

Concern for maintaining public order was nothing new. The Middle Ages had seen the establishment of a legal system that for centuries remained heavily biased in favour of the ruling classes. Initially, although perhaps unsurprisingly, the crimes that risked the higher sentences were those in which the ruling classes were the victims, and those with the lighter sentences were more likely perpetrated by the ruling classes. So crimes like theft, which were against property – of which the lower classes had little or none and the ruling classes plenty – were deemed more serious. And although William the Conqueror had outlawed execution, it was the Normans who gave us the word 'murder' which comes from Norman *mudrum* which meant, specifically, to kill a Norman.

One of the more colourful medieval punishments was the ducking stool, one of which, according to Victorian historian Stephen Glover, stood at the bottom of St Mary's Gate. Presumably the water into which the unfortunates were dunked was that of Markeaton Brook.

Conditions in prisons like those in the Market Place and on Willow Row were notoriously awful. Those responsible for serious crimes were usually sent to Nottingham, but in 1552 a new county gaol opened near St Peter's Bridge at the end of the Cornmarket. The cells were cramped, dirty and foul-smelling. Near Markeaton Brook they were liable to flooding and there was more than one fatality by drowning. Sewage flowed into the gaol and many prisoners died of typhoid, known then as 'gaol fever', before they even reached trial. In 1756 the county gaol moved to Friar Gate, on a site later occupied by the Howard Hotel. Remnants of the old cells and the exercise yards are still in existence and now form a small museum and cafe. In recent years it has been suggested that the condemned and debtors' cells themselves remain intact, but records indicate that there was never a specific condemned cell at either the Friar Gate or Vernon Street gaols – the most convenient cell at the time would have been used. Vernon Street was one of the earliest prisons to feature separation of debtors, felons and those on remand from other criminals. At Friar Gate prisoners of all kinds were normally billeted together, sometimes five or six to a tiny cell. Built to house 21 prisoners in seven cells, the Friar Gate gaol was almost always full to overflowing and consequently it was not long (1826) before the new county gaol was opened at nearby Vernon Street. The old prison was handed over to the borough.

The last person to be hanged at Derby was William Edward Slack, who went to the gallows in Vernon Street on 16 July 1907 after being found guilty of the murder of Lucy Wilson, who he had killed with a hatchet in Chesterfield. Henry Pierrepoint was the last hangman to ply his trade in Derby.

During World War One, Vernon Street became a military prison before its conversion to a greyhound stadium in the 1930s. After the track closed in the mid-1980s the complex lay derelict before being converted to the elegant Vernon Gate business and housing complex in the late 1990s.

Whilst the early Norman kings had preferred maiming or blinding to execution, the death penalty had been reintroduced in the 12th century and little time had been lost in utilising this new punishment. Derbyshire's earliest recorded execution took place in the middle of the 14th century, but there are certain to have been unrecorded executions before this date. By the time of the Tudor era, execution victims stood at around 2,000 a year in England alone.

One of the most hideous punishments was not administered following a guilty verdict at all – it was given to those who refused to plead in the first place. Legally known as *peine, dure et forte* it is more familiar to us as pressing to death. It was not unknown for an accused man or woman to simply refuse to say whether they were guilty or not and the courts used pressing as an effective inducement to comply with their wishes. Perhaps the authorities

were all the more enthusiastic because the estate of those convicted, normally the property of the government, could be handed over only if a plea had been made.

The accused would be taken to a pitch-dark room, usually a cellar, where they had to lie naked on the ground with a large flat stone upon their bodies while 'a weight or iron as great as you can bear and greater' was placed there. The longer the accused refused to plead, the more weight he or she had to bear.

The victim was permitted only three morsels of bread on the first day, then three draughts of stagnant water on the second, and three more morsels of bread and so on. In 1665 the last pressing to death in the country took place at County or Shire Hall on St Mary's Gate. Here an unknown woman met her brutal death because she steadfastly refused to submit. Claims have been made by some that she was a mute, perhaps even deaf, and that she could not have pleaded even had she wanted to, which adds yet more pathos to the appalling tragedy of her

The Shire Hall in St Mary's Gate, scene of the last pressing to death in England.

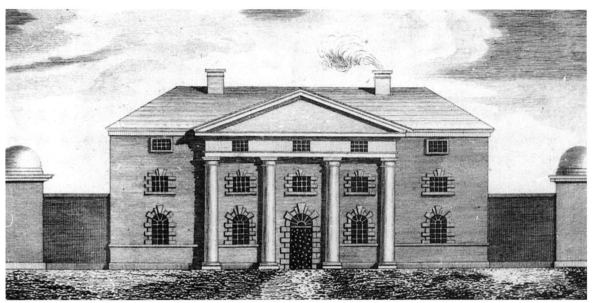

The county gaol in Friar Gate. The cells now form part of a museum.

case. But there is no evidence to support this theory, and probably some confusion has arisen from records stating that she was 'mute of malice', which is simply a legal term for refusing to plead.

For those who did plead there was the ordeal of a trial at the Assize courts. Assizes took place twice-yearly at Derby, in spring and summer, to try all serious cases. For many years the location for these was the original Guildhall in the Market Place. During a small outbreak of the Plague in 1645, the court had moved to private premises on what is now Friar Gate and in 1660 the forbidding Shire Hall was opened on St Mary's Gate, and continued to serve the town as Assize, County and Crown Courts until the opening of the new combined court building in the Morledge in the 1990s. Plans are now under way to revive Shire Hall as an active court as part of the new magistrates' court complex.

It was at Shire Hall that George Eliot set the trial of Hetty Sorrel in her popular novel *Adam Bede*. Hetty is a working-class woman who finds herself unmarried and pregnant and stands trial for the murder of her child. Although the details perhaps owe more to Eliot's imagination than to hard fact, the following passage from that book at least conveys something of the mood of the court. 'The place fitted up that day as a court of justice was a grand old hall... The midday light that fell on the close

pavement of human heads was shed through a line of high-pointed windows, variegated with the mellow tints of old painted glass. Grim dusty armour hung in high relief in front of the dark oaken gallery at the farther end, and under the broad arch of the great mullioned window opposite was spread a curtain of old tapestry, covered with dim melancholy figures, like a dozine indistinct dream of the past.'

Derby itself saw more than one real-life 'Hetty Sorrel'. Infanticide was one of the least forgiven of all crimes and, sadly, one of the most prevalent. In addition to the turmoil experienced by any new mother, a single mother faced almost unbearable pressures from society as she tried to protect herself and her child from scorn and disapproval and to support her offspring with little outside help. Many women resorted to abandoning their babies, even leaving them to die, sometimes desperate enough to hasten the infant's end themselves. Two who must have surely struggled with such a dilemma were Mary Dilkes, who was executed on Nuns Green for murdering her child, and 24-year-old Susannah Moreton who was convicted of the same offence but was reprieved on the morning of her execution.

If one examines only the numbers of executions and imprisonments in the town, one might imagine that Derby in the 17th, 18th and 19th centuries was a violent, hateful place. But that is far from the truth.

Under what became known as the Bloody Code, a huge number of offences – as many as 200 or more – were listed as capital crimes. Murder, of course, was one of them, as were many other serious offences such as robbery and rape, but many were at most minor offences, and many more are ridiculous by today's standards. Among the offences which called for the death penalty were poaching, damaging royal forests, counterfeiting and forgery, and even more incredibly, shoplifting, vandalism, letter-stealing and even keeping the company of gypsies.

Clearly many of the crimes, such as sheep and cattle stealing, theft and burglary, were driven by desperation and would have been committed, in most cases, by members of the poorer classes. There was nothing in the way of welfare for the very poor, save the humiliation of parish support, or later of the workhouse. These desperate men and women were far from being 'career criminals', rather they stole only when they needed something. They might steal food or valuable objects which could be sold on and the money used to pay off a debt or purchase some essential item for their families. With the stakes so high, any prospective wrongdoer would have to have a very good reason to literally risk their necks. Some observers argue that these draconian punishments served only to increase the severity of crimes committed, the offender reasoning that he or she might, literally, as well be hanged for a sheep as a lamb.

With so many hanging offences on the statute books it would have proved quite impossible to carry out every execution – every gallows in the country might well have been in non-stop use. The solution was to commute death sentences to transportation to the colonies, or life imprisonment. Around 50 per cent of those convicted had their lives spared. Whether one was lucky enough to avoid the hangman depended largely on the whim of the judges. If five people were condemned on one day, perhaps one or two might be executed as an example. Those with influential friends seemed to benefit more than others, as did those with families who would otherwise become the financial responsibility of the parish. Most of those executed were men, and a single, working-class man would find himself a far more likely choice to set an example to others.

As another discouragement to those considering a life of crime, the bodies of the executed could now be taken from the gallows and fastened inside an iron cage and hung from a prominent tree. Known as gibbeting, this gruesome procedure involved the body being shaven of hair and painted with a preservative tar. The slowly decomposing body might remain there for 20 years or more. There were at least two gibbeting sites in Derby – at Bradshaw Hay, which now lies in the grounds of the DRI; and at what is now the corner of Loudon Street and Normanton Road. Those who were not sent for gibbeting were usually sent for dissection. Often this took place in public; in Derby many such displays were held in Shire Hall. A physician would often perform the dissection in front of a group of anatomy students. Executions themselves had long been performed in public but in the 18th and 19th centuries it became a public 'entertainment'.

The Tudors had been the first to exploit the 'entertainment' potential of public execution days. They had established an almost ritualistic procedure that could regularly draw crowds numbering into thousands. Spectators would flock from surrounding towns and villages to watch the condemned being dragged through the streets from the gaol to the execition site fastened to a sledge-type device. Accompanying clergymen and local dignitaries performed a religious ceremony. This continued until the days of the Bloody Code when the ceremony was pared down, mainly for expediency. The gallows were placed high above the street, well above head height, affording everyone an excellent view. A statement of confession was read out. More often than not this was provided by the clergy who had been attending the condemned. It fulfilled a number of purposes, the purging of the soul not necessarily the most important. A public confession helped to justify the authorities' actions. Since the prisoner almost always blamed some moral inadequacies such as alcohol abuse or womanising, the Church's standpoint was also bolstered. And, of course, it added a greater depth of drama to the occasion.

The increasing regularity of executions under the Bloody Code did nothing to discourage spectators They packed the streets around Friar Gate where the executions took place. First in an area believed to be right in the middle of the street towards its Ashbourne Road end, then in front of the old county gaol, on the site which later became the Howard

The county gaol in Vernon Street, pictured in 1904. The last public hanging took place here in 1862; the last judicial execution of all in 1907.

Hotel, and later outside the new county gaol on Vernon Street (now the Vernon Gate development). There may also have been an early gallows at what is now Bradshaw Way, since records note a 'Gallows Baulk' in that area. At Vernon Street it is still possible to see evidence of those days of public hangings. To the side of the entrance is a grilled door in front of a small doorway. This is where the condemned would first enter the execution arena.

Far from being the speedy method of later years, hangings up to the late 19th century were tortuous. No account was taken of the weight or height of the body, so when it dropped there was usually not enough force to break the neck, or even to cause immediate unconsciousness. Death might take as long as 20 minutes as the victim was slowly strangled. The arms and legs of the prisoner were often bound to prevent the thrashing that usually accompanied the struggle against death and, in later years, a hood was placed over the head of the victim to hide facial contortions. Often the executioner would have to pull on the legs to expedite the process. It is often said that our 21st-century souls have been de-sensitised by the images of violence and destruction portrayed in some television dramas

or, indeed, in news programmes, but is is hard to imagine any of us being willing to witness such an awful sight as a man or woman being slowly strangled on the end of a rope. Yet literally thousands of our forebears not only regularly attended hangings, they participated in what became almost a fairground atmosphere. On public hanging days, Derby's inns did their best business of the year. Street traders, musicians, entertainers, food hawkers and pickpockets all gathered too. There were even souvenirs available for purchase, including a printed copy of the confession along with the life story of the accused and the details of the crime and the trial. Crowds could even buy gingerbread effigies of the condemned.

On days when a particularly notorious murderer, or several murderers together, might be on the gallows, crowds numbering 20,000 to 40,000 flocked to see the spectacle. Later, special trains were laid on to bring people from far and wide. On one occasion there was a mass fight at Derby station as a huge crowd tried to get on the same train at the same time. It was scenes like these and concerns for public safety as well as moral decency that eventually led to the abolition of public executions.

TRIALS AND EXECUTIONS

LIKE most large towns and cities, Derby has seen its fair share of sensational trials which have ended in the execution of the accused. John and Hannah Hewitt had a stormy, violent marriage. The husband was known to often beat his alcoholic wife. In 1732 he began an affair with Rosamund Ollerenshaw, a serving girl at the Crown Inn on Friar Gate. With the help of Rosamund's employer, Ellen Beare, the pair plotted the murder of Hannah. Precisely who performed what part of the plan is not clear, but Hannah died of arsenic poisoning shortly after eating a meal cooked by Ellen and served by Rosamund. Immediately suspicion fell on the lovers and on Mrs Beare, who was a notorious figure known to arrange a number of illegal services, most notably the performing of abortions. Rosamund claimed that Ellen had not been part of the plot and so, unlike the lovers who were executed on Nuns Green, she escaped with her life. She did stand trial for supplying the poison and for performing an abortion. She was sentenced to two one-hour sessions in the pillory and three years' imprisonment. During her first pillory session Ellen escaped and when she returned for her second, she wore several layers of thick clothing and padding to protect her from the stinking refuse hurled at her.

Around this time, the Crown Inn ceases to exist in records, apparently replaced by the Old White Horse, presumably a renaming of the inn to avoid association with Ellen Beare.

The murder of Mary Vickars
Forty-two years later, in December 1774, a Mrs Mary Vickars was disturbed by strange noises in her Tenant Street home. Going to investigate, she was confronted by two burglars, Matthew Cocklayne and George Foster. Cocklayne knocked her to the ground with an iron bar and the men stole £300 and, after threatening Mrs Vickars' maid, escaped from the house, narrowly avoiding a passing group of musicians. The two fled along Full Street and on to Nuns Green before splitting up to meet again in Liverpool. Here they learnt that Mrs Vickars had died of her injuries and that they were wanted for murder. The men sailed for Ireland where they continued in their chosen trade for some time before another robbery went wrong and Foster was shot dead. Cocklayne was arrested and returned to Derby for trial. Found guilty, he received the death penalty and was hanged from a tree on Nuns Green. At the request of Mrs Vickars' family his body was tarred and displayed in the gibbet at Bradshaw Hay. His remains hung there for many years and in 1791 a youth in Derby produced what was claimed to be Cocklayne's skull.

The Pentrich Revolutionaries
Perhaps the most well-known multiple hangings in Derby were those of the Pentrich revolutionaries in 1817. Jeremiah Brandreth, William Turner and William Ludlam were the local ringleaders in a disastrous plot to overthrow the government at a time when much of England was in a state of poverty following poor harvests, economic decline and rocketing unemployment.

Brandreth had been meeting regularly with a London man, William Oliver, who encouraged Brandreth and his friends to take part in a coup with the intention of establishing a US-style federation. Oliver claimed that hundreds of thousands of men across the country were ready to march on London where at least 50,000 more waited. After months of planning Brandreth led around 300 men towards Nottingham, believing that he would be joining up with a massive force. But the coup never had any chance of success. There were no hundreds of thousands, nor thousands, nor even hundreds. For Oliver was operating under a different agenda. He was a government spy appointed to infiltrate the rebels and relay their secrets to his contacts within the government. Many even suspected that Oliver had been sent to provoke the rebels into action.

With Oliver's constant updates, government forces were more than ready to disperse the small uprising. The rebels had travelled only as far as Giltbrook, near the present IKEA store at Eastwood, when word reached them that the army was preparing to confront them. Most scattered and fled. In all, 35 of them were captured. Turner at Codnor, Ludlam at Uttoxeter and Brandreth at Bulwell after weeks on the run and an aborted attempt to flee the country. All 35 were brought to the county gaol at Friar Gate and charged with high treason. Twelve were freed when no evidence was presented, six more received short prison sentences, another three were transported for 14 years, 11 more were given life imprisonment and four, one of whom was reprieved, were sentenced to be hanged, drawn and quartered, although the quartering was never carried out. Six thousand locals watched as each man was hanged and, in turn, beheaded –

the head of each being held high for the crowd to see. Their bodies were buried together in an unmarked grave at St Werburgh's Churchyard.

The last public spectacle

Derby's last public execution is one of its better known. In 1862 Eliza Morrow – a young, good-natured, flirtatious woman – had been involved in a romantic but turbulent relationship with Richard Thorley. Eliza had been a friend of both Thorley and his wife, and after Mrs Thorley's death the pair had begun meeting regularly. But Thorley had long had a reputation for violence and the death of his wife at so young an age had propelled him into dark moods and alcohol abuse. Thorley jealously guarded Eliza and was angry when he saw her flirting with other men. In particular, Thorley suspected that Eliza had been entertaining an Irish soldier at her home at Court No 4 in Agard Street. He had confronted Eliza in a noisy argument, but eventually had left. Clearly Thorley was not satisfied and he returned later that day and slit Eliza's throat. He ran from Agard Street to Abbey Street, where he called at the Old Spa Inn for a glass of ginger beer,

explaining away his blood-stained, bandaged hands as the result of an earlier fight. But several people had already placed Thorley at the scene of the crime and the police were already on their way. Thorley was arrested in Canal Street and his trial was one of the most dramatic held at Derby, particularly notable for the damning testimony of 11-year-old Charlie Wibberley. An estimated 20,000 people flocked to what would be the town's last public execution. The last execution of any kind in Derby took place on 16 July 1907 within the walls of the county gaol in Vernon Street. Thereafter prisoners were sent to Nottingham for execution.

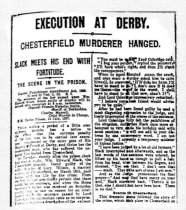

How the Derby Mercury reported the last judicial hanging at Derby. William Slack murdered Lucy Wilson with a hatchet at Chesterfield in 1907.

LESSONS FOR LIFE

THE philanthropists of Derby were not just concerned with the physical well-being of their fellow Derbeians – in line with the rest of the country they were also aware of the need for greater education for all and for the importance of leisure to the working man and woman.

Although Derby School had been in operation for several centuries, there had been little in the way of official education for those not fortunate to attend that establishment. All but the youngest of children were likely to be of working age and their only day of rest was Sunday. Churches of all denominations established their own free Sunday Schools, and it was here that the majority received their education. Of course, the whole point of a church teaching reading and writing was to encourage study of the Scriptures, but a happy side-effect of the ever-increasing array of churches and chapels in the town was the immediate improvement in basic literacy among young Derbeians.

In addition to the Sunday Schools, a few church schools were opened such as the National Schools in Traffic Street and Curzon Street and the Diocesan School on the corner of Vernon Street and Friar Gate. In addition, the

HERBERT SPENCER – DEFENDER OF LIBERTY

HERBERT Spencer was born in Derby at a house, now demolished, on Exeter Street on 27 April 1820. The Spencers later lived at 8 Wilmot Street (also since demolished). Herbert's father George took over his father Matthew's academy and taught Herbert until the age of 13. Herbert was the only child of nine born to survive beyond infancy.

Like so many philanthropists of the 18th and 19th centuries the Spencer family were Nonconformists – in their case Methodists with Quaker sympathies. From an early age Spencer was taught that every individual should be treated with equal respect regardless of their position in the world. His father felt so strongly about this that he refused to lift his hat in deference to anyone and called all men 'Mr' whether they be 'Reverend', 'Sir', 'Doctor' or 'Esquire'.

The senior Spencers passed on to Herbert their ideas for education and he firmly believed that children should be given as much freedom as possible during their education, rather than being subjected to a rigid, disciplined regime.

Throughout his life Herbert Spencer was a passionate defender of liberty and was active in the anti-slavery movement stating: 'No one can be perfectly free till all are free; no one can be perfectly moral till all are moral; no one can be perfectly happy till all are happy.'

At the age of 15 he had his first article (about boats) published.

Herbert Spencer, the Derby-born philosopher who coined the phrase 'survival of the fittest', more commonly attributed to Charles Darwin.

'I found my article looking very pretty... I began shouting and capering about the room... And now that I have started I intend to go on writing things.'

And so he did, writing throughout his life many articles, papers and books on subjects as wide ranging as sociology, psychology, education, ethics, biology and politics. More than 1,000,000 copies of his various works were sold in Europe and

North America during his lifetime. His work was translated into at least five languages. His books became standard texts at Oxford and Harvard and his theories were studied at most of the major universities.

Despite his success, Spencer eschewed a luxurious lifestyle. In 1837 he had taken a job with the railways and returned to Derby in 1841. He spent several years working as a sub-editor at *The Economist* and although he was eventually able to establish a professional writing career, he chose to live in relative simplicity.

His first book, *Social Statistics*, was published in 1851 and much of it was devoted to his assertion that human progress, such as industrialisation, had occurred naturally at will, without government intervention. He stated that it had been humans who, feeling free to do so, had chosen to develop farmland and subsequently to build cities because they so desired, not because of any government's intervention. And that the most remarkable and important human achievements had been solely the result of human spontaneity.

Spencer believed passionately that every individual should be free to do as he or she wishes. In his chapter 'The Right to Ignore the State' Spencer says: 'If every man has freedom to do all that he wills, provided he infringes not the equal freedom of any other man, then he is free to drop connection with the State, to relinquish

protection and toward paying for its support. It is self-evident that in so behaving he in no way trenches upon the liberty of others, for his position is a passive one, and while passive he cannot become an aggressor.'

Spencer was also adamant that there should be no trade restrictions, no nationally subsidised Church, no central banks and no government postal monopolies. In its purest form, Spencerism also left no room for any kind of State assistance for those unable to support themselves. In a perfect example of the phrase which Spencer first coined – 'survival of the fittest' – he believed that the best-equipped to succeed would flourish naturally. This left behind those less able and some of Spencer's theories have become unfashionable since the establishment of the Welfare State. 'We have the unmistakable proof that throughout all past time, there has been a ceaseless devouring of the weak by the strong.'

In his book of 1884, *Man Versus the State*, Spencer was critical of the way that laws and rules and government initiatives often backfired. He cited an example in London where 21,000 sub-standard homes had been demolished and replaced by 12,000 better properties, leaving the residents of the 9,000 deficit effectively homeless.

Respected by many of the leading lights of the day, Spencer was a close friend of Mary Ann Evans (the novelist George Eliot)

and steel magnate Andrew Carnegie. Many had suggested that Spencer and Evans might marry, but the relationship appeared to remain a platonic one based on mutual interests and beliefs.

Carnegie had been so impressed with Spencer's theories that he actively pursued a correspondence with him.

'Few men have wished to know another man more strongly than I do to know Herbert Spencer,' he said. In 1891 Carnegie gave Spencer a grand piano as a symbol of his regard.

Oliver Wendell Holmes doubted that 'any writer of English, except Darwin [Charles] has done so much to affect our whole way of thinking about the universe.'

The ever forward-thinking Spencer witnessed the severe Derby flood of April 1842 and had designed a flood prevention system that was rejected by the borough. Ironically, this was the same system finally adopted by the town after another disastrous flood some 90 years later.

In later years, Spencer suffered debilitating health problems which may have included depression. He was regarded as something of a hypochondriac and an insomniac, and regularly used opium. He was able to write for only a few hours a day. Becoming reclusive and increasingly eccentric, he took to wearing earplugs to save himself from having to listen to others. He died in Brighton in 1903.

British Girls' School on Chapel Street taught sewing and knitting as well as the 3Rs. The Lancastrian School on Orchard Street was reserved for boys only.

The cost for a week's education at these establishments ranged from 1d to 3d per student. For the children of the more wealthy families, education was usually provided either by public schools such as Repton, if they were particularly wealthy, or by private academy or tutor, of which there were several. The most notable of these was that established in 1789 by Matthew Spencer at 4 Green Lane. Spencer had been well acquainted with – and been inspired by – the members of the Derby Philosophical Society and his academy, which numbered the Darwin, Strutt and Whitehurst children among its pupils, became noted for its diverse curriculum that included the detailed study of science and art subjects in addition to the usual English and Mathematics. Spencer's knowledge and passion for learning was inherited by most of his family, most famously by his grandson Herbert, the philosopher.

As the population expanded and the spread of knowledge became paramount, there was a move towards universal education. From 1833 the government did issue grants to help in the establishment and running of schools. In 1849 a Ragged School was opened to cater for the children of the very poor.

But it was as late as 1870, when the Elementary Education Act became law, that universal free education became available. Under the watchful eyes of the Derby School Board, all children were expected to attend school until the age of 12. Several 'Board Schools' were opened around the town and surrounding suburbs and villages. Among the earliest of these were Abbey Street and Gerard Street Schools near the town centre (demolished in the 1970s), and Ashbourne Road School (now Ashgate).

Another educational establishment of the 19th century and one of which Derbeians can be justly proud was founded by William Roe as the Midland Deaf and Dumb Institute and is now known as the Royal School for the Deaf and the College for Deaf People.

Roe's work with the deaf had begun many years before. From the age of 20 he had spent much of his spare time teaching uneducated deaf adults at his father's house in Kedleston Road, Derby. As news of

The Royal Institution for Deaf and Dumb in Friar Gate. The building was opened in 1894, although the institution itself was founded in 1879.

The former Bishop Lonsdale's college for training schoolmistresses on Uttoxeter New Road. Pictured here in 1918, more than 80 years later it remains virtually unaltered.

Roe's work spread, parents began to bring their deaf children to see him and in 1873 Roe became a committee member of the Derbyshire Association for the Deaf.

The aim of the association was to make deaf children more independent and self-confident so, from premises at Becket Well Lane, children were given an education, some being sent to London and Birmingham for more formal training. There was as strong an emphasis on physical education as there was academic studies, and Roe's students won the National Physical Recreation Society's All England Challenge Shield in its early years.

Eventually Roe's work became so time-consuming that he decided to work full-time with the association. In 1880 he began raising funds to build a dedicated institution in Derby, and by 1883 a site had been acquired on Friar Gate. Work was completed by October 1894 at a cost of £12,000. Just three years later, Queen Victoria in her diamond jubilee year, granted the 'Royal' title.

Among the many famous visitors to the Institution were Lord Baden-Powell, who had a particular interest in the Scout group based there, and Alexander Graham Bell, inventor of the telephone, whose wife was deaf.

The Institution was eventually renamed The Royal School for the Deaf and began to branch out in its activities. By 1935, at 93 Friar Gate (now demolished), the Roe Memorial Home for the Adult

Deaf was opened and in 1962 the school became the first organisation in the UK to establish further education for deaf people, with the opening of the College for Deaf People. In 1972 the School and College relocated to larger premises at Ashbourne Road.

The Royal School for the Deaf is still regarded as one of the premier such establishments and teaches a bilingual approach of both British Sign Language and written and spoken English to its students. Students on the site are either resident on campus or at the University of Derby. Studies are undertaken both at the college and at the mainstream colleges in the area. Facilities at both the school and the college are state-of-the-art and are constantly being updated and improved. One in four members of the professional staff are deaf and pupils study for GCSEs, other vocational certificates and participate in the Duke of Edinburgh Award Scheme. The school caters for 120 deaf and partially-hearing children from ages 4 to 16, who attend daily or weekly classes which follow the National Curriculum. Some children are day students, but many live within the school, during the week, in one of three residential houses. The college has 100 students and has a residential tutorial support unit.

The sudden expansion of the education system in the mid-19th century created an urgent need for schoolteachers. In 1850 the Bishop of Lichfield, John Lonsdale, opened a college for 'the Training of School Mistresses' on Uttoxeter New Road. It was the first higher education institution in Derby and has continued to flourish, changing its name to Bishop Lonsdale Teacher Training College in the 1950s when it moved to a campus at Mickleover. It then became part of the Derby College of Further Education, having absorbed what was known as Kedleston Road Technical College and the College of Art on Green Lane. This had been the first purpose-built college of art in the country. Throughout the 1980s the Derby College of Further Education had petitioned for polytechnic status. By the time the application was accepted, further educational reforms had done away with the distinction between 'Poly' and 'Uni' and so the University of Derby welcomed its first students in the early 1990s. It now stretches over several sites including the city centre, Mickleover, Kedleston Road and the former Britannia Mills, catering for more than 12,000 students. The College of Art is also home to the Metro Cinema – the city's only specialised outlet for independent and cult film.

The education of the adult population was also among the concerns of the improvement commissioners back in the 19th century, and efforts were made to expand the knowledge of every adult in a variety of ways. One of the most notable, and successful, was the Mechanics' Institution which was opened in 1825. Founded, yet again, by the Strutts (this time Joseph and his nephew Edward, as well as Dr Douglas Fox), its aim was to provide working people with access to a range of information, education and culture that had previously been restricted to only the fortunate few. For some time the Institution met in a house in the Wardwick, but in the 1830s a purpose-built hall was opened on the site. This elegant building has been recently renovated and restored by developers who have opened the Old Institute bar and restaurant there.

Derby historian Stephen Glover described the building in the 1840s as 'An elegant and spacious room in the Grecian style… 16 windows, 12 branch gas lights and a handsome chandelier. The room is ornamented with many valuable paintings presented by Joseph Strutt.' Twenty-first-century visitors to the Old Institute have plenty of evidence to support Glover's claims, for the ornate ceiling and many other decorative features are still in stunning condition.

By 1840 the Institution had more than 800 members, an increase of around 500 since its inception. Members were able to take advantage of classes in Reading, Writing and Arithmetic as well as

Bemrose School on Uttoxeter Road. Opened as a boys' grammar school in 1930, it became a comprehensive school in the 1970s, as did Derby's other grammar and secondary modern schools. The grammar schools to disappear along with Bemrose were Derby School (for boys) and Homelands and Parkfields Cedars (both for girls). Central School, a 'technical grammar' school which later became Henry Cavendish, also went comprehensive.

Art, French and Science. There were regular lectures on all kinds of scientific subjects and a library of over 600 books. In 1839, part of the Great Exhibition was held there, and the lecture hall also served as a ballroom. Many famous people visited the Mechanics' Institution, including Charles Dickens who appeared in 1852 with his players and made many return visits to read from his various works. Franz Liszt also performed, as did Johann Strauss in 1838.

According to an advertisement of the time:

'Mr Strauss, the celebrated waltz composer from Vienna, with his unrivalled orchestra composed of 28 Artistes, will have the honour to give a Grand Evening Concert on Tuesday, October 9th 1838, in which he will introduce a selection of his compositions as performed by him at the courts of Austria, Russia, France, Holland, Belgium and at the Coronation in London. Tickets 7s [35p] each. Family tickets to admit four £1 1s [£1.05].'

The cost of such entertainment might have been beyond the means of the working classes, but there were plenty of other opportunities for the working man or woman to 'improve' themselves.

THE ATHENAEUM SOCIETY

The graceful sweep of the Royal Hotel, Post Office and Derby & Derbyshire Bank building at the corner of the Cornmarket and Victoria Street. The complex was completed by 1841.

I N the late 1830s, some of Derby's major benefactors, among them Edward and Joseph Strutt, established a company called the Athenaeum Society to oversee a new development of land on the corner of Victoria Street and the Cornmarket.

The Derby & Derbyshire Bank had purchased a tract of land on which to build their new premises. Facing on to the Cornmarket, the building remains and still serves as a financial establishment, its original purpose clearly visible on a frieze in the stonework on the building.

A competition was arranged to determine the architect of the new development. Out of 52 applications it was Robert Wallace, architect of the bank, who was chosen to complete the task. As work was already under way on the bank, the decision ensured the complete co-ordination of the corner, and finally saw the completion of the work which had begun with the culverting of Markeaton Brook.

Within the Athenaeum was a new Post Office which then stood on the Victoria Street end of the bank. The grand Royal

The Royal Hotel corner at the head of the Cornmarket. An annexe to the hotel is pictured over the F. W. Woolworth building on the opposite side of Victoria Street.

Derby Museum and Library, financed by Michael Thomas Bass MP in 1879. An extension was built in 1915. Much of Joseph Strutt's private collection was moved here.

Hotel straddled the corner and was built on the site of the old Red Lion and White Lion public houses. In its heyday it was a premier location for visitors. The Athenaeum itself was home to a news room where the latest editions of some 18 different newspapers were available to read. Here, too, was the Town and County Museum.

According to Stephen Glover's account in 1843, Derbeians were able to see exhibits as varied as fossils and rare minerals, skeletons, stuffed animals and birds from across the globe and even 'the dress of an Indian Chief, a richly-carved Canoe from the South Sea Islands, the Bengal Tiger, the Mexican Deer, the Lion's Cub, a great variety of foreign snakes and several cases of insects etc'.

All for the price of 6d (2½p). The Derby Philosophical Society met within the walls and brought with them their own 'capital library, with mathematical and philosophical apparatus, specimens of fossils etc'. Joseph Strutt himself owned a large collection of artefacts at his house at the bottom of St Peter's Street, just across Albert Street from the Royal Hotel. The public

were permitted entrance to his house on Sunday afternoons. Strutt had numerous fine pictures by artists such as Holbein, Rembrandt, Reynolds and Titian, as well as marble and bronze sculptures and a 'very perfect' Egyptian mummy. Much of Strutt's collection is now in the hands of Derby Museum and Art Gallery and some pieces remain on general show.

THOROUGHLY MODERN DERBY

IN 1828 a new town hall, or Guildhall was built on the Market Place. It was Grecian in style with a grand portico entrance. The architect was Matthew Habershon and it cost £7,000 to build. In October 1841 a devastating fire destroyed much of the building's fabric. The interior was completely lost and only the outside walls and the central interior one survived. There was little choice but to rebuild. Henry Duesbury was asked to design a replacement, and whilst this is very different in style from its predecessor, it did make use of the surviving structure. The present-day Guildhall utilises the wings of the original almost intact, and the portico with arches beneath was transformed into the clock and bell tower we see today. The rear of the Guildhall,

Victoria Street with the Post Office Hotel to the right and looking towards the Strand and the Wardwick. Markeaton Brook, now culverted, once flowed along here.

Derby Guildhall as rebuilt after the devastating fire of 1841.

which adjoins the Market Hall, was undamaged and remains to Habershon's design. High upon the front of the Guildhall are two bas relief sculptures by Bell. One depicts judicial proceedings, the other municipal, indicating the primary uses of the new building, a role it continued to fill until the opening of the Council House in the middle of the 20th century. Across Derby other important improvements were being made. In 1820 the Derby Gaslight and Coke Company was formed to install the first gas-powered street lighting in the Market Place. Eleven years later the Commission spent £564 17s 2d on street lighting throughout the town centre and by 1836 there were

210 gas lamps in operation. Whilst most of these were been erected in areas where the wealthier Derbeians had their homes and businesses, the lighting was of benefit to all. The Improvement Commissioners were also responsible for the building of seven new bridges and, in 1839, the culverting of Markeaton Brook beneath the streets. A section between St James' and St Peter's bridges was completed, and what was once Brookside became Victoria Street in honour of the young queen. The brook continued under what was now named Albert Street, after Victoria's consort. The bridges were buried beneath the street and traces are still visible where the streets rise up noticeably to

The Market Hall around the time of its opening in 1866.

accommodate the bridges below. This is particularly true of St Peter's which is located under the pedestrian crossing between the Cornmarket and St Peter's Street. In times of heavy rain the rushing brook can still be heard beneath the road surface.

The brook's course through the town had long been problematic. Always susceptible to flooding, particularly following prolonged heavy rain, it was now being recognised that such waterways presented a serious health risk too. Whilst sanitary conditions improved considerably, it seems that the culverting measures were not yet effective enough as the flood of 1 April 1842, which the *Derby Mercury* called 'probably, the most calamitous inundation', was to prove.

In 1878 the elegant Strand and Strand Arcade were opened. The arcade was intended as a copy of London's Burlington Arcade. In 1864 a new market was opened. Built on land between Albert Street, the Guildhall and the Morledge, it connected with the Market Place through archways beneath the Guildhall and housed hundreds of stalls. Some were in the Market Hall itself, which has recently been restored and is still in use, and some were in covered and uncovered annexes surrounding the new hall.

One casualty of the Victorians' plans for Derby was part of the Jacobean House in the Wardwick. Until the 1850s it had five gables but then Becket Street was driven through and three of the original gables were lost, as was most of its gardens which included a Robert Bakewell wrought-iron gate. The house dates from either 1611 or 1677 – the date carved on the pediment over the entrance is impossible to decipher either way – and for many years it was used as a cafe and then by an estate agent. Recently there have been suggestions that it could return to leisure use.

The health of a town

The lot of the average Derbeian had improved immeasurably since the Improvement Commissions and there was almost universal employment. A report of 1849 into conditions in Derby, following the Public Health Act the previous year, found working conditions were excellent:

'The ten or dozen silk mills now in active operation are all well ventilated… in no instance was there observed a neglect of cleanliness. Generally on each floor are separate water closets for males and females, the construction of which cannot but be approved… All the inhabitants of Derby are engaged in some profitable employment, and nothing can exceed the order and cleanliness observed in the larger workshops and manufactories… did the same conditions exist in the workmen's families, there would not be much to complain of.'

And here was the problem. Whilst there was no doubt that conditions and opportunities for the working class had greatly improved, living conditions were still unsatisfactory.

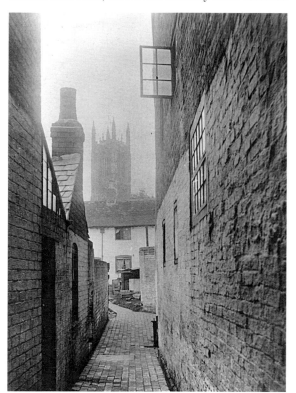
Court off Walker Lane, pictured in the early 1870s.

The Derbyshire Royal Infirmary, pictured in the 1930s.
The buildings are connected by glass corridors.

The Old Spa Inn, Abbey Street, built on the site of a spa originally intended to rival that of Buxton.

The flushing toilet

Thomas Crump, a 19th-century manager of the Derby Gas Company, invented one of the earliest flushing toilets. He registered his patent just a few weeks after Thomas Crapper, who went down in history as the official inventor and thus it was Crapper not Crump who gained a place in the vocabulary of English slang.

The report continued: 'No efficient arrangements have been carried out to prevent the vast accumulation of filthy matter on the several yards and courts belonging to private individuals, and which is found to be productive of excessive disease and premature mortality… Few towns have more need of the provision of the Public Health Act being supplied to them than Derby.'

The borough was urgently instructed to make the following provisions: lay new sewers and water pipes, abolish cesspools, replace privvies with water closets, clean up lodging houses, move slaughterhouses to the edge of the settled area, regularly collect refuse, ventilate public buildings and prevent over-crowding.

We can only imagine how appalling conditions must have been for Derbeians of that era. In all it took more than 40 years for these requirements to be completed, and disease and infection continued to pose a serious threat to the population even beyond that. Even minor viral diseases continued to be a mass killer until the introduction of effective antibiotics after the 1920s.

Perhaps the most important change brought about by the Improvement Commission was the

Derby's spa waters

The Old Spa Inn in Abbey Street was originally part of an 18th-century spa complex built by Dr William Chauncey around a mineral spring. He built bath houses and sleeping quarters and intended the complex to rival that of Buxton. Ultimately, the scheme failed and the buildings were converted first into a house and then into the present-day pub.

In 1727 the novelist Daniel Defoe visited Derby and drank 'Chaleybeate', or mineral water, from a spa in Allestree.

establishment of a formal healthcare system.

It was William Strutt who, in 1806, began fundraising efforts to build a hospital for all Derbeians. Prior to this, aside from Erasmus Darwin's charitable clinic there had been little in the way of formal healthcare for the masses. The wealthier had access to private doctors, of course, but those on low or no income had to rely heavily on home remedies and the kindness of others. So when Strutt's Derbyshire General Infirmary opened in 1810, a new standard of healthcare was available to all the people of Derby.

Florence Nightingale, heroine of the Crimean War, lived for a time at Lea Hall near Matlock. She was consulted over the construction of the Derby General Infirmary.

The Infirmary was extended both in 1849 and in 1869, the latter extension including the Nightingale wing, which was constructed only after lengthy consultation with Derbyshire's nursing heroine, Florence Nightingale, and incorporated many of her pioneering methods. Most notably, the new wing featured a modern operating theatre. As medical science developed, it was discovered that the innovative ventilation system designed by another of the Strutts – this time George – assisted rather than prevented the spread of disease and infection, there being no possibility of cleaning the vents of germs and dirt. One nurse had even died of typhoid and 17 others had fallen seriously ill. Even before this concerns had been raised about the apparent insanitary conditions.

'The interior of the hospital has been most ingeniously frittered away in the formation of narrow, ill-ventilation much interfered with... the water closets seem, with curious infelicity, to have been squeezed into the most objectionable nooks, to have little ventilation, except what they get from the corridors and... are certainly not sweet.'

The foundation stone of the rebuilt hospital was laid by Queen Victoria in 1891 and on the same day the hospital was granted the title of Derbyshire Royal Infirmary, and the DRI has continued to serve as one of the mainstays of healthcare in Derby into the 21st century.

In 1877 a new hospital was established, dedicated to the care of Derby's children. The Derbyshire Hospital for Sick Children originally occupied No 4 Duffield Road. In 1883 it moved to nearby North Street as the Derbyshire Children's Hospital. It served the community for more than 100 years before being transferred to state-of-the-art premises at the City Hospital site on Uttoxeter Road. The new hospital – one of only two children's hospitals to be built in the 20th century – was officially opened by Queen Elizabeth II on 18 July 1997. Built at a cost of £15.2 million, with an additional £1.5 million raised by the public through the Kite Appeal, it is one of the most up-to-date children's hospitals in the world. Utilising ideas from doctors, nurses, parents and patients, the new hospital has many unique features including the first dedicated children's intensive care beds, and reception desks designed with seats and steps especially for young patients and their siblings. Out-patients and future patients are invited to tour the hospital to ensure that their stay there is as comfortable and pleasant as possible.

Founded between the wars, the Derby City General Hospital is now the home to the city's only maternity unit, a highly-regarded special care baby unit, the specialist geriatric unit and a host of other facilities. It is also the site of the planned 'super hospital' which will see all acute services moved there.

Care for the mentally ill had been the sole responsibility of a private establishment known as Green Hill House on what is now Green Lane. It followed traditional lines of treatment and residents were treated more as inmates than patients. Conditions were poor and harsh and in December 1848 one patient, Samuel Tomlinson, was murdered by another. In 1851, a pioneering new establishment was opened at Mickleover. It was named the Derbyshire Paupers' Lunatic Asylum, but present-day Derbeians would recognise it as Pastures Hospital, which closed at the end of the 20th century. It was set on almost eight acres (3.2 hectares) of land and was designed to accommodate 300 patients, extended to 700 later in the century.

It featured beautiful landscaped gardens, a hospital farm and workshops and was one of the first of its kind in the world. During its early years it received visitors from across Europe who modelled their own institutions upon it. In 1888 a borough asylum was opened – on land behind the Union Workhouse (later the Manor Hospital, generally for geriatric patients) on Uttoxeter Road – which is now known as Kingsway Hospital.

Together the hospitals of Derby, combined into the Southern Derbyshire Acute Hospitals NHS Trust, provide a level of healthcare of which Derbeians can be rightly proud, with some of the top specialists and units in many areas including rheumatology, neurology, renal dialysis, and the world-renowned Pulvertaft Hand Clinic. Some 40 years ago John Collins founded the 'Derbyshire Flying Squad' – a small, specialised mobile unit to provide emergency on-scene medical care to the victims of serious accidents. Initially utilising taxi cabs to get to accidents, it was the first of its kind in the world and has since been the inspiration for dozens of similar services world-wide which still fill an essential role in 21st-century emergency treatment.

A Place of Trees – Derby Arboretum

THE 19th century was to see one more significant improvement granted to the people of Derby and it was the first of its kind. Although workers in the town were generally well-paid in comparison with many towns, few could afford the luxury of regular recreation. Even though the railways had come in 1839, the prohibitive fares meant that only a small minority could hope to escape the pollution of the towns on a regular basis. When Joseph Strutt decided to donate an 11-acre (4.4-hectare) park to the townspeople of Derby, on what was then the edge of the residential area and at a cost of more than £10,000, he provided not only a place of great beauty but a new lung from which to breathe fresh air in contrast to the stale air of rapid urbanisation.

'It is of the first importance to their health on their day of rest to enjoy the fresh air, to be able, and exempt from the dust and dirt of the public thoroughfares, to walk out in decent comfort with their families,' said Strutt.

Derby Arboretum showing the fountain and well laid-out gardens and walkways.

Joseph Strutt was 75 years old when the Arboretum, or 'place of trees', was opened in September 1840, and he had spent much of his life dedicated to improving the lot of the working classes. He knew that it had been partly due to the hard work of his family's employees that he had been able to enjoy such a comfortable existence for so many years.

He said, "I will only add, that as the Sun has shone brightly on me through life, it would be ungrateful in me not to employ a portion of that fortune which I possess in promoting the welfare of those amongst whom I live, and by whose industry I have been aided in its acquisition.'

The Derby Arboretum was unique. Whilst there had long been parks open to the public, it was the first in an urban area and the first to be designed for and owned by the public. It was truly the first public park. But, true to his aims, and the aims of his family and fellow entrepreneurs, Strutt was determined that not only would the Arboretum provide air and light for the whole population, it would also be a stimulating place, a place of great beauty and interest.

To design this park Strutt employed John Claudius Loudon (hence Loudon Street at one edge of the park). Loudon was a Scottish landscaper of great repute. He had written many books and papers on horticulture, which were among the most influential publications of their time. His *Encyclopaedia of Cottage, Farm and Village Architecture* of 1833 helped to shape the middle-class British suburb. Loudon had designed a radical plan for London which involved the designation of mile-wide rings of housing and industry, alternated with half-mile wide zones of parkland (effectively inventing greenbelts), a pattern which would continue until the city reached the sea, ensuring that no person be more than half a mile away from an 'open airy situation'. His idea also included huge ducts beneath the ground through which all utilities – gas, water, ventilation and heating – could be laid, as well as cheap universal public transport, self-contained food production and even waste recycling. Loudon was also the founder of

In 2001, Derby was awarded the prize for best city in the East Midlands in Bloom competition. Markeaton and Darley Abbey Parks were granted judges' special awards. Darley Abbey is the home of the National Collection of Viburnum and Hydrangeas.

the first *Gardener's Magazine* and the inventor of the practice of 'carpet bedding' in which plants are put in the ground the instant they begin to flower and removed the instant they decay, to be replaced by others. It is a tradition continued to this day in the gardens of Derbeians and in the spectacular public flower beds around the city, which have resulted in several awards.

The Arboretum is considered by many to be Loudon's most important work, and it proved to be his last of any size. Throughout the project Loudon battled ill-health and exhaustion and was financially ruined at the time of his death.

Some 6,000ft (1.8km) of gravel walkways were created, consisting of one major central pathway with a fountain as a focal point, plus a circuit path to take in the whole park. These main walkways were 15ft (4.5m) wide, whilst those interconnecting were shorter and narrower and led the visitor to particular features. The trees were planted on undulating mounds of 6ft to 8ft (1.8m-2.4m) in height, with the effect that the whole of the park could be seen from any one point, but other visitors on other paths could not, and so could not cause a distraction. The entire park boundary was originally enclosed by 6ft-high grassy mounds, so as to block out the view of the urban area beyond.

Some 1,000 trees were planted, thousands of evergreens, and a hundred different types of roses, all according to type and all labelled for the information of the visitor. The whole garden was punctuated by seating, statues, fountains and ornaments including the famed 'Florentine boar' which survived the attention of several generations of clambering children, only to disappear during World War Two. This marble carving of a wild pig had been brought to the Arboretum from the garden of Strutt's home, Thorntree House. Introduced later were cannons used at Sebastopol in the Crimean War, which were donated by Lord Palmerston in 1857, and a very large glass conservatory called the 'Crystal Palace' which was erected for indoor dancing and other activities. It cost £3,000 and the subscription fund was headed by the Duke of Devonshire. It was named after the London version which was designed by Sir Joseph Paxton, gardener to the Duke of Devonshire at Chatsworth. Appropriately, Paxton was meeting members of the board of the Midland Railway at Derby station in June

Sir Charles Fox
Wardwick-born Sir Charles Fox became an eminent engineer and was responsible for the construction of the station roofs at St Pancras, Euston, Paddington and Waterloo, as well as Joseph Paxton's Crystal Palace. Fox also constructed the first narrow gauge railway in India, the Medway Bridge at Rochester, Kent, and the Thames bridges at Richmond, Barnes, and Staines. Two of Sir Charles's sons became noted engineers too – Sir Douglas worked on the Mersey Tunnel and the other, Sir Francis, on the Liverpool Overhead Railway and the bridge over the Zambesi at Victoria Falls. While working there he discovered a new breed of gladioli flourishing in the mist of the Falls enabling horticulturalists to introduce yellow and orange varieties into British gardens. In 1906 he proposed a scheme for an undersea tunnel linking Britain to France, which was rejected due to fears of invasion.

1850 when he sketched the initial designs for the Great Exhibition of 1851.

There had been a great movement in horticulture to recreate an 'idealised' version of nature. One that would improve upon nature and create a 'picture-perfect' view for the observer, the emphasis being on aesthetics rather than science. In contrast it had always been Strutt's intention that the Arboretum should not just provide fresh air and beauty, but that it should be of scientific value too. Loudon shared this view and employed what was called the 'gardenesque' style in Derby. Here he used many non-native trees and plants and emphasised their unfamiliarity by deliberate planting. Loudon intended that the 'look' of the park should be maintained and that, should a tree top 50ft (15.2m) in height, it should be cropped or replaced. Two lodges in Elizabethan and Tudor styles were built and there were also pavilions which featured public conveniences, as well as rooms where members of the public could eat their own food indoors. Here was placed a copy of Loudon's *Arboretum Britannicum* for reference.

The opening day of 16 September 1840 was declared a universal holiday in the town. On that first day the park was open only to factory and mill owners and managers. Each was presented with a souvenir pamphlet which set out the aims of the Arboretum, as well as providing a botanical catalogue of the plants on show. A celebratory tea was provided and guests were then invited to Joseph Strutt's house in town. The next day some 9,000 millhands and factory workers were invited to attend. There was a parade and banners were displayed with such slogans as 'Seek Truth, Honour Science' and 'From Art & Science True Contentment Grows'. On the third day, it was the turn of 6,000 children and their parents. Games were laid on in a nearby field.

Initially visitors were charged for entry. A year's admission cost 7s (35p) and for a single day's admission the cost was 6d (2½p) for adults and 3d for children. However, in line with Strutt's intentions, admission was free for all on Sundays (except that the park was closed to everyone from 10am to 1pm, presumably to encourage people not to miss church and Sunday school) and Wednesdays and 'open to all classes of the public... subject only to such restrictions and regulations as may be found necessary for the observance of order and decorum'. In 1882 all admission charges were dropped.

In 1845 'Arboretum Field' – the portion of land to the south-east and bordered by Rose Hill Street and gardens on Reginald Street – was purchased to extend the park. It was here, in 1888, that Derby Junction FC reached the semi-finals of the FA Cup by beating mighty Blackburn Rovers, recent winners of the trophy.

Joseph Strutt's many contributions to Derby were well appreciated, and when Loudon and Henry Duesbury designed a new main entrance to stand at the Osmaston Road side of the park, facing on to Arboretum Place, it featured a statue of Strutt himself.

A programme of special attractions was held annually on the anniversary of the park's opening, this later being moved to mark Strutt's birthday earlier in the year. Military bands played, there were hot-air balloons, knife-throwers, wire-walkers and trapeze artists. The event was attended by people from all over the area, and some came from as far away as Birmingham, Manchester and Leeds – arriving in the town on cheap railway day-trip tickets. In all, there are reputed to have been some 250,000 people in attendance. On one occasion, however, the

A floodlit Arboretum highlights the statue of Henry Royce.

celebrations turned sour. An out-of-town balloonist became entangled in the trees and subsequently crashed. The ever-loyal local people, feeling sure that such an accident would not have occurred had a local balloonist been employed, began to riot, the police were called in and were pelted with stones by the dissatisfied mob.

Over the years time, and to some degree pollution, eroded much of the park's beauty, yet it remained a favourite haunt of so many Derbeians who shared fond memories of childhood summers spent there. In recent years a programme of conservation and restoration has been implemented – new trees and plants being set, paths improved and the fountain repaired. Much of the charm and beauty of the Arboretum has been restored and, once more, it makes a tranquil oasis away from the bustle of the city, particularly in summer and autumn when the wealth and variety of colours are so pleasing. A 'Tree Trail' is available from the Derby Tourist Information Centre, listing 40 of the more interesting specimens, each of which have been individually numbered. Some of the most notable are: the Caucasian wing-nut (its leaves were once used by fishermen to intoxicate fish); the Indian Bean Tree (from the Mississippi, its durable wood was used for railroad sleepers); the Red Oak (a North American tree, the bark of which is used to tan leather); and the Wych Elm (native to Britain, its wood was once used for the manufacture of archers' bows).

Less than 40 years after its opening, the Arboretum was surrounded on all sides by intensive urbanisation. And the conditions described by the Public Health report had only just been attended to. No doubt airborne pollution caused the premature demise of several of the less hardy species.

ENTERTAINING DERBY

I F the late Victorian and early Edwardian eras are notable for anything, it must be the sudden explosion in popular mass entertainment. For hundreds of years, though, there had been nothing in the way of leisure time as such. And those diversions which were available would likely be distasteful to our modern sensibilities. In addition to seasonal fairs, horse races and such, there were regular cockfights in town and several venues served this purpose – Cockpit Hill for instance, as well as Nuns Green and a number of yards to the rear of several town pubs. This brutal sport, and that of dog fighting too, were particularly popular at fair times and on market days when the town would attract many visitors from the surrounding area. We can assume, also, that these contests were officially sanctioned since rents were paid to both the town and the church for the hire of land for this purpose.

For those with more genteel tastes there were the Assemblies, held regularly at the Assembly Rooms in the Market Place, which proved a popular venue, not only for meetings but also for concerts, balls and the like. The Assemblies were held once a fortnight and additional special events were arranged for race days etc. Usually they involved a grand meal which was followed by dancing and other entertainments which went on well into the early hours. The end of the evening would be marked by a supper. Entry to such delights, however, was restricted to the gentry and the very wealthy – not by the admission charge of 7s (35p) or so, but by the very rules of the establishment which were specific in outlining the type of people who would or, to be more precise, would not be considered eligible.

Initially, there had even been two separate assemblies – one for the gentry, built in 1714, which occupied a building on the corner of the Market Place and Full Street, on the site of Derby's modern Assembly Rooms, and another for the burgesses of the town, probably in the old Moot Hall on Irongate. Eventually, it was decided that this division was not at all egalitarian enough and plans were laid to build a new combined Assembly designed by Joseph Pickford. But even the new establishment, which opened in 1765, was strict in its admissions policies.

When a grand celebration was organised to mark the defeat of Napoleon, the leading lights were invited to a grand ball at the Assembly Rooms, ordinary men of the town were given meals at local inns, 4,000 children were given buns in the Market Place, and their wives and mothers had to be content with 1s 6d (7½p) with which to buy food which they had to eat at home.

The only exception to this class rule seems to have been one Henry Franceys who had an apothecary's shop on the south side of the Market Place, which many older Derbeians will remember as the premises of Cope and Taylor. The rules of the Assemblies even stated specifically that 'no Shopkeeper, or any of his or her Family shall be admitted, except Mr Franceys'. Clearly Mr Franceys had been singled out for special consideration. He certainly mixed in rather elevated circles for a man in his position. Many of his clients were members of the very best Derby families and this may be the clue to the reasons for his acceptance. As apothecary to the gentry, he would have been party to some of the secrets, medical and otherwise, that his clients might prefer to remain just that, and so acceptance into the well-to-do was doubtless assured.

Pickford's new Assembly Rooms survived until 1963 when a severe fire caused irreparable damage. The frontage was re-erected at the National Tramway Museum at Crich. Ironically, its predecessor, the 1714 building, survived until the early 1970s, being demolished only to make way for the modern Assembly Rooms of 1977.

Although theatrical performances took place in various venues around the town, it was 1773 before a formal theatre was established. The Theatre Royal on Bold Lane occupied a building more recently used as a Youth Court. When it had first opened, many local churches had protested because theatre was considered a serious threat to the moral hearts and minds of the population.

The first performance at the Theatre Royal had been *She Stoops to Conquer* by Oliver Goldsmith, and many of the better-known actors of the day graced the stage. In 1833 Paganini gave a concert there. The Theatre Royal closed in 1862 when, following a long period of deterioration, it lost its licence, leaving the town without a formal theatre.

That situation continued for more than 20 years, despite the formation of a committee to establish a new theatre. It was not until the intervention of Andrew Melville, a noted actor, writer and producer, that Derbeians were again able to enjoy the latest plays. The Grand Theatre, on Babington Lane, opened its doors for the first time in March 1886. Only six weeks later, however, disaster struck. On 7 May, just prior to a performance, part of the scenery caught alight. Despite desperate attempts by Melville and several others to extinguish the flames, the blaze quickly took hold and the theatre had to be evacuated. Tragically two people – one an actor, the other a carpenter – had been unable to escape and died in the fire. Watched by many dozens of onlookers the fire ripped through the building. By the time it had burned out, virtually all but the façade of the theatre had been destroyed. Undeterred, Melville rebuilt his theatre – this time bigger and better than before – and sensibly incorporating more sophisticated means of fire-proofing.

Six months later the Grand reopened and continued to serve the town for more than 60 years. Melville wrote and starred in many of those plays performed at the Grand, but the theatre also attracted some of the biggest names in the country. In 1901 the famous actress, renowned beauty and mistress of the Prince of Wales, Lillie Langtry, performed there. She was some years past her heyday and had long been replaced in the affections of the new King Edward VII, but she was still a famous name. In 1922 Ivor Novello, by then an established film star, appeared in *The Rat*. During

Andrew Melville's Grand Theatre in Babington Lane. After closing as a theatre in the late 1940s it eventually became a dance hall and night spot and is currently McCluskey's.

World War Two many big-name stars appeared in productions which came to Derby prior to debuting in London's West End: John Gielgud and Peggy Ashcroft in *Love for Love*; Anna Neagle in *Emma T*; and in December 1941, two years after her success in *Gone With the Wind*, Vivian Leigh appeared in George Bernard Shaw's *The Doctor's Dilemma*.

Other stars who performed at the Grand included Arthur Askey and Vera Lynn. In addition, some of the best known names of post-war British entertainment cut their professional teeth there. Max Bygraves made his revue debut and Frankie Howerd appeared well down the bill, only to return a year later as the star of *Ta-Ra-Rah-Boom-De-Ay*. Others who appeared there early in their careers include Benny Hill, Harry Worth and Reg Varney. Even Sydney Chaplin, brother of Charlie, featured at the Grand, as did Lionel Blair who performed there as a teenager. To supplement the more 'serious' theatre, circuses, ice shows and water shows were also held there. In 1924 the Grand would also be the venue for the first public performance of a dramatic adaptation of Bram Stoker's *Dracula*, opening the way for scores of vampire plays, films and television programmes. The Grand closed in 1950 and lay empty for seven years, at which point it was transformed into a dancehall, a role it has loosely filled to this day, becoming a disco and later a nightclub.

The outskirts of town were not without their popular venues either. At the Cavendish, at the meeting point of Old and New Normanton, stood the Derby Pavilion. Originally a temporary marquee built in 1905, it was rebuilt in timber four years later on the site of what is now a supermarket, and served for many years as a venue for 'concert party' and 'end of the pier' style shows. The structure burned down in the late 1920s, to be replaced later by a cinema..

But while the more outlying areas had their own entertainments, it was still the town centre that could boast the greatest variety. In 1861 the Corn Exchange on the corner of what is now Albert Street and Exchange Street opened. The first-night crowd of 1,200 was treated to a performance by Jenny Lind, the Scandinavian soprano known as 'the Swedish Nightingale'. Later 'turns' included the D'Oyley Carte Opera Company who presented *Iolanthe*. In 1907 Marie Lloyd, the great music hall performer, appeared there. Famous for her bawdy delivery – punctuated by knowing nods and winks – of

The Midland Electric Theatre in Babington Lane, the first purpose-built cinema in Derby.

reasonably innocent-sounding songs like *Don't Dilly Dally on the Way*, *The Boy I Love is up in the Gallery*, and the perhaps less innocent-sounding *She'd Never Had Her Ticket Punched Before*, which were full of saucy innuendo, Marie Lloyd brought the house down.

Eventually the Corn Exchange passed into the hands of Charles Morritt – a renowned hypnotist and theatrical act in his own right. Under Morritt's guidance, public entertainment in Derby would now enter a new era. On 21 September 1896, Morritt's Empire brought the first moving pictures to the people of Derby. The cinema had arrived and life would never be the same again.

Going to the pictures

THE first exhibition of what would become the 'movies' had been held in France in December 1895, when the Lumière brothers had presented their 'Cinematagraph' to 30 or so mesmerised Parisians. In these days of blockbuster films packed with computer-generated imagery, it is hard to comprehend the impact of those first moving images, for most people had yet to take the static photograph for granted.

When Charles Morritt brought those first flickering frames to excited Derbeians in the autumn of 1896, the advertisement in the *Derby Daily Telegraph* heralded the 'Greatest Sensation and Innovation ever placed before an audience'. And so it was to prove.

Film shows such as these, featuring a series of short clips of horse races, ponies and traps, trains steaming toward the camera and even local sights (as Morritt's first offering had) quickly became a regular event. Initially film shows were held in any convenient venue, a regular home being introduced as late as 1904 when the Temperance Hall (now the Derby City Church) on Curzon Street began screenings.

The very nature of celluloid itself meant that it was highly flammable and frequently caught fire, sending panicking audiences rushing out into the streets. Across Britain there had been numerous such incidents and several fatalities. In 1909 Parliament introduced an Act intended to improve safety for cinema-goers. Projectors had to be placed in fire-proof boxes and wider aisles and a specified number of exits provided. This meant it was often necessary to create purpose-built premises. Derby's first picture house was the Midland Electric Theatre, 'the smartest electrical theatre in the provinces'. It stood at the bottom of Babington Lane until the 1960s and later became known as the Picture House and then the Ritz, specialising in X-certificate films.

It was a luxurious palace, filled with exotic greenery and featuring the kind of velvet-clad seats familiar to any cinema-goer right up to the multiplex era. There was a roaring open fire to welcome customers and in later years refreshments, in particular tea, was provided. Later still the balcony was transformed into a cafe.

The Midland proved so popular that it was soon joined by several more cinemas. By the outbreak of World War One, Derby boasted no less than six picture houses – the Midland, the Spot, the Victoria, the Alexandra, the White Hall (which later became the town's first Odeon, on the site of the present BHS store in St Peter's Street) and the Normanton Picture House.

But cinema was not just limited to the town itself. Film shows would often visit surrounding villages. Many of these took place in local halls and it was one such exhibition that ensured Derby's place in cinematic history. On 7 February 1900 the Infant Schoolroom in Mickleover, now Mickleover Community Centre, was the venue for a 'one night only' demonstration of the 'Bioscope', another type of projection. What made this particular event so significant, though, is that prior to the 8pm showing on that evening of '100 Images …Tour Round the World' there was a special children's performance given earlier that day. This is the first recorded instance of a children's cinema matinee performance in Britain.

In its opening programme, on 27 July 1910, the Midland showed a colour film. The owners had secured the exclusive rights to a process known as Kinemacolour which added artificial tinting to film by way of coloured lenses and filters. Clearly this was a primitive system by today's standards, but was hailed an astonishing success by a writer in the *Derby Daily Telegraph*.

Less successful was The Spot's attempt at adding sound to its films. Here a series of phonograph cylinders were intended to be played alongside the moving images, so providing a soundtrack. But it proved impossible to synchronise the two elements and the experiment lasted barely a week.

Soon offerings were extended to actual linear stories and live musicians were usually in attendance to help advance the story and to provide mood, atmosphere and drama. As the cinematic offerings became more sophisticated, so did the surroundings. Many picture houses featured ornate external architecture and even more sumptuous interiors with grecian figures, decorative plasterwork, rich colours, drapes and curtains, spectacular chandeliers and lots of gilt and gold leaf touches. Derbeians lapped up this luxury, not only appreciating the splendour of the picture houses themselves, but wholeheartedly allowing themselves to be caught up in the big-screen action, romance and drama. This was pure escapism and it was almost addictive. Long queues formed every night at every cinema as Derbeians flocked to see the latest pictures.

Ask any Derbeian over the age of 50 about their youth and they will undoubtedly talk enthusiastically about one, two, three or more trips to the pictures each week. Whether it be Saturday morning matinees to see the latest instalment of *Flash Gordon*, lazy afternoons spent with dads and pals watching the US Cavalry battle it out with Red Indians, or weepie evenings watching Bogart and Bergman fall in love, the cinema was the place of dreams and imagination. It was also a meeting place and there must be hundreds of Derby couples who spent much of their early romance bathed in the reflected limelight.

Eventually every neighbourhood had its own picture house, such as the Sitwell at Spondon, the Popular in the West End, the Cosmo near the Rowditch, the Rex at Alvaston, the Essoldo and the Majestic at Chaddesden and the Cavendish at, not surprisingly, the Cavendish.

The fascination with cinema continued well beyond World War Two and in the late 1940s and early 1950 queues snaked around the streets, but began to decline the instant television became widely available. One by one the old picture houses closed. Some, like the Gaumont on London Road, attempted to supplement their dwindling takings by putting on pop concerts in the 1960s. Among those appearing in Derby were Cliff Richard, Gene Pitney, Roy Orbison and the Kinks. By the 1970s only the Odeon (formerly Gaumont) and the ABC (previously Regal) on East Street remained. By the mid-1980s it was only the Odeon. Then, just when it seemed cinema was dead and ready for burial, two US companies decided to build modern multiplexes in the town. The Showcase, on the former Normanton Barracks and the AMC (now UCI) at the Meteor Centre, revolutionised cinema-going for a new generation. Clean, glitzy and modern, these establishments opened just in time for the birth of the modern blockbuster with special effects and three-dimensional sound. Now the whole family could attend, and each could find a film to suit his or her tastes.

Sadly the old Gaumont (Odeon), by then the Cannon, was closed in the late 1980s after a ceiling collapsed in the auditorium. But Derby was not without a city centre cinema. In 1981 the Metro cinema had opened on Green Lane in the converted lecture hall of the College of Art, now part of the University. Specialising in arthouse movies, independent films and foreign titles that otherwise would not have been available to Derbeians, the Metro is still flourishing, despite having space for only around 120 customers. It is in great contrast to the multiplex giants, being compact and intimate. It may not present the more mainstream titles, but watching a film at the Metro is every bit as special.

In the mid-1990s there had been speculation that the Metro might take over the old Gaumont on London Road, but this has recently been converted to a nightclub. There is hope that the city centre might be home to a new multiplex as part of the proposed Riverlights scheme, with either a new company coming to the city or the relocation of the UCI. And speculation continues over the possibility of the relocation of the Metro to the proposed arts complex on the former police station on Full Street. Whatever decision is made, it seems the future of the cinema in Derby is undoubtedly assured.

Acting talent

Derby has produced a number of successful actors, the most successful of which is **Alan Bates**, who was born in Allestree in February 1934. After studying at RADA, he made his West End debut in 1956, aged 22. Later that year he was launched to stardom in John Osborne's *Look Back in Anger*. For the next four years he worked successfully on the stage and, in 1960, made his big screen debut in *The Entertainer* alongside Sir Laurence Olivier. A year later he appeared in one of his most popular films *Whistle Down the Wind*, a captivating film in which he plays a man on the run from the police. Two young children

become convinced that the stranger hiding in a barn is Jesus Christ. Since that time he has appeared in more than 50 film and television roles whilst continuing to appear on the stage. Other notable works include: *A Kind of Loving*; *The Caretaker*; *Zorba the Greek*; *Georgy Girl*; *Women in Love*; and as Claudius to Mel Gibson's *Hamlet* in 1990. On television he has taken roles in *The Mayor of Casterbridge*; *Voyage Round My Father*; *Hard Times* and in 1995 *Oliver's Travels*. In 1971 he received a Tony Best Actor award for his work in Simon Gray's *Butley*. Alan Bates still visits his home town and is a great supporter of Derby Playhouse.

A face familiar to television audiences in the 1950s and 60s was **Eric Lander** who, although born in Rugby, with his family moved to Derby during World War Two. His father was a minister at Ashbourne Road Methodist Church and the family lived at Vernon Street and later Radbourne Street. Eric Lander attended Bemrose School and later became an apprentice at Rolls-Royce. But acting was always his first choice and he became a member of the forerunner of the Royal Shakespeare Company, acting with such names as John Gielgud. He came to national prominence in *No Hiding Place*, a TV detective drama that starred Lander and Raymond Francis. It was said that at one time Lander received more fan mail than Clint Eastwood, then appearing on TV in *Gunsmoke*, and Lander was voted 'the sexiest man on television'.

One of the Derby-born actors best known to modern television audiences is the late **Kevin Lloyd**. His portrayal of scruffy detective 'Tosh' Lines in more than 400 episodes of *The Bill*, made him one of the most familiar and well-loved faces on British television. Never one to hide behind the mantle of stardom, Kevin Lloyd could regularly be seen out and about in the city centre and was always approachable to his many fans. He was a passionate Derby County fan and a proud Derby man and would work both his beloved Rams and his Derby roots into his work at every opportunity. Kevin Lloyd had established a successful stage career before moving into television and had been preparing to appear in a stage version of *The Cherry Orchard* alongside Sir Laurence Olivier in Los Angeles, when Lord Olivier died. He took a number of small roles in a variety of television series from children's programming to sitcoms and a large number of dramas including *Z Cars*, *Blake's 7*,

Derby-born actor Kevin Lloyd.

Bergerac, Juliet Bravo, Boon and *Casualty*, before moving on to featured roles in *Dear John* and *Auf Wiedersehen Pet*. He earned a regular role on *Coronation Street* playing Don Watkins, the manager of Mike Baldwin's Graffiti Club, before joining the cast of *The Bill*. Very much a Derby man, he elected not to move to London and eventually the strain of travelling each day to work, whilst living in Duffield, became too much. His private life hit the tabloid headlines as his marriage broke down and at the time of his death, in May 1998, he was seeking treatment for a serious drinking problem.

Although Kevin Lloyd is probably Derby's best-known showbiz celebrity in recent years, there are other familiar faces with Derby connections. Although not a native of Derby, **Julia Watson**, best known for her portrayal of Baz in *Casualty*, spent most of her childhood in the town. Born at her grandparents' home in Wales, she and her mother moved to Derby when she was three months old, to join her father who worked at Rolls-Royce. The family

A MUSICAL LEGACY

RONALD Binge was born in Derby just before World War One. He had proved a talented musician from an early age and performed as a cinema organist whilst still a very young man. His passion for music eventually led him to London where he became a composer of 'light' music for silent films and later composed both original songs and his own arrangements of popular standards for Mantovani. Amongst his most famous compositions were *Elizabethan Serenade, Sailing By* and *Spitfire*. Between 1955 and 1963 Ronald Binge had his own radio show known as *String Song*.

Born in Derby in 1913, Ronald Pountain worked at the LMS as an apprentice electrician. Under his stage name of **Denny Dennis** he spent five years with the Roy Fox Orchestra and toured extensively across Britain and Europe. He was with the BBC at Bristol during World War Two before going on to entertain troops. In 1948 he became the first British singer to tour the USA with Tommy Dorsey, whose previous featured singers had included Frank Sinatra. Thus Derby-born Denny Dennis appeared at venues such as Chattanooga, Atlanta, Orlando, and the Café Rouge in New York City. Many have suggested that had he remained in the US, Denny Dennis might have enjoyed even greater fame. Denny's brother Eric was also a musician. Under the stage name of **Barry Gray** he played with Roy Fox and Harry Roy. He married one of the four daughters of Frank Rowley, a Derby insurance agent, but in 1941, aged 31, he died in the icy waters of the Atlantic when the merchant ship on which he was serving was torpedoed by a German U-boat.

In recent years a numbers of artists and bands with Derby connections have enjoyed brushes with fame, including Whitetown, whose single *Your Woman* made number one in 1997.

lived at Westbourne Park, Mackworth, and she attended Reigate School followed by Parkfields Cedars. Her first forays into drama were in Derby in school and youth productions. She joined Derby Shakespeare Company when at senior school.

Former Derby bank clerk **Gwen Taylor** recently starred in her own sitcom *Barbara*. Previously she has been seen in popular comedies *A Bit of a Do* and *Duty Free*. A versatile actress she has also guested in a number of a dramas, most notably *Inspector Morse* and *Holby City*.

Jane Rossington has risen almost to iconic status in her role as Jill Harvey in *Crossroads* for the entire run of its original series from 1964 to 1988. She reprised the role for the first few weeks of its recent revival.

Derby's love affair with television and the movies goes back much further, to the very birth of Hollywood itself. **Fred Stanley**, born in Derby 1891, moved to Hollywood where he became a writer for 1920s silent movies including 1928's *Riley The Cop,* which was one of the first films directed by the legendary John Ford.

Born in Derby in 1883, **William A. Burton** moved to Canada just before the outbreak of World War One and arrived in Hollywood in 1922. He, too, wrote for the silent movie industry, as well as writing several plays. In the late 1920s he returned to Britain, becoming Scenario Editor for British Instructional Films. His greatest contribution was perhaps the critically-acclaimed film *Shiraz*, an historical romance. He later returned to Hollywood and with his wife co-wrote a novel *The Years Between.*

Probably the busiest actor to have come out of Derby, **Frank Conroy** made upwards of 80 Hollywood movies. Born in Derby in 1890, he continued working right through the 1930s, 40s and 50s and appeared alongside some of the greatest names in Hollywood, as well as working on some of the classic movies of all time. He worked in several *Charlie Chan* films, as well as featuring in *Grand Hotel* starring Greta Garbo and Joan Crawford. He appeared in *Manhattan Melodramas* as the attorney to Clark Gable's character Blackie. The film itself has claimed its own place in history as the one which arch-criminal John Dillinger watched just moments before being shot dead by police officers. Conroy also played opposite Gable in *The Call of the Wild*, as Loretta Young's husband. He also had an important role in the controversial 1951 version of the death row drama *The Last Mile* with Mickey Rooney.

Joan Rice was born in Derby in 1930 and became one of the best-known British leading ladies of the 1950s. She gained the greatest recognition for her role as Maid Marion to Richard Todd's Robin Hood in the Walt Disney live action film *The Story of Robin Hood and his Merrie Men* in 1952.

Former Derby School pupil **Ted Moult**, born in Derby in 1926, a member of a family whose name was familiar as drapers in the town, became one of the nation's best-loved TV characters, first through his appearances on the panel game *What's My Line*, and later when he appeared in *All Creatures Great and Small* as well as a series of memorable advertisements for Everest double glazing. He was also a farmer and many a young Derbeian spent a weekend picking strawberries at Moult's 'pick your own' farm at Ticknall. He died tragically, by his own hand in September 1986.

Although **James Bolam**, best known for his role as the Geordie Terry Collier in the popular sitcom of the 1970s and 1980s *The Likely Lads*, was born in the North-East, he attended Bemrose School and initially took a position as a trainee accountant with Ling's in Derby. Another former Bemrose pupil **Michael Knowles** rose to fame as Captain Ashwood in *It Ain't Half Hot Mum* and in *You Rang M'Lord?*

Former presenter of *Tomorrow's World* **Judith Hann** was born in Littleover and is the daughter of former Derby County player and trainer, the late Ralph Hann.

THIS SPORTING LIFE

THE late Victorian-early Edwardian era was also marked by the sudden rise in the popularity of organised spectator sports. The ever-expanding rail network had opened up the whole country and it was now possible for the first time to organise formal competitions in all manner of sports and for people to travel from village to towns and from town to town to watch and compete.

Horse racing at the Nottingham Road course. The grandstand which replaced the one in this picture was itself scheduled for demolition in 2001.

Poster advertising horse racing on Nuns Green in November 1779.

Horse racing had long been popular among Derbeians and for many years these had taken place on Sinfin Moor, but had relocated to the Holmes following the enclosure of the lands at Sinfin. In 1848 a new racecourse was opened just to one side of the Nottingham Road. The Racecourse, as it is still known to this day, served as such for some 90 years until the outbreak of World War Two precipitated its closure. After the war the Borough Council decided that the type of people attracted to the town during

meetings were less than desirable and the whole area was converted to local football pitches, leaving the nearest racecourses at Nottingham and Uttoxeter. The Derby track was the scene of many famous victories and all the best jockeys rode there. It was also featured a straight mile, a rarity in the world of racing. Remarkably no photograph of racing taking place has ever been uncovered and so we must rely upon the limited physical evidence left behind, such as the old judges' box and the Grandstand which until recent times remained intact.

For more than a century it had been a recognisable and unique feature of the County Ground, occupied since 1872 by Derbyshire County Cricket Club, although like so much of the ground, the Grandstand has suffered from repeated cycles of alteration and neglect. At the start of the 21st century, work began on what it seemed would be the demolition of the Grandstand but this was halted for a while, leaving a fine old structure without its familiar dome and thus characterless. Despite the construction of a small pavilion and basic stands, as well as land being used for a health club, the ground has been allowed to fall into sufficient disrepair that in the summer of 2001, one national newspaper journalist stated that Derbyshire's County Ground 'repelled visitors with its seediness'.

Derbyshire Cricket
Records tell us that cricket was first played in Derbyshire in the middle of the 18th century. At that

time it was played purely on an informal basis and it was not until the next century that organised competitions took place. In 1836 the South Derbyshire Cricket Club was formed. Initially playing its home matches at Chaddesden, the club later moved to the Holmes, but was forced to relocate to the Racecourse in 1863 when parts of the Holmes began to sink and much of what remained was used for the new cattle market. South Derbyshire's first game on what was to become the County Ground was against Rugby School 2nd XI that year.

South Derbyshire and the Australian Aboriginal touring team at Derby in September 1868.

In September 1868, South Derbyshire met a team of Australian Aboriginals who were touring England that year – 10 years before a white Australian team first visited these shores. The 14 men in the squad were members of the Djabwurrung people from the Lake Wallace area of Victoria and had been coached by Tom Wills, who is also credited with the invention of Australian Rules Football. With exotic names like Red Cap, Two Penny, Dick-a-Dick and Mosquito, and displays of 'Australian' and 'native' sports like spear and boomerang throwing, they were guaranteed to fascinate the curious crowds. Dr W. G. Grace gave particularly high praise to two stars of the team – Johnny Cuzens, known as Yellanch, and Johnny Mullagh. Their fielding was noted as being of a particularly high standard and it was felt that hunting in the outback had prepared them for this. But to most of the spectators and reporters of the day their cricketing skills seemed of less importance than their 'impressive' physiques. One man, known as Tarpot, was particularly noted for his ability to run backwards at great speed. Their behaviour impressed many, in particular one writer for *The Times* who declared them to be 'perfectly civilised' and 'quite familiar with the English language'. Sadly

many of the team suffered ill-health during the tour and one man died. It is also thought that several developed drinking problems whilst so far from home and their loved ones.

In 1870, the Gentlemen of Derbyshire beat their Kent peers at Tonbridge and a team styled 'Derbyshire' beat MCC Club & Ground XI. On 4 November 1870, at the grand jury room in the Guildhall, Derbyshire County Cricket Club was formed. A number of local men had been influential in the formation of the club, most notably John Cartwright, Col Sir Henry Wilmot and the Boden brothers. The first president was the Earl of Chesterfield, who was succeeded by Hon W. M. Jervis. Derbyshire CCC's first match came on 25 May 1871 when they defeated Lancashire by an innings and 11 runs. In 1874 members of the press declared Derbyshire 'county champions', although they had played only four games, and other counties were elected champions by other journalists.

In 1887, despite having been relegated to second-class status for a time, they secured the services of Australian Test player F. R. 'Demon' Spofforth, who had married a Breadsall girl the previous year. In February 1890 there were angry scenes at the AGM, reminiscent of more recent years perhaps, when several players were accused of keeping late nights and even turning up for a match drunk. The most serious allegation, however, was against assistant-secretary and former captain Samuel Richardson, who fled the country after being accused of embezzling club funds. He was next heard of living in Spain where he had changed his name and taken a job as personal tailor to King Alfonso.

In 1882, William Chatterton stepped out at the Newlands Ground in Cape Town to become Derbyshire's first-ever England Test player.

Derbyshire's fortunes ebbed and flowed either side of World War One, but in 1936 they achieved what no other Derbyshire side has ever done – they won the County Championship. Led by the amateur A. W. Richardson, a member of a well-known Derbyshire family with tannery business interests, the side included batsmen Denis Smith, Stan Worthington, Albert Alderman, Harry Storer (later to manage Derby County), all-rounder Leslie Townsend, pace bowlers Bill Copson and Alf Pope, spinner Tommy Mitchell and wicketkeeper Harry Elliot. It was one of Derbyshire's shining moments and it would be

45 years before a Derbyshire team would bring another trophy back to the County Ground.

In the meantime Derbyshire supporters would have to content themselves with watching some of the greatest players to represent the county. The post-war years saw the emergence of a great pair of opening bowlers in Cliff Gladwin and Les Jackson – both already well into maturity after losing seven seasons to the war – and players like Arnold Hamer, Donald Carr, Derek Morgan, Harold Rhodes, Edwin Smith and George Dawkes.

In the 1970s, Derbyshire still had their England Test stars – Mike Hendrick, Alan Ward, Bob Taylor and Geoff Miller – and the club received a boost when South African Test star Eddie Barlow was appointed captain in 1976.

In 1981, with a side combining wiley old pros with up-and-coming youngsters, Derbyshire won what was arguably the most exciting one-day Final in history when they defeated Northants at Lord's to lift the NatWest Trophy off the last ball of the match. By now New Zealander John Wright and South African Peter Kirsten, perhaps two of the most elegant and exciting batsmen ever to play in English cricket, were the new batting stars. In 1982 Kirsten established a club record of eight County Championship centuries in a single season.

The following year, after the sudden resignation of former Lancashire and England player Barry Wood, the Derbyshire committee took the bold step of appointing 22-year-old Kim Barnett as captain. Barnett had barely established himself in the first team and there were many who doubted his ability to take hold of what had become the hot-potato of the Derbyshire captaincy. But Barnett was utterly dedicated to the Derbyshire cause and was to prove the most successful captain – and the most prolific batsmen – in the club's history.

Barnett's reign was to signal the start of the most successful period in Derbyshire's history. There were some exceptionally talented younger players like John Morris, Devon Malcolm and Chris Adams, and older, more experienced, professionals like Alan Warner, Philip DeFreitas and the Dane Ole Mortensen. This was the team that would go on to win the Refuge Assurance Sunday League but one overseas player, South African Adrian Kuiper, proved to be a most significant factor in 1990. In a limited-overs season that seemed to provide drama and thrills at every turn, all-rounder Kuiper proved to be a vital member of the Derbyshire team. His spectacular batting displays, often hitting several boundaries an over, were short but very sweet and they gave the side the necessary impetus to go on week after week claiming tight victories. No cause was ever considered lost and the title was won in the last game of the season, at home to Essex. Like so many matches that season, it went right down to the last over. The champagne flowed and the trophy was held aloft by a triumphant Kim Barnett.

Three years later, on an overcast July day, Derbyshire were again victorious. This time they had captured the Benson & Hedges Cup after a rain-interrupted match that it had almost seemed would run over into the following day. Again supporters celebrated, and it seemed as if yet more success would soon be theirs to savour. But that day in 1993 would be the last measure of success for a team on the verge of breakdown. One by one, established players left the club to pursue their careers with other counties. Some left for reasons of ambition and the promise of captaincy elsewhere, some due to clashes of personality. Committee members left too and, rather than any preventative action being taken, the discord that had been brewing for some time was allowed to ferment and ultimately led to a dramatic showdown.

Barnett had stepped down as captain, but remained as a player. He had been replaced by former Australian Test star Dean Jones, who brought in his own support staff determined to revolutionise training methods etc. Jones's first season in charge saw Derbyshire reach their highest position in the County Championship for many years, but rumours spread that some of the senior professionals were less than enthusiastic about the new regime and factions began to form. The ugly disagreements that followed became the focus of the following season and resulted in the abrupt resignation of Jones and his coach Les Stillman and the temporary appointment of DeFreitas as captain. Over the following seasons, several key players left, including Barnett and DeFreitas. There were those who suggested that the club would benefit from breaking with the old guard, but any doubters of Barnett's positive influence need only to look at his record as both batsman and captain to dispel such thoughts.

In more recent years Derbyshire's playing

fortunes have sunk to an almost embarrassingly poor level, and more players have left for pastures new, many of whom were bright young stars and intended to be the foundation on which the club would build its future.

The birth of the Rams

While Derbyshire County Cricket Club has never been assured of a secure future, the early years found Derbyshire's finances in serious strife. The committee looked to alternative means of income and one solution was to create a new outlet for the competitive energies of the town. For some years it had been apparent that one particular sport had been capturing the imagination and enthusiasm of England's sporting public. And in Derby itself the game of Association Football was steadily gathering momentum. In March 1884, some 7,000 spectators had entered the County Ground to watch Derby Midland take on Staveley in the Derbyshire Cup Final. Convinced that there was significant profit to be made from this sport, the cricket club held a meeting at the Bell Hotel in Sadler Gate, where it elected to form its own football team - Derby County.

'The Derbyshire County Cricket Club has decided on the formation of a football club under Association Rules and desires to render football worthy of the patronage blessed upon it by the public by endeavouring to arrange matches with first-class clubs which will enable the public to witness matches in a higher order than have hitherto been played in Derby.'

It was a simple enough announcement in the *Derby Daily Telegraph* in September 1884 and although it immediately laid claim to some superlative entertainment, it bore no hint of the impact which the formation of a football club would have on so many Derbeians over the next century, nor of the passions it would unleash. Derby County – the cricket club wanted to call it Derbyshire County FC but the Derbyshire FA refused – was born.

Derby County's first game took place on 13 September 1884 against Great Lever at Bolton. Derby lost 6-0. It was an inauspicious start and the club had to wait until its fifth game – against St Luke's in the Derbyshire Cup – before it recorded a victory. But there was soon steady improvement as many of the better players from other local teams joined the club, which went on to win 14 and lose 11

Steve Bloomer, arguably Derby County's greatest player. He joined the club in 1892 and went on to score 332 goals in 525 appearances as well as winning 23 England caps. Bloomer was football's first true superstar.

out of 34 matches in its first season. As seven of these defeats came in the first 15 matches of the inaugural season, the improvement is clear. The following November, Derby beat the great Aston Villa team in the second round of the FA Cup. Derby County had arrived.

There were now three established teams in the town, Derby County, Derby Junction and Derby Midland, and all were vying for the services of the same players. In 1888 the Rams, as they were to become known, were elected founder members of the Football League and so attracted the best players and the biggest crowds. Subsequently they also made more profit. It was not long before Midland fell into serious debt and were in danger of folding. The Rams, meanwhile, had unexpectedly lost large sums of money, embezzled by club secretary Samuel Richardson who had also served Derbyshire CCC in the same way. In 1891 the football and cricket clubs went their separate ways and the Rams absorbed

Midland with all their assets, including one which would prove particularly valuable in the shape of Steve Bloomer, who was to become Derby County's most famous player.

The club continued to play at the County Ground on the Racecourse, where watching any sport was only for the most enthusiastic and hardy of souls. Even today, with the development that has taken place in recent years, the Racecourse and County Ground are draughty on all but the steamiest of days. In those days, with little protective shelter, the wind blew straight across the ground and one game even had to be abandoned due to high winds. Only those few who were lucky enough to be permitted access to the football half of the two-sided pavilion were afforded any degree of shelter. The rest had to stand surrounding the pitch, which was located approximately where the modern scoreboard now stands. Because there were no raised viewing areas, when there was a big crowd present, it was necessary to stand a long way back in order to ensure an unobstructed view. Facilities for players were little better, though apparently good by the standards of the day. According to Steve Bloomer, 'We didn't have a lot of high falutin' gadgets in those days, but we did have plenty of good fresh air and nice cold water and what many a club might have envied us in those days of infancy was the turf we played on.'

It may surprise some Rams fans to discover that there were no familiar white shirts and black shorts to begin with – early strips utilised the cricket club's colours of chocolate, amber and pale blue, later players wore black and white stripes, and at one point a red and white halved shirt was worn with black 'knickerbockers' and socks.

Modern fans, weary of the stereotyping of football fans as hooligans, are only too aware of the rather dated reputation that comes with their hobby. In those early years too, football had earned a reputation for disruption. The Rams' train carriage had been pelted with bricks by Walsall fans – perhaps proof that those looking to misbehave had latched on to the sport as a convenient vehicle from its very earliest days.

The Rams, themselves, however, have avoided acquiring such a reputation and it is well recognised that despite being amongst the most passionate and loyal of supporters, or perhaps because of that fact,

Rams fans are regarded as being among the more peaceable and tolerant in the country. Perhaps the same cannot be said of the men behind the scenes. The club has endured more than its fair share of board-room wrangles, scandals and controversies.

Players, too, have sometimes proved controversial. Among the most notorious of these was centre-half Archie Goodall. Both Goodall and his brother John represented the Rams in those early years and whilst the older sibling, an England international, was known as 'Johnny All-Good', Archie, who was capped for Ireland, gave his employers and supporters plenty of cause for concern. Once he was hauled before the magistrates accused of punching a spectator, long before Eric Cantona did his infamous 'karate' kick on a fan. Archie also disappeared shortly before he was due to take the field for the 1898 FA Cup Final and was found outside the ground trying to sell the tickets he had invested in. On another occasion Goodall refused to play extra-time in a United Counties Cup Final, claiming that he was contracted only to play for the 90 minutes of normal time. Goodall had numerous outside interests and even toured the United States and Europe with his strongman act which he had perfected in his Wolfa Street home. All this eccentricity aside, Goodall was an excellent player, his record of 85 goals in 211 games a good one, even in the days of more attacking centre-halves.

The Rams' move to the beloved Baseball Ground came in 1895, although they had played there previously when racing at Nottingham Road had prevented them using their usual pitch. The first game on the Baseball Ground as the Rams' official home came on 14 September 1895, Derby beating Sunderland 2-0 with Bloomer getting both the goals. It was about this time that the famous gypsy curse is said to have been placed on the club. Legend has it that a group of gypsies were evicted from the ground and in return cursed the club never to have success. It is true that until 1946, when the club had the curse 'removed', the Rams did not win a major honour, but it is also true that in the first 10 years of their tenure at the Baseball Ground, Derby reached three FA Cup Finals, and four more semi-finals as well as finishing runners-up in the First Division in their first season at the Baseball Ground. Doubtless today's Rams fans would be more than content with such 'failures'.

Relegated for the first time in 1907, Derby County

see-sawed between the First and Second Divisions until 1926 when they were again promoted to the top flight of English football. In the years that preceded and followed World War Two, Rams fans would have much to cheer about.

Homes of football

Informal football games had long been played in Derbyshire. Indeed, fiercely-fought local 'derby' games are so called after the Shrovetide matches between the parishes of All Saints' and St Peter's. This was an unruly, rugged and primitive form of the game and had become so riotous that by 1845 the authorities banned it altogether. At nearby Ashbourne, Shrovetide football continues to this day in much the same vein.

The choice of Pride Park for the England-Mexico international in May 2001 was not the first time the national team had played in the town. In 1895 England met Ireland at the County Ground, and those two countries met in Derby again in 1911, this time at the Baseball Ground.

International matches were not the only important football games played in the town. In 1886 some 12,000 spectators saw Blackburn Rovers beat West Bromwich Albion in the FA Cup Final replay at the County Ground and both that venue and the Baseball Ground staged FA Cup semi-final matches. Two years after their Cup Final victory in Derby, Blackburn Rovers met minnows Derby Junction (from Junction Street Sunday School) in the FA Cup quarter-finals at the Arboretum Field in front of 4,000 people. Against the odds Junction pulled off a remarkable victory to win 2-1. Alas, they lost their semi-final to West Bromwich Albion.

Football was not the only sport at which the great Steve Bloomer excelled. He was an accomplished player of the game which was Francis Ley's pet love, baseball, and was described as the 'best second baseman in England'.

Ley had travelled to the United States on business and had seen baseball for the first time. He immediately fell in love with the game and, together with US sports equipment magnate A. G. Spalding, set about introducing the sport to England. Derby became something of a baseball hotspot and at his 12-acre (4.8-hectare) sports complex Ley built a baseball field on the site of the future football ground. The field was set out in similar principle to a rounders field, the catcher stood at what is now better known as the Osmaston End-Popside corner and, indeed, this area of the football ground was known as 'catcher's corner' for many years. Elsewhere in Derby there are accounts of children playing baseball in parks and on greens. For several years the Derby baseball team was the best in the country, winning the English Cup three times in the 1890s. Ley managed to attract a number of Americans to play for Derby and when his club began to run away with the title so early in the season, there were accusations of cheating from other clubs. For reasons which may never become clear, and although baseball had attracted large crowds, it failed to become the major sport many had predicted.

England meet Ireland at the Baseball Ground in February 1911. The Popular Side – where the Ley Stand was erected in the early 1970s – is still uncovered.

INTO A MODERN ERA

IN common with the rest of the nation, the people of Derby were in sombre mood in January 1901. Queen Victoria, their monarch of more than 60 years, was dead. The mayor sent condolences on behalf of the town and among the solemn reports that filled the pages of the *Derby Daily Telegraph* was one simple line that perhaps summed up the silence that had fallen over the town: 'Theatre will be closed tonight.' As the funeral service at Windsor began, a solemn civic procession made its way from Derby's Guildhall to All Saints, watched by hundreds of mourning Derbeians who must surely have looked back 10 years earlier to when the queen had made her great State Visit to Derby.

The arrival of Queen Victoria in Derby was one of the most eagerly anticipated events in living memory. Overnight the town had been specially and spectacularly decorated throughout. There were

Queen Victoria visited Derby four times, in 1843, 1849, 1852 and her State Visit of 1891.

'Venetian masts' and floral garlands lining the streets where the royal procession would travel. At junctions there were monograms, crowns and enormous hanging baskets. According to the *Derby Express* more than 'a million yards' (which equates to a staggering 568 miles) of bunting were used and three miles of barricades were erected. Each house and business along the route had their own decorations in addition to those organised by the borough. Everywhere there were flags, floral arches, canopies and colourful illuminations of every kind.

In the Market Place, in front of the Guildhall, a dais was erected and here the queen appeared before specially invited guests. The rest of the population had to line the route to catch a glimpse of their monarch, which they did with great enthusiasm. At the Infirmary, Victoria laid a ceremonial foundation stone with a golden trowel, but those who waited at the exit gate were denied their opportunity to see the queen when the procession took a wrong turn and retraced its path through the entrance gate. At the end of the day, as she waited in a 'retiring room' at Derby Midland station, and before leaving the jubilant town for the journey to Scotland, Queen Victoria knighted the mayor, Alfred Haslam, who had paid for much of the lavish celebration. Later a celebratory banquet was held on the lawn of the Midland Hotel for invited guests only.

In many ways it was the death of Queen Victoria which heralded a new era in Britain. The 20th century was only three weeks old and that year would see Marconi make the first radio transmission, from Cornwall to Newfoundland. The early days of the new century would see the power of electricity take over from that of steam, and it would see the birth of popular music with the development of ragtime jazz in the US. It seemed that every month there would be some innovation to completely transform everyday life, and yet as Britons looked to the future they also looked back upon a reign packed with changes that had been every bit as remarkable as those that would follow.

The coronation of Edward VII was set for 26 June 1902 and detailed plans were put into action to turn the whole country into a riot of colour and

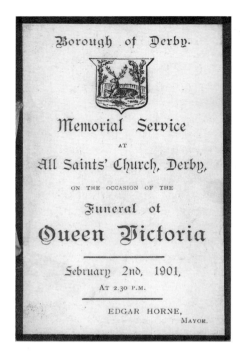

Far left: Like all major towns and cities Derby held a memorial service for Queen Victoria. *Left:* The wreath sent by the town to the funeral of Edward VII. It was made by Thomas Rowley & Co of Green Lane, who also made wreaths for the funerals of Queen Victoria and George V.

celebration. The *Derby Daily Telegraph* declared that everything was in 'apple pie order' in the town. Indeed, all over the town Derbeians were preparing food for public teas and dinners, hanging bunting and flags and eagerly anticipating the celebrations. Suddenly word spread that the king had fallen ill and needed urgent hospital treatment – the coronation would have to be postponed. Assurances were made to a shocked nation that the new king would soon be back on his feet ready for a rescheduled coronation.

However, so much planning had already gone into the festivities that Edward VII ordered that those celebrations should go ahead on the original coronation day. That day was warm and fine and the whole town celebrated the forthcoming event, as bands played in all the parks and a public firework display took place at Chester Green.

The actual coronation day, some six weeks later, was a much more low-key affair and spoiled by rainy weather.

The Derwent Hotel on London Road is decorated for the State Visit to Derby of Edward VII in 1906.

MARCHING OFF TO WAR

THE building of Normanton Barracks had begun in 1874, on a piece of land on the edge of the village of Normanton. The first soldiers arrived three years later, and in 1881 the barracks became the headquarters of the newly-amalgamated Sherwood Foresters, whose home it was to be through two world wars. It was here at Normanton Barracks, now demolished to make way for the Foresters Leisure Park, that troops would amass for what was to be the 19th century's final major conflict. The Boer War had broken out in South Africa in October 1899, the inevitable result of dispute after dispute between British and Boer settlers culminating in the many British, who had emigrated there to work in the gold and diamond mines, being refused full political rights. In the light of almost immediate British setbacks at the hands of the Boers, many Derbyshire reservists were ordered to report to Normanton Barracks by 6 November, ready to sail for South Africa.

As the first batch of men arrived they were greeted by huge crowds of onlookers and well-wishers. And as the first group left on 7 November, they were cheered by more enthusiastic Derbeians. A half-day holiday had been granted on the morning of the 8th, and factories and schools closed to allow workers and children to join the throngs lining the route from the barracks to the Midland station. At 9am the second group of soldiers were saying their emotional farewells to their wives and children, their parents, siblings, sweethearts and friends. At 10am the men fell in and, led by three bands, the khaki-clad soldiers marched smartly out of the barracks gates. Their route took them through streets strewn with Union Flags, past waving, cheering neighbours and past sobbing loved ones. The procession made its way down St Thomas's Road and Pear Tree Road, along Normanton Road where one soldier carried his tiny baby while his wife walked beside him holding his rifle.

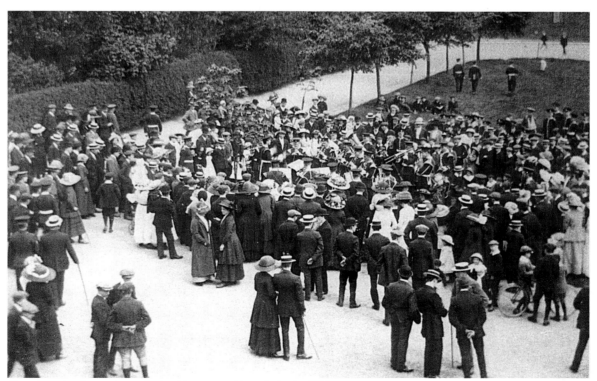

Crowds gather for an 'open day' at Normanton Barracks in the 1900s.

Sherwood Foresters band at Normanton Barracks in its final years as a regimental depot.

As it turned into Hartington Street and then Osmaston Road the crowds became increasingly excitable. The procession passed beneath a banner strung across Bradshaw Street (now the widened Bradshaw Way) proclaiming 'Success to the Soldiers of the Queen'. As the men reached London Road chaos broke out as onlookers rushed over to the soldiers to wish them well or give them an encouraging pat on the back. By the time the parade reached the station, the risk of crushing was bordering on critical. The Midland Hotel had to be used as a temporary ambulance station where fainting spectators could be cared for. It became near impossible to issue kit and equipment, such was the panic as desperate men, women and children fought to get one last glimpse of their loved ones. Even when all the soldiers had been safely admitted to the station the commotion was so great that the stationmaster feared he would be unable to get the train away safely. At 11.15am, however, the train gathered steam and gently slipped out of the station, the National Anthem playing, and leaving a solemn gathering of families and friends behind.

The *Derby Daily Telegraph* had proclaimed that this occasion had been 'the chance of a lifetime to see one's fellow workers march off to fight for Queen and Country'. Sadly the first half of the following century would see this event repeated not once, but twice.

A SKILLED WORKFORCE

ALTHOUGH Derby had long been recognised for its industrial prowess, it was soon to reinforce its position as one of the most important engineering towns in Britain. When a new business arrived, it was one which was to become one of Derby's primary employers – Rolls-Royce

Henry Royce had developed an early interest in electrical and mechanical engineering, pioneering a street lighting scheme for the city of Liverpool in 1882. He started his own company as early as 1884, and in 1903 modified and improved his own second-hand Decauville motor car which he had found irritatingly unreliable, building his first car from scratch by April 1904. In May of that year he met the Hon Charles Rolls, owner of a company that was already selling high-quality foreign cars in London. Rolls was a motor car enthusiast and had won a number of driving trials, along the way setting a world land speed record of 93 mph, at Phoenix Park in Dublin.

The two agreed to produce a range of luxury cars which would be sold exclusively by C. S. Rolls and Co under the 'Rolls-Royce' name. The first cars were ready for the public by December that year and the Rolls-Royce company was officially founded two years later. At this time Claude Johnson joined the board as managing director, an appointment which proved vital in the company's history as it was as much Johnson as Rolls or Royce who was the creative force behind the scenes and it was he who continued to guide the business onward after the death of its founders. Two years later Derby was chosen as the location for the new company headquarters and this began an intimate relationship between the town and precision engineering that would continue into the 21st century.

That year also saw Rolls-Royce launch its Silver Ghost, although this name was not used until the following year. The Silver Ghost was described as 'the best car in the world' and riding in it was described by *Autocar* magazine as 'being wafted through the landscape'. During World War One, Rolls-Royce cars were deemed so reliable that they were used as staff cars, ambulances and even armoured cars. Other models produced at Derby were the

Two names inextricably linked with Derby: Sir Henry Royce and the Hon C. S. Rolls, pictured in 1903 in the racing car in which he set a record over one kilometre.

Phantom and the Twenty. Demand for the cars was such that in 1908 a new purpose-built factory was established at Nightingale Road and production continued here until 1946 when all motor car manufacture was transferred to Crewe.

This left the Derby factories to concentrate on the work that had begun just prior to the outbreak of World War One – the design and building of aero engines. Royce designed his first aero engine – the Eagle – in response to the needs of the armed forces. The Eagle and its cousins the Hawk, Falcon and Condor proved so successful that Rolls-Royce powered more than one half of the total British and allied air power used in World War One. The Eagle engine also powered Alcock and Brown's first direct transatlantic flight and the first flight from England to Australia – both in Vickers Vimys.

Silver Ghost 40/50hp cars being assembled at no.1 shop at Nightingale Road in 1911. A ride on one of these was described as being like 'wafted through the landscape'.

The Rolls-Royce works at Nightingale Road. The original works there were built in 1907-08 but were extended later.

When Charles Rolls died in an air accident in 1910, the company had become very much the child of Henry Royce and in the late 1920s the 'R' engine was developed to provide power for Britain's entry into the prestigious international Schneider Trophy seaplane competition. The 'R' set a new airspeed record of more than 400 mph in 1931 and went on to set more world records on land and water too. Most significantly, though, it provided the company with the basis for the Merlin engine.

Royce had begun the work on the Merlin but it was not finished until after his death in 1933. Completion of this engine proved not only to be crucial in the development of the company and in Derby's industrial future, but also in the very history of Europe, for it was the Merlin which would power the RAF during the Battle of Britain in 1940, and in many bombing raids over the Rhur in the years which followed. In 1940 Merlin-powered Spitfire and Hurricane fighters gave Britain vital air superiority

which averted the threat of a German invasion. For its reliability and adaptability the Merlin is probably the most famous of all aircraft engines and besides the Spitfire and Hurricane fighters, Halifax, Lancaster and Wellington bombers and the Mosquito fighter-bomber, as well as the American Mustang and a host of others were powered by Merlin engines. Modified versions of the Merlin were used in land-based combat vehicles and tests were undertaken to assess the engine's potential as a torpedo.

Alongside the Merlin, Rolls-Royce were the first to build Sir Frank Whittle's gas turbine engine. In June 1941 a test plant was established in Derby and by the end of the year the company had been commissioned by the British government to develop and produce this engine. The earliest versions of these to go into mass production were the Welland and the Derwent, which both quickly passed the required endurance and safety tests and were put into service powering the Gloster Meteor towards the end of the war. Later models also took the names of British rivers and included the Dart which was the first jet engine to go into civilian service with the Vickers Viscount in 1953; the Avon which provided the power for the De Havilland Comet and was the first turbojet to fly across the Atlantic; and the Conway which was the first turbofan engine with the Boeing 707 in the 1960s.

But in more recent years it has been the RB211 that has provided the main income for the company. Its development, though, almost resulted in the closure of the company. By 1971, the escalating research and development costs of the RB211 had far exceeded the agreed amounts, and with the company contractually obliged to sell the engine at a fixed price, bankruptcy was a certainty. Only extreme emergency intervention by the British government saved thousands of Derby jobs, not just at Rolls-Royce itself but also at several local companies for whom Rolls-Royce was the main customer. The whole company was nationalised and broken up into several divisions, assuring its continuation. Despite the early teething troubles, the RB211 has become the mainstay of modern civil aviation. With more than 2,400 engines currently in service with dozens of operators, it has completed more than 75 million flying hours and a 535 model run by Icelandair holds a world record, having completed more than 40,000 hours on wing.

An RB211 engine, the project which brought the company to bankruptcy but, ironically, the one on which the company's subsequent success was built.

And it is not just in the air that Rolls-Royce engines reign supreme. More than 20,000 commercial and naval vessels use Rolls-Royce equipment – a remarkable figure which includes no less than 400 ships in 30 navies and, in particular, the Royal Navy for which Rolls-Royce supplies nuclear propulsion systems for the submarine fleet.

Rolls-Royce is also a world-leader in generating systems for power stations where it has used modified aero engines as generators.

The future now seems relatively secure, although following the company's return to the private sector in 1987 a number of mergers, acquisitions and closures have significantly reduced the size of the Derby workforce. The new Trent engine continues alongside the RB211 series in leading the way in power engineering and the company have opened a state-of-the-art training facility at their main site and are working on the development of engines for the new 'superjumbos'. At this moment some 2,400 corporate and utility operators and 100 armed forces use Rolls-Royce precision engineering – something of which Derby is deservedly proud. The terrorist attacks in the United States in 2001, though, had a profound effect on the commercial aircraft industry and, inevitably, Rolls-Royce looked to be affected.

Commercial success
Throughout history the settlement of Derby has become renowned for its innovative industrialists and its skilled workforce. The textile, porcelain, railway and engineering industries are best known, but Derbeians have excelled in many different areas of industry and commerce. Although Derby's near-neighbour of Burton upon Trent is widely recognised as Britain's 'brewing capital', Derby was itself once a thriving brewing town. In the 17th century, the town was one of the country's major brewing centres with as many as 76 malthouses at one point. And although the brewing industry has faded over the years, there have been other industries and individual companies that have continued in the proud tradition of their forebears.

The food industry is not one automatically associated with Derby but one of the country's best-known manufacturers owes its origins to the people of the town. In the late 19th century a young man named Matthew Walker was employed in Mr Hodgkinson's high-class grocery shop. At the turn of the 20th century, Walker had opened his own business on Exeter Street. From here he sold Christmas puddings made to an old family recipe and, by the outbreak of World War One, these were in high demand among Walker's customers. Now, of course, Matthew Walker have relocated to Heanor and supply many supermarket own brands as well as

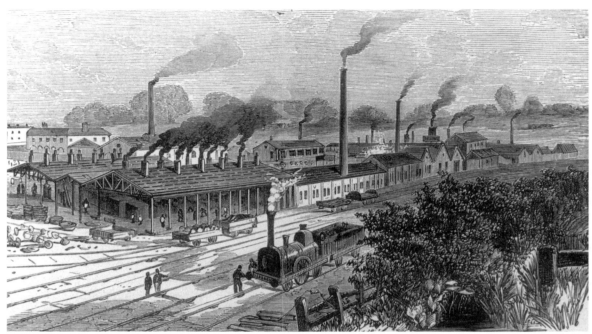

The 19th century saw Derby's burgeoning industrial base. *Top:* James Eastwood's foundry at Osmaston Road in the 1850s. *Bottom:* Haslam's Union foundry at City Road in the 1890s.

their own much-loved range of puddings which are sold in many countries.

It is a little-known fact that from 1820 to 1891, at 98 Friar Gate in Derby, Mr Jacob Schweppe from Switzerland ran one of his first three English factories producing Schweppe's soda water.

And modern Derbeians are now helping to contribute to one of the most successful food businesses in the country. S & A Foods was founded by Perween Warsi and her husband in 1987. Dismayed by the poor choice of supermarket-bought Indian snack food, Mrs Warsi decided to produce her own. The company soon grew into a thriving cottage industry and from that into what has been called the UK's fastest-growing independent food manufacturer. Now producing a large range of high-quality 'ready meals', S & A Foods is one of Britain's most important success stories. At Derby the business employs around 1,500 people and has an annual turnover reckoned to be approaching £100 million. In 1996 Perween Warsi was named Woman Entrepreneur of the Year and a year later received the MBE in recognition of her achievements.

Although virtually unknown outside of the Derby area, Bird's the Confectioners are certainly a company of which locals can be proud. Their famous claim 'we never sell a stale cake', and the familiar scent emanating from the local Bird's shops have delighted generations of Derbeians since the end of World War One. Now there are around 40 branches and all sell the same familiar range of delicious traditional favourites.

Old favourites of a different kind were once produced by Hampshire's, first at their Silk Mill premises and then, following a serious fire there, at Sinfin Lane. Hampshire's were founded in 1895 and produced some of our best known domestic, cosmetic and food products such as Wasp sticky fly paper, Supersoft and Loxene shampoos and hairspray, Snowfire, Zubes throat sweets and Creamilla ice cream powder. In 1965 the company became Reckitt and Coleman and began to manufacture familiar products such as Mr Sheen, Harpic and Windolene.

The Bemrose Corporation was founded in 1826 by William Bemrose in Wirksworth, relocating to Derby soon after. From the first offices in Irongate, Bemrose's soon established themselves as a leader in all kinds of printing, becoming the official printer for the railways. Today the firm, now an international business, specialises in security printing, gift vouchers and also calendars.

One company which has carried the city's name far and wide is that of clock manufacturer Smith of Derby, which can trace its origins back to the days of John Whitehurst. Smith's is now the largest UK firm specialising in the manufacture and restoration of public clocks. In 1893 Smith of Derby produced the clock known as Great Tom for St Paul's Cathedral. Smith clocks are also seen throughout the world atop high-profile buildings such as the Savoy Hotel in Moscow, the Hyatt-Regency Hotel in Belgrade, the government building in Kuwait City, skyscrapers in Chicago and in St Petersburgh in Florida; and the company recently installed six large clocks for

TO THE SOUTH POLE WITH CAPTAIN SCOTT

IN 1912, the attention of many Britons was fixed firmly southward as news was eagerly awaited of the adventures of Captain Robert Falcon Scott as he attempted to reach the South Pole. For Derbeians there was extra cause to follow Scott's progress – the town had its own representative with the expedition party.

Dr George Clarke Simpson was born in Derby in September 1878, at 44 East Street. The son of a local alderman and JP, Arthur Simpson, he had attended the Diocesan School before furthering his studies at university. Simpson had been serving with the Indian meteorological service and joined Scott's expedition in a similar role. One of the main purposes of the trip to the Antarctic was to undertake atmospheric research, and that was Simpson's sphere. Simpson had sailed aboard the expedition's boat, the *Terra Nova*, to South Africa where they were joined by Captain Scott. When they arrived in Antarctica, Simpson and several others remained with the base camp to complete his research while Scott and the others set out for the Pole. Fully intending to remain with the expedition until its conclusion, Simpson received word that his deputy in India had been taken ill, and he briefly returned to Derby in June 1912 before sailing for India. Little did anyone realise that the last of the party had perished three months earlier. That news would have to wait for the return of the *Terra Nova* in February 1913. In tribute to his colleague, Simpson named his first child Scott. Dr Simpson later went on the become Director of the Meteorological Office and President of the British Meteorological Society. He died in January 1965.

Disneyland Paris. They have also completed restoration work on clocks at Windsor Castle, Kensington Palace, St Pancras station and Westminster Abbey.

DERBY AND THE GREAT WAR

AS the 19th century turned into the 20th, Europe had been transformed into a political tinderbox waiting for the spark which would set off a full-scale conflagration. Britain, preferring to concentrate on matters of empire, had remained aloof from the political machinations that for decades had boiled on the European mainland, particularly in the Balkans. However, during the long, hot summer of 1914 it became clear that Britain could ignore the situation no longer.

On 28 June that year, in Sarajevo, a 19-year-old Serb named Gavrilo Princip, a member of Young Bosnia, a nationalist organisation seeking union with Serbia, shot dead Archduke Ferdinand of Austria-Hungary, and his wife Sophia. That was the spark. On 28 July, Austria-Hungary declared war on Serbia and as Russia mobilised in support of the Serbs,

Germany declared war on Russia on 1 August. On 2 August, the Germans demanded right of passage through Belgium, which Belgium naturally refused. On 3 August, Germany declared war on France and the following day invaded Belgium on their way to crossing the French border. Bound by treaty to protect Belgium's neutrality, and concerned about threats to the Channel ports, Britain had little alternative but to take up arms. War with Germany was declared on 4 August 1914.

The full enormity of an all-out European war was yet to emerge but already the *Derby Telegraph* predicted, 'Empire Faced With A Life And Death Struggle.' The effects were felt in Derby immediately as the same edition of the newspaper announced that the price of bread had gone up by a halfpenny per loaf. Soon there were shortages of flour and sugar,

THE GREAT ZEPPELIN RAID

FOR the people of Derby, the war was to come a lot closer to home on the night of 31 January and 1 February 1916 when German Zeppelins let loose their bombs over the workshops and stores of the town's railway industry.

Prior to World War One there had been two separate aviation technologies. The emerging aeroplanes were relatively flimsy in construction, heavier than air and strong enough only to carry one or two persons per craft. The airship, however, was lighter than air and so able to transport several tons in weight. They were magnificent too, and none more so than the giant German blimps of the Zeppelin Company. The Zeppelin was massive yet elegant with a gentle, sweeping

The engine shed after the bombing.

movement accompanied by the steady drone of their great propeller-generated power. But upon the outbreak of World War One, this awesome sight of wonder was to be turned into one of terror when the German

army and navy developed Zeppelins as weapons of destruction and began aerial bombing raids of Britain.

And they were effective too, since the Zeppelin could fly safely in most conditions and was particularly menacing under cover of darkness, whereas the fixed-wing biplanes of the British forces were often grounded since night-flying was still extremely dangerous. Even those who could intercept a Zeppelin were at a disadvantage. The Zeppelins were well armed and held a relatively stable position in the air, allowing gunners time to take aim before firing. British tactics relied upon quantity rather than quality of targeting and gunners found it hard to inflict any significant damage even when they did pepper the bulkheads with gunfire, until a 'mixed ammunition' system was utilised which caused the hydrogen gas which powered the Zeppelins to mix with oxygen and then explode.

The first Zeppelin raids had concentrated on coastal Britain. In January 1915 the east coast had been targeted and in May that year came the first raids on London. Quickly the raids became more daring, eventually stretching as far north as Edinburgh. The Midlands were not to escape either, and in particular neither was Derby. On that late January night, 10 German Zeppelins crossed the Channel and travelled across England headed for the city of Liverpool. Although repeated bombing raids had led to restrictions on lighting across the country, this was far from complete and since the Loco and Carriage and Wagon Works' war work was considered of prime importance, they were only required to comply during

Bomb damage at no.18 boiler shop at Derby Loco Works following the Zeppelin raid of 1916.

special alerts. And although such an alert had been given when the Zeppelins had first appeared in the skies of Derby at around 7pm, by the time they returned, having failed to reach their target, the lights of the railway were shining out like a beacon in contrast to the rest of the blacked-out town.

Although no official order had been given, each individual workshop had elected to turn on its lights, convinced that the danger had passed. As each light went on, the next workshop turned on theirs and by the time the Zeppelins returned the whole area was illuminated. In all nine high explosives were dropped near No 9 Shed of the Loco Works, inflicting severe damage and killing four men: William Bancroft, Henry Hithersay, James Gibbs Hardy and Charles Henry Champion who died three days later from his injuries. A further five bombs were dropped on the Carriage and Wagon works and some fell near the gasworks at what is now Pride Park.

Just before being posted to Salonika during World War One, Bill Poynton of the Derbyshire Yeomanry poses for a family photograph with his wife Annie and daughter Beatrice. The Poyntons were a Normanton family and were living in Cameron Road when this picture was taken.

Macedonia in the case of the Yeomanry; at the Somme, Ypres, the Menin Road and Passchendaele in the case of the Foresters. Although those left behind as their loved ones, once more, marched off to war probably had no real comprehension of the horrors that were to come, they would have been little comforted by the words of one particular advertisement in the *Derby Telegraph*. Weston's chemist's shop on St Peter's Street asked, 'How can your boy stand at ease if he is worried by vermin?' The advertisement promised that the 'Kergold Belt' would provide 'six months' freedom from body pests' for just 2s 6d (12½p). Conditions in the trenches may have been well-documented in more recent years, but the horrific sights and stenches, the awful mud and filth, the relentless bombardment and continual terror encountered by the soldiers minute by minute are beyond our comprehension, of that there is no doubt. And perhaps we are little better equipped to understand the sense of loss and loneliness of those left behind. But though we may not realise it, we are still feeling the effects, both good and bad, of that conflict, and of the one which was to follow it.

The changes which World War One brought to daily life in Britain were to last far beyond the Armistice in 1918. For the first time the entire economy of the country was concentrated on fighting an enemy. Mass production went into overdrive. Industry and technology, while forced to assist the war-effort, also benefited from investment and advances were made at a rate probably far greater than would have been achieved in peacetime.

Factories abandoned their usual production and took on specialised war work. At the Carriage and Wagon Works in Derby, ambulance trains, army wagons and parts for rifles were all produced. And the Loco Works began to turn out field gun carriages and gun cradles as well as recycling 18-pounder brass shell cases. Here, too, as they would in the next conflict, women joined their men in the workforce. Hundreds of Derby women took jobs in the foundries and other heavy industries, and many kept those roles after the Armistice. In total in Britain by 1918 there were nearly five million women at work, which marked a significant rise from the figure of just over three million in 1914. Women were not permitted to serve in the armed forces but could take part in voluntary work. Eventually, as more and more men were called up, women moved into the less

and prices went up right across the board. E. H. Simpson & Son of St James's Street were advertising, 'Blue Serges are very dear and will be more so.' Rationing, particularly of petrol and food, was introduced at once, although regulations would be far less stringent than those imposed during World War Two.

The majority of Derby men who either volunteered, or later were conscripted, served with either the Sherwood Foresters or the Derbyshire Yeomanry, who were headquartered at Siddalls Road. Both the Foresters and the Yeomanry were to participate in battles across Europe, the most recognised of those being at Gallipoli (now Gelibolu in Turkey), Salonika (now Thessaloniki in Greece) and

War memorial in the Market Place, erected in 1924 to remember those who had fallen during World War One. The victims of later conflicts were commemorated and in September 2001 the memorial became a focal point for those wishing to leave floral tributes to victims of the terrorist attacks in the United States.

as well as cinema newsreels of events like the Battle of the Somme, depicting not only heroic and patriotic images but also wounded and dead British servicemen, all served to heighten the resolve of the British people.

With Britain in the grip of war and now under seemingly constant risk of attack from the skies, those who called themselves pacifists, who refused to join the fight under any circumstances, were feeling the considerable antagonism of the public, particularly of those who had watched their own loved ones march into battle and felt that pacifism was simply a synonym for cowardice. Those who could prove beyond doubt that they were morally or religiously opposed to war, rather than merely attempting to avoid conscription, were permitted to do essential non-combative work. However, particularly for those posted to the Medical Corps, life as a non-combatant was far from safe. For many it meant a posting on the front line and frequent trips into 'No-Man's Land' to retrieve wounded and dying colleagues, often coming under heavy fire themselves. It was certainly no place for cowards.

Some refused to take part in the war at all and were generally placed in detention centres. Many others were sympathetic to their cause and across the country were 'safe houses' where those wanting to avoid detention could seek refuge until it was safe for them to move on. Mrs Alice Wheeldon of 12 Pear Tree Road, Derby, ran one such refuge. Her son, William, was himself a conscientious objector and Alice and her daughters, Hettie, Winnie, Nellie, and her son-in-law Alfred Mason, were all pacifists. The family believed that Prime Minister David Lloyd George was personally responsible for the deaths tens of thousands of soldiers. They had told several people they thought the Prime Minister deserved to die for his actions and the family would soon find themselves accused of a murder plot and right at the centre of one of the most dramatic and astonishing political intrigues of the 20th century.

Alice and Hettie Wheeldon and Winnie and Alfred Mason were accused of plotting to assassinate Lloyd George. Alfred Mason was a chemist in Southampton and he and his wife sent Alice a package which was found to contain the poison curare. The Wheeldons claimed that they had intended to use the poison to drug the guard dogs at

traditional jobs such as munitions work – where 700,000 were occupied – coal stacking and engine cleaning, and in 1917 the Women's Royal Auxiliary Corps was formed. In more aesthetic matters, shortages in dress materials, as well as practicality, saw the hemline rise above the ankle for the first time.

Buildings and homes were requisitioned for vital government use and as thousands of refugees arrived in Britain from mainland Europe, Derby played host to many Belgians. World War One also saw a change in the use of propaganda. Whilst most of us are familiar with the 'Your Country Needs You' recruitment posters – displayed in particular in the early years of the war – there were also graphic and often horrifying accounts of enemy atrocities. These, a detention centre for conscientious objectors. But in March 1917 the authorities attempted to prove in court that the plan had been far more heinous than a simple rescue mission. It was claimed that the Wheeldons had intended to shoot Lloyd George and a member of his War Cabinet with air gun pellets coated in the deadly poison. There was enormous public interest as the trial began and the unimaginable scandal of a plot to murder the Prime Minister undoubtedly took some attention away from an increasingly unpopular war. Hettie was acquitted but her three co-defendants were convicted.

All three could most certainly have received the death penalty for their actions, but they escaped with short custodial sentences. At the request of Lloyd George himself, Alice was released after only nine months in prison, the Masons after less than two years. The leniency of the sentences perhaps lends credence to the theory that the Wheeldons were provoked into the action by an undercover agent of MI5. Alice Wheeldon died in 1919, just a few months after the Armistice. Her son William took up Soviet citizenship that same year, and he was joined by his sister Nellie who married socialist activist Tom Bell. Their sister Hettie married Arthur MacManus, the first chairman of the British Communist Party.

Great rejoicings

On Monday, 11 November 1918 came the news every soul in Britain had been praying for – the Great War was ended. Speculation of a cease-fire had been rife for several days. It was well-known that the tide had turned in favour of the Allies and that the German people were tired, starving and now standing alone in their cause, Austria-Hungary having already signed an armistice with the Allies. Earlier, there had been naval and military uprisings in Germany. It was also well-known that an offer of peace had been presented to Germany several days before, and since the abdication of the Kaiser the previous Saturday, anticipation had reached fever-pitch. There had been a huge crowd in the Cornmarket on the Sunday, waiting outside the *Derby Telegraph* offices for the latest news to be posted, but still no word had come.

Injured soldiers and their nurses pictured at the King's Ward, Derbyshire Royal Infirmary, in 1915.

When Derbeians awoke on Monday, though, it was to the joyous news that the Armistice had been signed at 5am French time, and that a full ceasefire would be enforced precisely six hours later. 'Great rejoicings in all free countries', ran the *Derby Telegraph* headline.

Immediately, calling-up papers were cancelled, restrictions on lighting bonfires and fireworks were eased and, for the first time in several years, church bells and public clocks could ring out night or day. Thanksgiving services took place all across the town – at St Alkmund's, St Thomas's and St Werburgh's, as well as at the Congregational Church in Victoria Street. The jubilation would soon subside, though, to be replaced by so much sadness particularly in the homes of the estimated 1,200 Derby men who had perished in the Great War.

The memorial in the Market Place was unveiled in 1924, its simplicity a lasting reminder of those ordinary men who gave their lives for the assured freedom of their families and friends. And outside the Midland Hotel stands a magnificent memorial, designed by Lutyens who was also responsible for the Cenotaph in Whitehall. It commemorates the fallen 2,833 employees of the Midland Railway, from right across the country. So many had been killed. In some cases villages were left without any young men, for all had joined the same fighting unit, and all had been obliterated in a single moment.

VALOUR OF NO ORDINARY KIND

DERBY'S **Jacob Rivers** was a true hero – an ordinary man thrown into extraordinary circumstances and responding with outstanding courage. Born in 1881 to a poor family from Bridge Gate, he attended Orchard Street School. In 1899 he had joined the Royal Scottish Fusiliers and served in India. On his return to Derby he found employment as a labourer with the Midland Railway but at the outbreak of war, aged 33, he was one of the first to volunteer. It was on 12 March 1915 that Rivers and his company of Sherwood Foresters found themselves essentially trapped by German forces at Neuve Chapelle in France. In the words of the *Official Gazette* of 28 April:

Private Jacob Rivers VC.

'Private Rivers, on his own initiative, crept to within a few yards of a very large number of the enemy who were massed on the flank of an advanced company of his battalion, and hurled bombs on them. His action caused the enemy to retire, and so relieved the situation. Private Rivers performed a second similar act of great bravery on the same day, again causing the enemy to withdraw. He was killed on this occasion.'

For his remarkable acts, Rivers was posthumously awarded the Victoria Cross which was accepted by his widowed mother, Adeline.

The *Derby Daily Telegraph* reported: 'In a war like the present, in which every man at the front is proving himself as an undoubted hero, the winning of the Victoria Cross can fall to the lot of but a small proportion of those engaged. Its possession therefore, bespeaks valour of no ordinary kind but represents courage allied with resourcefulness of the highest type.'

Rivers, of course, was not the only Derby man to have exhibited such uncommon valour. In 1855 **Robert Humpston**, who was born in the town in 1832, the son of a local tobacconist, had been awarded the VC for his actions whilst serving with the Rifle Brigade in the Crimean War.

'On 22 April 1855 in the Crimea, Private Humpston and another private, on their own, attacked and captured a Russian rifle pit situated among the rocks overhanging the Woronzoff Road. The pit was occupied every night by the Russians and its capture and subsequent destruction was of great importance.'

Humpston and his colleague had also been able to regain control of the vital water supply. He received his VC from Queen Victoria in Hyde Park on 26 June 1857, the first-ever VC investiture. In addition to his VC, Humpston was also awarded the French Legion d'Honneur. He later served in India during the Mutiny.

The second Derbeian to win the Victoria Cross was **Henry Wilmot**, who was born at Chaddesden Hall in February 1831, the son of Sir Sacheverel Wilmot. Educated at Rugby School, Henry Wilmot had served in the Crimea with the Rifle Brigade (Prince Consort's Own) before being appointed Deputy Judge Advocate in India in 1857. On 11 March 1858, in heavy fighting around Lucknow during the Indian Mutiny, Wilmot won his VC.

'…Captain Wilmot's company was engaged with a large number of the enemy near the Iron Bridge. That officer found himself at one stage at the end of a street with only four of his men opposed to a considerable body of the enemy. One of his men was shot through both legs and two of the others lifted him and although one of them was severely wounded they carried their comrade for a considerable distance, Captain Wilmot firing with the men's rifles and covering the retreating party.'

After serving in China, Wilmot returned to Chaddesden and became Conservative MP for South Derbyshire before succeeding to the baronetcy. He died in April 1901.

Three years after Jacob Rivers's VC, another Derbeian earned the highest honour. Born at Fern Bank on Trowells Lane in 1892, **Charles Hudson** was the son of a colonel with the Sherwood Foresters and had attended Sandhurst before running a tea plantation in Ceylon. Like Rivers, he joined up immediately upon the outbreak of war in 1914. Serving on the Asiago Plateau in Italy towards the end of the war, he found himself the only surviving officer of a battalion that had been unexpectedly taken out by the enemy, but Hudson did not hesitate.

'On 15 June 1918 near Asiago, Italy, during an attack when the enemy had penetrated our front line, Lieutenant-Colonel Hudson collected and personally led various headquarter details such as orderlies, servants, runners, etc to deal with the situation. He rushed a position with only men, shouting to the enemy to surrender, some of whom did. He was severely wounded by a bomb which exploded on his foot and although in great pain gave directions for the counter-attack which was successful, about 100

prisoners and six machine guns being taken.'

Hudson also received the Italian Silver Medal for Valour - the Valore Militaire – and in later years earned the Military Cross, the Distinguished Service Order and bar and the French Croix-de-Guerre, as well as being mentioned in despatches on no less than six occasions. When the Unknown Warrior was laid to rest in Westminster Abbey in 1920, Hudson was part of the honour guard. He became chief instructor at Sandhurst, achieving the rank of major-general, and spent two years as aide-de-camp to George VI.

Rivers, Humpston, Hudson and Wilmot were undoubtedly great heroes, their acts of courage something for every Derbeian to be justly proud, but during World War Two another Derby man was performing acts of incredible courage almost daily.

Harold Lilly had been born in Spondon in 1888. During World War One he had seen action on the Somme and as lieutenant-colonel was serving as commanding officer of the 1st/5th Battalion Sherwood Foresters when Malaya and subsequently Singapore fell to Japan in January and February 1942. He and his troops were captured and imprisoned at Changi jail, later being forced to march 85 miles from Singapore through mosquito-infested jungle in searing heat and

unbearable humidity to Wampo where they were put to work on the infamous Burma Railway. He was placed in command of 1,500 PoWs, almost a third of whom were to die during the three-and-a-half years that followed, either from their injuries, from their living conditions, or from their ill-treatment by their captors. Lt-Col Lilly was remembered by all those under his command for his continual efforts to protect his fellow prisoners from punishment, often taking severe beatings on their behalf. He also worked constantly to improve conditions, managing to secretly obtain essential medical supplies from locals outside the camp. Lilly's men, and the Malayan volunteers he also helped, held him in high esteem and he even earned the respect of several of his Japanese captors.

Although he survived his captivity, his health had suffered irreparable damage and he died just nine years after his liberation. His parents, who had died during the war, were never to know the fate of their son nor of his heroism.

Henry Hewitt, born in Uttoxeter Road, was killed during a heroic attempt to rescue trapped miners at Cadeby Main Colliery near Rotherham in 1912. Mr Hewitt was a skilled mining engineer and became HM Inspector of Mines.

DERBY AND THE GENERAL STRIKE

ANATION left to mourn a lost generation was a fertile ground for political change. Increasing numbers of people were adopting a pacifist line and many more were joining the more radical parties. Whilst Derby has never been a political hotbed, it had been the first place in England to elect a Labour MP. Richard Bell, a native of Merthyr Tydfil, served the people of Derby between 1900 and 1910. He had been the second Labour MP in Britain, beaten only by Keir Hardie who had been elected the previous day. Bell was succeeded by Jimmy Thomas, a much-loved and colourful character who was to serve Derby for more than a quarter of a century during some of the most turbulent years in modern times. Jimmy Thomas had long been associated with the trades unions. At the time of his election as MP for Derby, he was chairman of the National Union of Railwaymen, a union with which he has been largely credited with creating. He went on to play a prominent role in the General Strike of 1926.

The General Strike had begun with a crisis in the coal industry, mine owners wanting to cut wages but the unions refusing to accept this. The miners had threatened an all-out strike and had enlisted the support of most of the country's major unions. When no resolution could be reached, the TUC called upon all workers in all unions to prepare for strike action. Those working in the health, food and sanitation industries were exempt. In Derby, just as matters were coming to a head, the annual May Day service was being held in St Werburgh's where Canon Alfred Blunt caused more controversy by preaching what was perceived by many to be a pro-socialist sermon, although Canon Blunt denied this, claiming that he had merely been advocating brotherly love and support. Although negotiations continued right up to the deadline, no agreement could be reached and a strike date was set for 4 May 1926. Immediately the government declared a state of emergency.

As the General Strike began, the country came to a standstill. Factories fell silent and all public transport ceased. Across Britain emergency centres were opened; at Derby one was based at the Guildhall. Here volunteers were organised to run essential services. Information was almost impossible to acquire, there being no newspapers, and crowds would gather daily outside the offices of the Derby papers the *Telegraph* and the *Express* for the posting of important news. By 12 May the government was declaring that the strike was over. Many unions did return to work, but the dispute was far from ended. Several unions were still dissatisfied with their lot. The miners' strike, which had begun the mass walk-out, was not resolved until December. Another continuing dispute concerned railway workers and here Jimmy Thomas, a man whose name was familiar to Derbeians, was deeply involved.

The man who leaked the Budget

Jimmy Thomas was one of the 20th century's most colourful political figures, the Welsh train driver who became a prominent Cabinet member before finding himself the centre of a national scandal which forced him to resign in disgrace.

Thomas had first come to Derby in 1906 as an official of the Amalgamated Society of Railway Servants, to speak in support of Richard Bell's re-election as Labour MP for the town. It was Bell who Thomas would replace four years later. In January 1910 he polled 10,189 and together with Sir Thomas Roe became one of the town's two MPs.

Thomas enjoyed a reputation as an outstanding trade unionist. Whilst MP for Derby he led the national rail strike of 1919 and obtained terms which at that time were regarded as of great material benefit to the men he represented. Two years later, however, he was in the news for a different reason when he took the railwaymen along with other transport workers in not supporting the miners, thus splitting the traditional union triple alliance.

In Ramsay Macdonald's 1929 Labour government, Thomas was Lord Privy Seal and began a public works programme which cost £42 million. In 1931, with a growing financial crisis, King George V asked Macdonald to form a National Government and Thomas was one of the Labour men who agreed to serve in it, as Secretary of State for the Dominions. Five years later, however, his career lay in ruins. As Colonial Secretary in Stanley Baldwin's National Government, Thomas was at the centre of an

Derby MP Jimmy Thomas prepares for a newsreel interview.

extraordinary political scandal when he was found guilty of disclosing Budget information, particularly matters relating to income tax, to a friend and another MP.

Thomas, who had vehemently protested his innocence, resigned first his Cabinet post and then his Derby seat. Only a year earlier, already an honorary freeman of the town, he had been asked to the King's Hall to receive a collection totalling £2,750 – which he gave to Derby hospitals – and a gold watch and chain. Mrs Thomas was presented with a 149-piece Royal Crown Derby dinner service.

Jimmy Thomas died in London in 1949, best remembered as the man who leaked the Budget. With his Privy Councillor's uniform and dropped aitches, some thought him an amusing figure, but he was held in high regard in Derby.

At the height of his powers he once commented: 'The most enjoyable meal I ever had was to open my wife's basket on a snappy winter's morning on the footplate of my engine and find a pound of juicy steak which I fried myself on my shovel. You come to a meal like that with an appetite which no public banquet can command.'

PROMINENT POLITICIANS

Michael Thomas Bass MP.

Michael Thomas Bass was MP for Derby from 1848. He was the grandson of the founder of the famous brewery that bore the family name. A Liberal, he reflected the very philanthropic ideals popular in the town at the time, and served seven periods in office. He helped to found St Christopher's Railway Orphanage in the 1870s and took up the cause of the railwaymen when they campaigned for shorter working hours. He financed the building of the Library and Museum and donated land to the town which is now known as Bass's Rec.

The **Rt Hon Sir William Harcourt PC** served Derby as MP from 1880 to 1895, following a period as MP for Oxford and as Solicitor General. He served as Chancellor of the Exchequer and introduced death duties, and was also Home Secretary and from 1886 was deputy to Prime Minister William Gladstone.

Samuel Plimsoll was elected in 1868. He was the wealthy owner of a flourishing coal mining business and had become very concerned by the lack of safety precautions taken in the industry. In particular he was alarmed by the habit of shipping companies sending old, unseaworthy vessels, dangerously overloaded with coal, halfway around the world. In 1873 he published *Our Merchant Seamen* to draw public attention to the problem. He also invented a new device to prevent the overloading of vessels. As a ship became heavier with cargo it would also become lower in the water. A symbol was painted on the side of the ship indicating a line above which the water must not rise. Once the water reached this point, the ship was full. The symbol became known universally as the Plimsoll Line and it has been credited with saving hundreds of lives. In 1890 Plimsoll published *Cattle Ships* which exposed the danger and cruelty of the sea trade in cattle. He retired as Derby's MP in 1880 but continued to campaign for the cause of the seamen and later railwaymen.

Like many of the men who represented Derby in parliament **Philip Noel-Baker** was not a native of the town. He was elected in 1950 and served that position for 20 years. He had already led a colourful and productive life, having competed in the three Olympic Games and winning a silver medal for the 1,500 metres in the Antwerp games of 1920. His involvement in sport was something he continued during his political career. In 1952 he became commandant of the British Olympic team and in 1960 became president of the International Council of Sport and Physical Recreation with UNESCO. A Quaker by upbringing, he was an ambulance driver during World War One and was awarded the Italian Croce di Guerra and was also instrumental in the establishment of the League of Nations. During his political career Noel-Baker held many important government posts. He was Minister of State at the Foreign Office from 1945; Secretary of State for Air; Secretary of State for Commonwealth Relations; and, from 1950, Minister for Fuel and Power. He was an expert in international relations and was awarded the Nobel Peace Prize in 1959 for his work during the Russian Famine, and for his continued efforts to promote peace. On receiving his award he stated: 'War is a damnable, filthy thing and has destroyed civilisation after civilisation - that is the essence of my belief.' He was a proponent of military disarmament and campaigned against the US involvement in Vietnam.

Philip Noel-Baker was not the only man with Derby connections to become an accomplished diplomat. In 1947 **Sir John Shaw** was appointed Governor and Commander in Chief of Trinidad and Tobago. He was the nephew of **Lt Gen Rt Hon Sir Frederick Shaw** who had been born in Regent Terrace in 1861 and educated at Repton. Sir Frederick Shaw had served with the Sherwood Foresters and had later accepted an appointment as Governor of Kandia in Crete. He later moved to the War Office and was awarded the French Legion d'Honneur, the Serbian White Eagle and the Chinese Wen Hu.

Sir Robert George Howe was the most distinguished diplomat to have been born in Derby. Born at 6 Carrington Street, the son of a loco driver with the Midland Railway, he had been awarded a scholarship to Derby School and graduated from Cambridge in 1915 from where he had entered the Foreign Office. He became the Third, then Second Secretary at Copenhagen. Then he moved to Belgrade, to Rio de Janeiro, to Bucharest and back to the Foreign Office. He was Assistant Counsellor at Peking in 1939-40, during the Chinese Civil War and the invasion by Japan, and was working at the British Embassy in Riga, Latvia, when the Soviets invaded, and was later posted to Addis Ababa in what was then Abyssinia. From 1945-47 he was Assistant Under-Secretary of State at the Foreign Office and from 1947-55 he served as HM Governor General of Sudan, after which he retired.

A TOWN OF SOME IMPORTANCE

IN 1917 the Church of England had proposed that Derby should be granted its own diocese. Some 10 years later, on 7 July 1927, the Diocese of Derby was finally formed, taking part of the Dioceses of Southwell and Lichfield. On that day, All Saints' Parish Church became Derby Cathedral. The official ceremony did not take place until 28 October, the weekend before All Saints' day, with the enthronement of the new Bishop of Derby, Dr Edmund Courtenay Pearce, taking place the following day. There had been much deliberation as to which church within the diocese should serve as the Cathedral. Others under consideration had included St Werburgh's, St Michael's at Melbourne and the famous crooked spire church at Chesterfield. That any other church should even be considered for such a prestigious role seems quite unimaginable when one considers the magnificence and grace of All Saints'.

Dr Edmund Courtenay Pearce, first Bishop of Derby.

DERBY CATHEDRAL

THE Cathedral Church of All Saints' is a dominating presence on the modern city skyline, being visible from several miles away on all approaches to the city. Although worship has taken place on this site since the tenth century, the oldest part of the present Cathedral, the Gothic tower, dates from the time of Henry VIII and was completed in 1530, after 20 years' work. It is a particularly fine example of its period and at 212ft (64.6m) tall it is the second-highest parish church tower in England – after the famous Boston Stump of St Botolph's in Lincolnshire. Over the centuries there have been several phases of building to the body of the church but throughout, the great tower of Ashover grit – a coarse sandstone quarried from Duffield Bank – has remained. Major alterations to the rear were made in the 18th and 20th centuries, nave and chancel respectively, the latter being constructed of artificial stone, although the building still appears as a whole, flowing structure.

The tower itself contains the oldest ring of 10 bells in the country. In fact the oldest – the tenor – is older than the tower itself, dating from the 15th century. The remaining bells date from the 17th century. The original clock was replaced in 1732. The shafts that drive the hands are made from mid-18th-century gun barrels, reputedly left behind by the army of Bonnie Prince Charlie. The main mechanism of the clock was replaced in 1927.

On a bright sunny day the honey-toned stone is a dramatic contrast to a deep blue sky. On a few selected days each year the tower is open to the public. The climb is certainly not for the fainthearted or the claustrophobic, and at 189 steps neither is it for the unfit. But for

Interior of Derby Cathedral, showing the Robert Bakewell screen.

one bay to the east (closer to the altar) but was moved in 1927 when the church became a cathedral. It provides a clear definition between nave and chancel, but is delicate enough to allow an uninterrupted view from one side to the other.

Bakewell's other works
Robert Bakewell, creator of the beautiful wrought-iron screen in Derby Cathedral, was one of the leading artisans of his day. Among the buildings decorated by Bakewell is the famous Radcliffe Camera in Oxford, as well as many important buildings in London.

those who can manage it, the view from the top is spectacular – on a clear day the whole city and beyond is visible. From here, too, it is possible to see in context the ancient trackways – now major streets – that meander still through the city centre. The dramatic Gothic tower often fools the first-time visitor into expectations of a dark, forbidding interior. Reality, of course, could not be more different. The over-riding impression is of light and space – the Sun streams in though the windows and the white plastered walls, with terracotta and rose, belie any preconceptions of sombreness. At Christmas illumination is provided by dozens of candles, their flickering light thrown back and forth between the graceful sweeping arches.

Although the three generations of the building are virtually indistinguishable from inside, the main body of the church was rebuilt in 1725 after the medieval fabric had decayed severely. The architect was James Gibb, the Scotsman responsible for St Martin's-in-the-Field in London. The resulting interior is one of the finest examples of Gibb's work. It is a calming, peaceful building - the simple, natural colours punctuated only by the spectacular modern stained glass windows, designed by Ceri Richards and representing All Saints and All Souls. The eye is drawn immediately to the magnificent and intricate ironwork of the Bakewell Screen. It was crafted by Derby ironsmith Robert Bakewell in 1725 at a cost of £500, to the design of James Gibb. Above the central gates is the coat-of-arms of the House of Hanover, the monarchs of the period. The screen originally stood

Beyond the Bakewell Screen lies the sanctuary area. It is perhaps the most magnificent feature of the whole cathedral. The Bishop's Throne was taken from a Greek church by the Turks in World War One and donated to the cathedral in 1927. The altar and sanctuary stand beneath the grand canopy. The lettering here represents the first two Greek letters of the word 'Christ'. Near the altar stand the cathedral banners which are for processional use.

There are a number of additional fascinating features within the cathedral and a walk around is always very rewarding. Details of a self-guided walking tour are available near the entrance and the friendly cathedral staff are always available and willing to answer any questions. Some of the most noteworthy features are as follows:

Near to the Bakewell Screen are the steps leading down to St Katharine's Chapel. The chapel was consecrated in 1978 and is used throughout the week for services and quiet prayer. It is usually open to all, and the small altar is made from local crinoidal limestone which has the appearance of fine marble but in fact contains the fossils of tiny primitive creatures captured there some 340 million years ago. The bronze crucifix was crafted by a local Derbyshire artist.

Just past the chapel, through the small gate in the screen at the end of the aisle, lies the Cavendish area belonging to the family of the Dukes of Devonshire. The main feature of this area is the rather ostentatious tomb of Bess of

Hardwick, Countess of Shrewsbury. Also visible are copper and brass plates commemorating some of her descendants, notably Henry Cavendish, the scientist who was the first to calculate the mass of the Earth; to identify the composition of water and to identify hydrogen. The family remains lie in lead-lined coffins in a chamber to the rear of the chapel.

The font, crafted from Greek Pentelic marble, was made as recently as 1974; however the design was a James Gibb original.

In front of the Bakewell Screen, to the centre of the nave, stand the mayor's pew featuring the symbol of the City of Derby – the Buck in the Park and, opposite this, the County Council pew featuring representations of industry, commerce, and agriculture.

Behind the screen is an old oak table, which was once the altar of St Michael's Church and now serves as an offertory table. The legs are carved with a notation of the table's donation by Joanne Edge in 1625. In the early 19th century, this area was used for parish meetings and, by the Corporation, for the choosing of the mayor.

The grand organ is located at the west entrance. It was rebuilt in 1938 and given a new case in 1963 and was a gift of the first provost. The gallery above affords an excellent overview of the cathedral.

Along the north aisle there are a number of memorials to local families, and in the corner near the entrance lies the Book of Remembrance. The flags, or colours, are those of the Grenadier Guards, and the local regiments of the Sherwood Foresters and Derbyshire Yeomanry, and there is also a memorial to the Burma Star Association.

On exiting the cathedral, beneath the tower, the visitor passes through glass doors bearing verses of Psalms 43 and 84. Above the door is the great west window which is decorated with four coats-of-arms: the Province of Canterbury, and the Dioceses of Lichfield and Southwell and the arms of the Diocese of Derby itself.

The Royal Show

The establishment of the Derby diocese brought a new sense of civic pride to the town. This had reached fever-pitch when, in 1933, King George V and Queen Mary visited the town to attend the Royal Show.

This prestigious event had taken place in Derby no fewer than five times since 1843. And each time the showground of old Osmaston Park, once part of the grounds of Osmaston Hall and now occupied by the Ascot Drive trading estate, had provided the location. Preparations had been under way for several days, the town's hedges trimmed neatly and several roads along the parade route benefiting from newly-laid surfaces. The weather was hot and bright and a recent heatwave had caused grave concern for the welfare of many of the animals. Three of the 1,000 hens at the showground had perished, as had a number of pigs.

But for the people of the town, the sunny weather was the perfect accompaniment to a perfect week. As the *Derby Evening Telegraph* was to report: 'The old borough of Derby lived today a story which might have been lifted straight out of a book of fairy tales, when, beneath a canopy of blue skies, amid a blaze of colour and with stately pageantry and splendour, the king and queen paid their official visit to the Royal Show at Osmaston.'

The royal couple had arrived by car from their base at Chatsworth and had transferred to an open carriage which was pulled by two beautiful grey horses. The *Telegraph* again, '…past cottages and mansions, and offices, shops and works, every window of which was framed with eager and smiling faces. From Allestree to Alvaston the royal route was gay with flowers, flags and bunting.'

As the king and queen arrived in the Market Place, the band of the Sherwood Foresters played the National Anthem.

At the showground the couple toured the displays and waved to the happy crowds. T. Rowley & Sons of Green Lane, who were usually entrusted with such important tasks, provided the queen's bouquet of mauve orchids.

In total the show attracted more than 100,000 visitors, many from outside the town. The *Telegraph* commented that at least one sightseer had arrived camera in hand determined to photograph all that Derby had to offer.

A new sports stadium

And there was much to see, for Derby was in the midst of a major redevelopment which, thanks to the intervention of World War Two, would take close on 20 more years to complete. The opening of the Municipal Sports Ground in August 1923 may be said to mark the beginning of a new era in the town. Known for many years as simply 'the Muni', it had been built as a public work, designed to help give work to the large numbers of unemployed following the end of World War One and the subsequent economic depression.

The Municipal was to prove controversial from the outset. Even as it opened, international cyclists claimed that the concrete track around the banking was unsuitable for first-class racing because high speeds were quite impossible due to what they considered the inappropriate positioning of the bends. The Derby public, however, were more than happy to take advantage of the opportunity to race their cycles or motorcycles free of charge, while out-of-towners could do the same for a charge of threepence an hour. The opening month, however, was marred by tragedy. On Wednesday, 12 September 1923, Baden Marples Masters, a 23-year-old newly-wed from West Bridgford, riding a 2½hp Blackburn-Massey machine, was thrown 60ft over the safety rails and landed on his head. He suffered severe injuries and died seven hours later at the Derbyshire Royal Infirmary.

Plans for the expansion of the Municipal Sports Ground continued. Later that year there was speculation that Derby County would move to the complex, but this petered out the following year when the Rams bought the Baseball Ground outright from the Ley family. Throughout the 1920s and 1930s the Municipal was an important regional venue for sporting events of all kinds, from athletics and soccer to outdoor boxing.

After World War Two, plans were set out to transform Derby's Municipal Sports Ground into a

The Municipal Sports Ground on Osmaston Park Road, a product of 1920s public works.

The Wembley of the Midlands? A model of what the Municipal Sports Ground might have looked like had futuristic plans been implemented in the early post-war years.

magnificent sporting complex of which the whole country, let alone the town, could be proud – a sort of 'Wembley of the Midlands'. It was intended to accommodate some 78,600 spectators in large grandstands. Below the stands would be swimming pools, indoor sports facilities, a gymnasium, changing rooms and also room for catering and dancing as well as administrative offices. And again the Rams were expected to move in. But this plan failed to become anything other than a glorious dream and the Municipal continued as it was, largely neglected, for another 20 years. In the 1960s the stadium benefited from the installation of floodlighting and once more became a focus of sporting attention as local football finals and schools events came to the arena. It was also home to the highly-regarded Derby and County Athletic Club. In 1974 the Municipal Sports Ground was joined by Derby Sports Centre and the Moor Lane Swimming Baths which were each built on a separate side of a large car park which did little to enforce the idea of a state-of-the-art sporting complex. Indeed, they were run by different council departments. In the 1990s, however, following local government restructuring, the entire complex was combined under the 'Moorways' name which brought it a little closer to the original idea.

On the right road

Back in 1924 radical plans had been drawn up to change the face of Derby's town centre. It was felt that several of the town centre streets would benefit from widening, and that a new ring road was needed to take road traffic away from the centre. The Central Improvement Plan (CIP), as the fine-tuned proposal of 1931, was named, had a number of simple aims: to improve traffic flow and roads around the town; to improve market facilities; to build a modern bus station; and to create a municipal centre, comprising town hall, magistrates' court and police station which would form one coherent development, with the river front becoming an attractive feature of the town.

Derby's borough architect Charles Aslin was set to work on the complete design. Beginning in 1931, land was cleared along the river bank and along the Morledge where a number of old wharves and industrial works were removed. Among the first and most notable old landmark to disappear was the Shot Tower, which helped to make way for the new Council House as the town hall part of the development was to be called. In addition, the Markeaton Brook culverting was completed, and the present-day Exeter Bridge also dates from the CIP. Initially, the development was intended to incorporate a fire station at the Full Street end of the scheme, but this never materialised.

First traffic lights
The first traffic lights in Derby were erected in St Peter's Street in 1929.

Derby in the 1920s, showing the Shot Tower still in situ, where the Council House car park now stands.

It is now the late 1930s and the Shot Tower has gone but work on the Council House has yet to be started. The new police station and magistrates court have sprung, up, though, and the bus station is to the extreme right of the picture.

In July 1932 work began on the new river wall, and in 1938 the construction of the municipal buildings got under way. The 'Open Market' was moved here from the Market Place and survived into the 1970s when the Eagle Centre opened. The Open Market on the Morledge served the town for decades, traders' cries echoing across the avenues of traditional market stalls. Crowds gathered to watch as goods, from crockery to cabbages, were tossed and juggled, the entertainment value of the traders' patter almost as important as completing the weekly shop. Those familiar sights, smells and sounds were lost when the market moved indoors, the unusual honeycomb

The magistrates court and police headquarters were part of the 1930s Central Improvement Plan.

Derby Council House, the last part of the Central Improvement Plan to be completed.

layout of the original Eagle Market apparently not conducive to the same atmosphere. The fact that Open Market stallholders had to endure some extremes of climate also helped produce some robust 'characters'.

Derby bus station, the subject of so much contention in the 21st century, was in its day a unique and efficient terminal. Its railway station-styled platforms were curved to take maximum advantage of a relatively small area. The canopies and refreshment facilities alone made it one of the best of its day and it is not without good reason that it will be remembered with great affection by many. Whether or not its uniqueness, either in form or architecture, is sufficient to merit its protection from redevelopment is open to much debate. What is certain is that in our modern era we have come to expect better facilities yet, more effective protection

from the elements and a greater degree of comfort than that provided by Aslin's bus station. If – and it seems this must be the case – the 1930s structure is to be replaced, then it seems entirely in keeping with the intentions of the CIP that a state-of-the-art bus station for the 21st century should take the place of one with its feet firmly in the middle of the 20th. Perhaps the incorporation of some element of the original may ease the transition from old into new.

Aslin's bus station pictured in 1935 when it was 'state-of-the-art'. Over 60 years later it remained unchanged and, to many, inadequate for the 21st century, although others wanted to retain it as it stood.

In common with the bus station it seems that most other elements of the CIP of the mid-20th century have been found to be insufficient for the needs of the 21st century. The police headquarters have moved to purpose-built premises at St Mary's Wharf and the reorganisation of the magistrates' courts in the city will soon leave the entire Full Street section of the CIP empty. And here, too, there are plans for major redevelopment. The Council has since found it necessary to relocate many of its key departments in the Heritage Gate complex in Friar Gate. However, the Council House itself remains very much the seat of local authority power and is also a familiar and important symbol of civic pride in what is now the City of Derby. As one of the last projects to get under way, work had advanced little on the new Council House when it was halted by the events of September 1939. For now, its completion would have to wait, there were more important things on the minds of all Derbeians.

AT WAR AGAIN

ON a sultry late summer Saturday evening in 1939, a violent storm erupted in the skies over Derby. It was a storm worthy of a warning from the gods, a portent of tempestuous times ahead. As thunder bellowed, rain lashed and forks of lightning exploded, five barrage balloons were brought down in flames. For this was a town, and a nation, on high alert. Defences at the ready, a fearful uncertainty hanging in the air. War had been feared, expected even, for several months. The promised halt to the Nazi expansion across Europe had never come. Ultimatums had been made and ignored, and finally defied. Preparations had been made should the worst come to the worst – sandbags placed around public buildings, gas masks issued. But the awful inevitability of war seemed to sink in only over that weekend in early September. Memories of the Great War still fresh in people's minds, many still mourned husbands, sons and brothers, and the very real possibility of sacrificing yet another generation was too much for many.

On Sunday, 3 September 1939, as Prime Minister Neville Chamberlain broadcast to the nation – '…and consequently this country is at war with Germany' – people stood in their front gardens and in the streets. With their families, their friends or with strangers. Some walked, some cried, all were sombre. None seemed to want to be alone, as if by gathering together they could garner strength and support and resolve to face whatever the coming months and years would bring. Just like they had at the outbreak of the Great War, all hoped it would be over by Christmas, but now few believed it. In the end, it would be six years before the country would know peace again. And in those six years there would be much sadness and grief. But there would be joy and humour too, and many friendships forged through shared hardships.

The people of Derby may have thought the war might come slowly to them, but they were jolted awake at 3.30 the following morning when the first air-raid siren was sounded. It was a false alarm, but no doubt awakened everybody's senses to the imminent danger. Within a few days of the outbreak of war, some 3,000 local children had been evacuated from the centre of town to the countryside. Derby, as the home of Rolls-Royce, feared heavy attack from the air and 60 buses took the children from evacuation centres and away from their sobbing parents. As the danger appeared to recede, many returned home and eventually Derby and its immediate area became a new home for children evacuated from other cities.

More than 9,000 air-raid shelters had been delivered to private homes and public shelters were established under the railway arches in Lodge Lane, in Full Street and in the crypt of the Cathedral. Trenches were dug at Derwent, Rykneld and Osmaston Recreation Grounds, each designed to accommodate dozens of people. There were practice air-raids and Derbeians were encouraged, at home and work, to be prepared for immediate evacuation to the shelters once the alert sounded. Windows across the town were taped to prevent shattering, blackouts were rehearsed and enforced, and auxiliary services such as the fire brigade honed their skills on abandoned buildings. Valuable records and museum artefacts were removed for safekeeping and volunteers were requested for the ARP and other auxiliary services. The first German plane to be spotted above Derby arrived on 6 December 1939. It was a Heinkel reconnaissance plane, and by this time a programme of camouflaging those buildings identified as key targets had been implemented. Derby artist Ernest Townsend had been called in to

Members of the Local Defence Volunteers (later the Home Guard) limbering up at the Baseball Ground in September 1940.

King George VI inspects Indian troops at Derby in August 1940.

paint trees on the power station, and other buildings were similarly treated. The blackout itself, apart from proving inconvenient in the extreme, was also credited with a huge increase in the number of road traffic accidents and people tripping and falling, and this was as true in Derby as it was elsewhere.

Yet despite all this disruption it became a 'Phoney War' until in May 1940 the German army swept through the Low Countries. Derby man Dundonald Jackson, a Rolls-Royce service engineer who had been working in Belgium, was forced to make a dash for safety with his wife and personal assistant under cover of darkness. As they hurried to the Belgian coast they passed hundreds of British soldiers rushing in the opposite direction to try to stave off the German advance. At one point the three were forced to take cover in a ditch while a German fighter machine-gunned the road. Eventually they reached the coast and managed to squeeze aboard a Belgian steamer jammed full of refugees. Despite coming under attack once more, the Jacksons made it back to their home in Swinburne Street where they found a town fearful of imminent German invasion.

A few days later those fears were heightened still further when Derby LMS station saw the arrival of the tattered remnants of the ill-fated British Expeditionary Force who had been plucked from the beaches and the sea at Dunkirk, having been beaten back to the coast by the oncoming Germans. One of the last to be lifted to safety had been Derby County centre-forward Jack Stamps, now a burly gunner in the Royal Artillery. Fate had lent a hand and Stamps would play an heroic role of a different kind six years later.

With the threat of invasion increasing daily, the government formed the Local Defence Volunteers, later to be known as the Home Guard, the 'Dad's Army' immortalised by television some 25 years later. Many of those too old to be called up into the armed forces joined the LDV, as did those too young, those in 'reserved occupations' whose work was deemed essential to the war effort, and those awaiting their call-up papers. A significant side-effect of 'invasion fever' was the internment of enemy nationals. At Derby LMS station, which had become a clearing centre for 'aliens', hundreds of nuns and members of other foreign religious organisations gathered to board trains to take them to the Isle of Man where they would spend the duration of the hostilities.

The first bombs

On 25 June 1940 the first bombs fell on Derby, and they claimed the first victims. At Mickleover, Mrs Elsie Henson, aged 39, whose parents lived in Shepherd Street, Littleover, was hit by bomb splinters in the head, chest and legs as she tried to enter the shelter at her home in Jackson Avenue. Her injuries were severe and six days later she died in Derby City Hospital, a few hundred yards from where she had been injured. Although most modern accounts give Mrs Henson as Derby's first civilian casualty, according to the Commonwealth War Graves Commission the first civilian death was that of Elizabeth Evans, 67, who died at her home in Violet Street on the 25th itself.

By August that year, air-raid alerts were coming almost nightly and Derby police had to prevent frightened Derbeians from camping out in their shelters. On the 14th of that month, Margaret Agnes Hutton died at her home on Hawthorn Street, and an overnight four-hour raid on 19/20 August, on Litchurch, left three dead: Annie Andrews of Litchurch Street died en route to the DRI just a few dozen yards away from her home; and Doris Bentley and her daughter Sheila of Regent Street died the next day in hospital. Because of reporting restrictions the *Evening Telegraph* was permitted only to mention a raid on a 'Midlands town', although for those who had survived the previous night there were plenty of clues as to precisely which Midlands town had borne the brunt. The report even featured a photograph of 'a well-known Midlands football ground damaged by bomb splinters' which was quite clearly the Osmaston Stand at the Baseball Ground.

Of course the town was fiercely defended by anti-aircraft fire whilst giant oil burners were designed to create a cloud of smoke which obscured the town from the air on bright moonlit nights. It was effective, but the foul odour that hung in the air at all times was less than popular. And above the smokescreen could still be heard the steady, sinister drone of German aero engines as bombers passed overhead bound for the northern cities of Sheffield and Manchester. From Derby, too, could be seen the terrible fires in the night sky as bombs rained down on the cities of Coventry and Birmingham.

Since Derby was suffering less than many other cities, many Derbeians found themselves drafted in to help both their near-neighbours and those towns further afield. Fred Gifford was a divisional officer in Derby's Auxiliary Fire Service, and spent many nights fighting fires across the country. He remembered one particular battle with a fire at Thameshaven which lasted for three days. 'We'd arrive in a town as complete strangers and be directed by local police to our own particular fire, through streets ablaze on either side. Then we had to find the nearest water supply and get on with the job. Map-reading was essential even to get to the town because all the road signs had been removed during the invasion scare. Often we'd fight fires with bombs still falling around us.' When Fred Gifford died in the early 1980s it was largely the result of the appalling conditions he and his fellow firefighters had endured in the Blitz.

Troops ploughing land near Derby Racecourse in March 1941.

A waste of money?

During World War Two, a local coal merchant was fined £1 10s (£1.50) by Derby magistrates for wasting petrol. His crime? He had driven his son to watch Derby County.

Heaviest raid

There were nights, however, when Derby did come under fierce attack. The worst of these came on the night of 15 January 1941 when 50 high-explosive bombs were dropped in two alerts, the first from 9pm to 1.17am, the other from 3.15am to 5.20am. A dozen bombs fell on the LMS station and although half failed to explode they caused extensive damage

and wrought havoc. A large part of the main roof collapsed and part of the bridge which connected the platforms was reduced to a mass of twisted metal which blocked the lines. A wall fell killing several people, among them civilians Arthur George Hallows of Breaston and his near-neighbour Cecil Edward Purser, a member of the local Home Guard. Also killed that night were 25-year-old Harry James Smith of Chaddesden, and Christopher Snailham and Victor Rutherford Farrington, both from the Bolton area, who were waiting for a train as were a number of soldiers also killed. One body was found seven months later when the rubble was finally cleared. Six people were killed at the Park Gates on London Road: Margaret Ann Jackson, 43; Ruby Manifold Priestley and Ronald Rowland, both aged 18; Arthur Geoffrey Watts, 27; and Gwendoline Bertha Young, 21. Edna May Payne, aged 20, died the next day at the DRI. More bombs fell near the Cavendish where another six people were killed, four of whom – Gladys Emily Foss, her husband Sidney, and Elsie May Jones and her daughter Christine Elsie – died in hospital later that day having sustained critical injuries at home in Kenilworth Avenue. At nearby Offerton Avenue, Rachel Ellen Percival and her daughter Brenda Ellen perished. The final victim of that January 1941 raid was Florence Brewster, who suffered critical injuries at her home on Madeley Street. She died in hospital on 5 April. In addition to those who lost their lives, some 48 others suffered significant injury and 1,650 houses were damaged. Because the names of victims could not be published in newspapers, crowds gathered around official notice boards which listed the dead. One other casualty that night was the Arboretum's bandstand which was severely damaged.

Terrible nights such as this saw the implementation of fire-watching. Many Derbeians risked injury nightly, stationed on rooftops alerting firefighters to potential risks across the town. By the middle of March 1942, Derby had more than 15,000 supplementary firefighters and as city after city across Britain began to suffer, preparations were hastened to deal with Derby's homeless in the event of air-raids on the Coventry scale. Soon, 30 emergency feeding and rest centres were equipped and ready to provide accommodation for up to 5,000 people. Two other casualties were air-raid warden Thomas Gerald Fitzgerald, who was killed outside his Shelton Lock home on 9 May 1941; and Arthur Adamson, who died at the Carriage and Wagon Works on 9 July the same year.

Food scarce

By now food shortages saw long queues, some forming as early as 8am. In March 1942, onions became so scarce that police had to be summoned to quell a disturbance in a queue for them. Queues formed for every conceivable foodstuff from sweets and biscuits to potatoes and cheese. Sometimes people joined a queue without knowing what was at the end of it. Other items also became scarce and Derbeians trudged from shop to shop searching for cigarettes. In September 1941 the Trent Bus Company, blighted by an enforced reduction in services, introduced travel permits with priority given to workers, schoolchildren, the Home Guard when on duty and patients attending hospital.

The day they raided Rolls-Royce

Despite Nazi propaganda that the Rolls-Royce factory was being flattened almost nightly, very little damage had been done to the Derby works, surrounding villages often bearing the brunt of the Luftwaffe's attacks instead. At Melbourne 10 were killed when a lone bomber ditched his entire payload over the village, and two more lost their lives at Long Eaton. Remarkably Rolls-Royce, the home of the Merlin engine – the power behind the Battle of Britain and the RAF's own bombing campaign over Germany – suffered only one significant attack. It came one overcast July morning in 1942 and, although it would

cause minimal damage to the works itself, it would become one of the most dramatic and poignant stories of Derby's war. From the start of the war, Royce's had employed a system of aircraft spotters on the main factory roof at Nightingale Road. During times of increased alert, an additional spotter and gun crews joined the main spotter. The changes of shift for the spotters and gun crews ran parallel with that of the workforce. At 7.30 the night shift stood down, but the day shift was not due to begin until 7.55, leaving the site undefended for some 25 minutes.

An RAF barrage balloon crew at Alvaston in 1941.

Alone on the roof was 21-year-old spotter Doug Bates, who recalled years later: 'About 7.40am I queried the noise of an aircraft in the south – we used to have a lot of trouble distinguishing that sort of thing because of the noise from the test beds at Sinfin – and the controller told me: "There's nothing on the board this side of Coventry." Ten minutes later there was an almighty roar and a Dornier skimmed No.6 Shop with his bomb doors open and his machine-guns blazing away. He was so low that he had to bank round the factory's water tower.'

Only one bomb was dropped on the factory itself, fractionally missing thousands of pounds' worth of vital machinery and instead falling on a store where former Sherwood Forester Fred Day was on Home Guard duty. Again speaking many years after the event, he recalled: 'When the siren sounded I went to the Central Stores to collect my rifle from the officer. When I went in the place was deserted except for a young girl called Olive Bates, who was sitting at her typewriter. I begged her to go to the shelter but she just sat there and suddenly a hole the size of a manhole appeared in the roof and there were bullets everywhere. I remembered my army training and pulled her behind some office furniture and told her to tuck her head down with her hands behind it. Then there was a blinding flash and the next thing I was waking up in hospital. They had dug me out about three in the afternoon. It some time later that they told me the girl had died when the bomb fell.' Olive Bates was 30 years old.

Derby's Chief Constable later commended the swift actions of the Home Guard and the eight millwrights who had worked frantically on the debris that had been the steel stores.

Elsewhere, too, chaos reigned. More bombs had been dropped over No 4 Gate in Hawthorn Street, where houses opposite were destroyed. Rescue workers had been quickly on the scene, but found 22-year-old Dorothy Lena Farmer dead, and her two-year-old daughter, Sylvia Mary, critically injured. Sylvia died three days later. Here, too, air cadet Doreen Cecilia Jenkins, 15, Margaret Eileen Finan, 21, Dennis Regan, nine, and Arthur Bacon, 37, a former Derby County player and then a policeman, all died. On 2 August, Doris Nield, another victim of Hawthorn Street, died in hospital. Only a family dog rescued from the rubble survived. For another family fate had intervened; they returned from holiday to discover their house flattened.

The lack of anti-aircraft gunfire allowed the Dornier's pilot to fly very low and effective use was made of the machine gun which sprayed the bustling streets at change of shift. Killed in the immediate area of the factory were George Henry Gratton, Dora Greatorex, Francis Robert Grimmer, Charles Levi Horn, James Peach and Joseph Taylor. Sidney Higgins, Joe William Hill, Arthur Frederick Base and Vera Mabel Doggrell died later the same day at the DRI. Frederick Cecil Isaac lost his fight the following day, and Cyril Leslie Lowe, 31, died at the City Hospital in October 1943, some 15 months after being injured in the raid. Ethel Esther Lawrence and Elizabeth Helen Franklin were hit at Marlborough Road and Abingdon Street respectively.

Forty more were seriously injured before the Dornier made its escape to the north, where it is claimed that its bullets hit a Corporation bus on Kedleston Road. A few days later, the BBC monitoring unit at Caversham Park near Reading picked up a

Damaged houses in Offerton Avenue after Derby's heaviest air-raid of the war, in January 1941.

radio transmission from Luxembourg. It was in German, for German audiences, and was made by one of the aircrew that had attacked Derby:

'My objective was the Rolls-Royce factory at Derby …We soon came to a railway line we'd been told to watch out for. We followed it and saw Derby before us. Suddenly we received a hit in the astrodome and felt a jar. A barrage balloon had touched us …At the same moment we saw the works below. The chief shouted: "Out bombs! Factory below us!" I pressed the buttons and the bombs fell. The wind was blowing in through the smashed astrodome and we couldn't hear much. We dived into the clouds as the plane had been badly damaged by the collision with the barrage balloon. The right wing had been smashed. We turned for home under cover of cloud …We were all in high spirits at having succeeded.'

The Dornier and its crew managed to limp back to its base in Holland.

In the intervening years there have many theories as to why Derby escaped so lightly when compared with other industrial communities. Suggestions have ranged from its location at the foot of the Derwent Valley, to unusual weather conditions, or even sheer luck. More recently it has been suggested that Derby might well have suffered more extensive damage had it not been for the work of British codebreakers at Bletchley Park utilising the Enigma technology to intercept secret German radio messages. The following mysterious message was intercepted in June 1940: 'Bent-leg beam at Kleve is directed to the point 53° 24'N 1°W".' Intelligence officers linked this with an overheard conversation between two captured Germans about a radio beam that could guide bombers to their targets. It was not long before the radio beam was detected and jamming measures implemented. If the story is correct, this simple discovery probably saved dozens if not hundreds of lives in Derby, for the beam was apparently found to pass directly over the Rolls-Royce works.

The Yanks are here

The Japanese attack on Pearl Harbor in December 1941 had brought the United States into the war and in September 1942 the first 'Yanks' arrived in Derby. Although both black and white soldiers came to the town, the US forces operated a strict policy of segregation during off-duty hours and different nights were set aside for black and white soldiers to travel into the town to visit its pubs. The Americans brought with them a hint of Hollywood glamour and were regarded by locals as both exotic and strange.

The last all-clear

As the spring of 1944 approached, the British people had been hearing of more and greater successes against the enemy. Air-raids had ended and personnel and equipment had been removed from the town. Military traffic had increased on the roads heading south and column after column of tanks and armoured cars snaked their way around the edge of Derby as overhead Dakotas towed gliders through the skies. Military camps around the town were all but empty and it became clear that something of very great significance was about to happen. For Derbeians there had been at least one false alarm when, on one April night, a huge air convoy lit up the skies overhead and speculation mounted that the longed-for invasion of Europe had begun.

As June 1944 came, the people of Derby went to bed each night afraid to even consider the consequences should the invasion they all expected fail. Listeners to the early-morning wireless programmes on 6 June heard only news of the fall of Rome which had been announced the day before. Still they waited, and waited. Then, just after 9am, came the brief announcement: 'Under the command of General Eisenhower, Allied naval forces supported by strong air forces began landing Allied armies this morning on the coast of France.'

Initial excitement turned to disappointment and then fear when, on 13 June, the first convoy of wounded soldiers arrived at Derby LMS station. For the days, weeks and months that followed the sad sight of so many casualties would become unnervingly familiar. From July to September, the southern half of England was terrorised by V1s and V2s, the German's new terror weapon, a rocket whose engine cut out before it fell to ground and exploded with devastating force. Some 8,000 evacuees arrived in Derby, fleeing these 'doodlebugs'. In August 1944, the first consignment of lemons to be seen in the town for three years went on sale, giving hope at last that life would soon return to normal. But on the last day of that month came a stark reminder of the horrors of war. For the people of Chellaston, including small children on their way to school, there was a miraculous escape when two RAF planes – a Tiger Moth and an Airspeed Oxford – collided over the village before the Tiger Moth plunged in flames on to the main Derby road. Barry Helliwell, then a seven-year-old living in South Avenue, Chellaston remembers the crash well.

'Another couple of minutes and we would all probably have been killed. The Tiger Moth came down on Derby Road with the pilot trapped inside. It was a fireball and people just knelt on the road and wept and prayed. There was nothing anybody could do.' Overhead the pilot of the Airspeed Oxford, which had half its wing torn off, managed to steer the machine clear of the village in an heroic and selfless attempt to save lives. Just before his plane crashed in a field off Sinfin Moor Lane the pilot bailed out, but he was far too low to save his own life.

In foreign fields

As the war seemed to be drawing to a close, thoughts returned to loved ones still fighting, some prisoners-of-war. In particular the local regiments, the Sherwood Foresters and the Derbyshire Yeomanry, had seen active service at Dunkirk, in Norway, the Western Desert, Singapore, Salerno and Normandy. The Yeomanry had written for themselves a special chapter in their regimental history by accepting the surrender of the Axis forces at Tunis in May 1943.

In stark contrast, Derby had been stunned in February 1942 when hundreds of local men serving in the 1/5 Battalion, Sherwood Foresters, were among the 60,000 fresh troops who had arrived in the 'impregnable' naval base at Singapore just before it fell into the hands of the invading Japanese. For months there had been little or no news of their fate and it was the following year before anxious relatives received confirmation that their loved ones were indeed in Japanese PoW camps. It was 18 months later that the first personal messages began to arrive, but even then there was scant information and the agony had lasted for many long months after that.

Victory celebrations

Anticipation of the end of the war had been slowly building for several days by the time news finally broke. And yet when word did come of Germany's unconditional surrender, it came from German sources only. People waited and waited for official word from the British government, but none came. Some decided that the celebrations could begin anyway; for others victory was not assured until official word arrived. The result was much confusion and more than a little irritation. At the LMS works management were forced to allow all non-essential workers to go home when a group took the unilateral decision to down tools. Word went out that, provided the victory announcement came during the evening, employees could remain on holiday. Many workers, confused by this arrangement, turned up for work anyway and had to be sent home again. When word did arrive, that this was truly Victory in Europe Day, it came so late that the following day was also declared a holiday.

At teatime on VE Day, the Harrison family of Middleton Street received a great surprise. Through the door, to the delight of his wife and family, came Corporal 'Sid' Harrison of the RASC. Forty-four-year-old Corporal Harrison had made his way home from a German PoW camp, where he had been since his capture in 1941.

The scenes of celebration in Derby Market Place at midnight on 8 May 1945 had reached chaotic levels. Thousands gathered to share this moment, to enjoy the official victory illuminations and join in spontaneous 'jamming' sessions with local musicians. Those with little or no musical talent simply picked up anything that would make a noise and hit it in time to the music. The whole occasion came very close to spiralling out of control. A US military policemen found himself surrounded and his equipment stolen. A saloon car was pushed around the streets before being ripped to pieces. At the Plaza ballroom, police were called to eject hundreds of gatecrashers to Sam Ramsden's private party. And

it seemed that every street in Derby wanted its own party. In Stockbrook Street blackout material was burned to the solemn accompaniment of a gramophone wheezing out *There'll Always Be An England*, and in Agard Street, on the edge of Derby's West End, a piano was wheeled into the street. On Osmaston Road, a shopkeeper had effigies of Hitler and Goering hanging from his premises, while in Brook Street another Hitler dummy bore the sentiment: 'Adolf, you've had it!' Although rationing severely limited the availability of party supplies, communities had saved up money and precious rations for the occasion. Flags were flown, bunting strung and joyous people sang and danced, little deterred by the violent thunderstorm around noon. The weather had been balmy for several days and by 9 May there was a three and a half hour wait for rowing boats on Alvaston Lake. Some 7,000 people sat in the Arboretum watching the Searchlights Concert Party, and at Normanton Park around 3,000 listened to the Borough Military Band. Cinemas and theatres were busier than usual.

Celebrations were tempered, though, by the daily updates of the atrocities committed by the Nazis in the concentration camps of Belsen and Buchenwald. For the first time newsreels were able to show the horrific evidence. And for many Derbeians the war was still raging. Hundreds of families had loved ones still fighting the Japanese in the jungles of the Far East, many still imprisoned there. Three months later came news that the first atom bombs had been deployed on the cities of Hiroshima and Nagasaki. Readers of the *Evening Telegraph* were informed that 'all living things were seared to death …the dead are uncountable …when buildings were hit, every living being outside simply vanished in to air because of the heat.' The world was still considering the awesome, terrifying damage that could be done to humanity from a single bomb when the Japanese emperor surrendered on behalf of his people. The A-bombs had become the ultimate test of whether the end could truly justify the means. But whatever viewpoints anyone chose to adopt, the war was over and life could return to normal. For some, of course, this could never be the case. Years of separation from family and friends had resulted in a lasting estrangement that could never be resolved. For others, particularly those who had been imprisoned in the Far East, they and their world had changed for ever, the result of continued barbaric treatment, appalling conditions and abject misery.

On the morning of 15 August 1945, Derbeians awoke to hear the bells of the Cathedral sounding out the victory peal. For many it was the first confirmation that the war with Japan was also at an end, the official news having been delayed until midnight. Housewives rushed to town to queue for fish, meat, bread, and even flags. By 9.30am demand for bread was so great that bakers were restricting supplies to one loaf per customer. There were

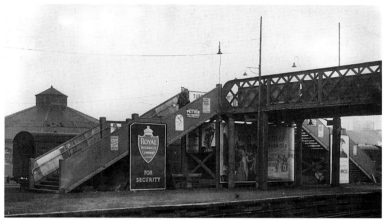

Despite the actions of the Luftwaffe, Derby LMS station was still open for business after the January 1941 air-raid.

angry scenes outside the Co-op's main store in East Street. It was closed and many of the women had not drawn their weekly rations of fat and other cooking requirements. A queue of 60 women waited for the Co-op offices in Albion Street to open so that they could draw their 'divi', only to be told that the Co-op would be closed for two days.

For the main part, though, Derbeians stuck to their tasks and of 180 Corporation bus employees on the early shift, all but 50 turned up for work. Buses ran to take night shift workers home, and staff to the City and Isolation Hospitals, before the bus crews themselves were stood down for the rest of the day.

With two-day leave passes in their pockets, hundreds of servicemen and women headed for the LMS station where queues for trains stretched down Midland Road as army and RAF personnel from bases around the town tried desperately to get home in time for the victory celebrations. A truckload of Afro-American troops made merry by 'careering around the town centre shouting and singing'. There had been scenes of wild excitement in the early hours of the morning outside Normanton Barracks. The midnight broadcast had been the signal for merrymaking and ATS girls stationed there had donned overcoats over their nightclothes and spilled out of the depot to celebrate. Members of the Sherwood Foresters band drew their instruments and soon a dance was in full swing on the barrack square as hundreds of nearby residents came out of their houses to join in. The vicar of Normanton arrived and civilians and soldiers joined in a service at the gates to the barracks. The men on the night

shift at the Carriage and Wagon Works, forced to remain at their posts, dragged the canteen piano into one of the sheds and began a sing-song which lasted until dawn.

On VJ Day itself, there were plenty of street parties. In Rivett Street, 30 children enjoyed home-made cakes and buns; the major feature of the party in Melbourne Street was a 7lbs (3.1kg) iced 'Victory Peace Cake' made by Mrs Ethel Wright; old age pensioners were invited to a children's party in King Alfred Street and enjoyed fruit, jelly, cakes and buns; in Goodwin Street, 161 happy faces testified to the quality of the fare bought by the £9 5s (£9.25) collected for the occasion; children in Offerton Avenue burned an effigy of the Japanese warlord Togo; the anti-aircraft battery on Kingsway loaned their canteen so that the children of the Westleigh Estate could stage their party; and on Chester Green there was a football match between local men and women who swapped clothes for the occasion.

Amidst the celebrations, though, there were also sombre moments. At midnight in the Market Place, a huge crowd sang *Abide With Me* before falling into a two-minute silence to remember the dead. And soon there would be the beginnings of reconciliation as in December 1945, the first Christmas of peacetime, German prisoners-of-war sat alongside local parishioners at Rose Hill Methodist Church on Normanton Road. After six long war-weary years, 148 air-raid alerts, some 50 civilian deaths, 152 high-explosive bombs, 164 incendiary bombs and nearly 4,000 houses damaged or destroyed, the people of Derby could finally regain their lives.

THE DAY THAT DERBY WON THE CUP

THE 27 April 1946 was to become one of the most important dates in history for the people of Derby. For it was on this day that Derby County secured the FA Cup for the first time in the club's history.

The 1946 FA Cup Final was the first peacetime Final after the end of World War Two and following the Rams' semi-final victory over Birmingham there was a desperate scramble for the 12,000 Wembley tickets made available to Derby supporters.

By the week of the Final the FA Cup was virtually the sole topic of conversation in the town. That this was the first post-war Cup Final meant that the Rams and their opponents, Charlton Athletic, were also the focus of attention for the entire nation. The LMS had laid on special trains to take fans to London and some had arrived in the capital as early as 1am on the Saturday. By dawn thousands of Rams fans had arrived and, determined to take in all the sights, they swarmed the streets, causing one observer to describe Piccadilly, where so many had gathered, as 'Little Derby'. Although all season ticket holders had been guaranteed a place at Wembley, on the morning of the Final tickets were going for up to 20 times their face value.

The team had been named two days earlier and many had been disappointed that the popular Sammy Crooks had been left out, manager Stuart McMillan not considering him sufficiently match fit to risk on such an important occasion. As it was, the players were in the middle of a stretch of four games in eight days as they tried to complete their league programme. Derbeians were well aware that the Rams could still secure the League South title – the Football League proper had not yet resumed after the war – but the romance of the Cup was all-consuming and it was difficult to be concerned about anything other than the Wembley game.

The Final itself was a steady affair at first. With no score after 80 minutes, the Rams had enjoyed the best of the play. Then silver-haired football genius Raich Carter sent a low throw-in to Reg Harrison, who passed the ball to Stamps. Stamps chipped the ball on to the head of Peter Doherty, who in turn steered it down for Dally Duncan to shoot from 10 yards out. After hitting Charlton defender Bert Turner, the ball was deflected past the helpless goalkeeper Sam Bartram and Derby were ahead. But jubilation among Rams fans was shortlived as a shot from Turner was deflected past Vic Woodley via the shin of Doherty. The last five minutes of normal time were frenetic and dramatic. Jack Stamps struck a shot so hard that the ball burst and landed harmlessly at the feet of Bartram and with the teams level after 90 minutes, the game went into extra-time.

Now Derby took control,

Derby County captain Jack Nicholas displays the FA Cup to cheering Derby supporters at Alvaston after the club won the trophy in 1946, for the only time in its history.

scoring after only two minutes when Stamps's cross-cum-shot from the left was blocked by Bartram and pushed into the path of Doherty, who just beat Duncan to slip the ball into the net to put the Rams in the lead at 2-1. Ten minutes later Doherty laid on a goal for Stamps, and the two linked up again early in the second period of extra-time to give Stamps his second goal, and Derby their fourth. Derby skipper Jack Nicholas received the trophy from King George VI and the celebrations began. Derbeians not fortunate to have been at Wembley that day had to wait until the following Tuesday to greet their heroes – the team had a league fixture at Southampton on the Monday. At Alvaston the victorious players transferred from their coach to an open-topped brewery dray for a celebratory parade around the town. A civic reception was laid on at the police station on Full Street (the Council House was not yet complete) and the players appeared on the balcony there to be congratulated by thousands of jubilant fans.

DERBY AGAINST THE ELEMENTS

AS anyone who experienced the high winds and rain of the winter of 2000-01 will recognise, there is very little to be done when Mother Nature decides to play rough. Although blessed by one of the most moderate climates in the British Isles and seemingly spared from most of the extremes of weather experienced by less fortunate parts of the country, Derbeians have long been forced to battle harsh weather conditions.

As early as 1587 there are records of serious flooding of the Derwent and, particularly, of Markeaton Brook, which caused noteworthy damage to St Mary's Bridge. In 1601 flooding caused the steeple of St Werburgh's to fall, which happened again in 1698. Nine years later another flood drowned three prisoners at the gaol on the Cornmarket when their brookside cells became inundated with floodwater. A year later, a worse flood still occurred and in September 1659 the 'lower parts of the town were almost drowned'. In 1673 three bridges were destroyed and in 1677, 1698 and 1740, St Werburgh's was again flooded, the floor being torn up on the latter occasion. That particular flood also swept cattle away and at Alvaston caused the death of a man who was drowned while trying to save his livestock.

One of the best-recorded of Derby's floods is the one that occurred on 1 April 1842. That morning many residents awoke to find Markeaton Brook flowing past, and in many cases inside, their ground-floor rooms. Following a sudden and sustained heavy rainstorm, the new culverts had been able to dispose of only around a third of the rainwater and the remainder had surged into the streets. The affected area spread as far as Friar Gate and Brook Street – where one woman was drowned. The worst-hit areas were Sadler Gate, the Wardwick and Cornmarket which were submerged beneath 6ft (1.8m) of floodwater. Today, on an exterior wall of the Wardwick Tavern, a marker records the maximum height of the flood. Although this marker is still a dramatic indicator of the depth of the floodwaters, it is important to consider that the modern street level is several feet higher than that of 1842. Where there are now steps down into the pub, in 1842 the steps

went upwards and so the relative depth of the flood is truly breathtaking. Many residents lost their valuables and a great deal of damage was done. Livestock were drowned and shopkeepers found their produce had been washed away. Even when the floodwater receded, Derby's problems were not over – the stinking, often glutinous mess which was left behind severely hindered repairs.

Derby's famous philosopher, Herbert Spencer, designed a new anti-flooding system for the town, but his advice went unheeded and his ideas ignored until another devastating flood hit the town in the 1930s.

That particular flood, in 1932, was caused by the fall of more than 3ins (76mm) of rain in 36 hours. Again it was the Markeaton Brook area that was worst hit, from the West End to the Derwent, and it was even more severe than that of 90 years earlier. Some 8ft (2.4m) of floodwater easily submerged all the markers from the 1842 event. Many people were trapped in their houses and several properties in Bridge Street saw the entire ground-floor level awash. Pavements and road surfaces were lifted and in St Werburgh's churchyard gravestones were dislodged. More than £400,000 of damage was done in the town centre. The next day, with the clean-up operation well under way, there was more damage. In the Cornmarket most of the businesses were still closed, but outside many people were milling around. As staff at the jewellers H. Samuel's busied themselves with cleaning and disinfecting their premises, gas was silently leaking into the basement. At 2pm the gas ignited and there was a massive explosion which sent debris outward into the Cornmarket itself. As staff sifted through shovelfuls of rubble to recover any gold, silver or precious gems, police stood guard. In all the shop reported losses of around £10,000.

Severe winters have been another repeated hazard. In 1875-76, for instance, Derby's poor died in the streets as snow and sub-zero temperatures gripped the town for weeks.

It began snowing on 13 December 1875 and continued throughout the next day as the town all but disappeared under a white blanket. Then

Above: May 1932 and the Morledge is under water in the last flood to inundate the town centre. *Below:* November 2000 and the Derwent laps against the highest step in the River Gardens. An inch or two more and the scene of 68 years earlier would have been repeated.

temperatures began to fall in what would be one of the worst winters Northern Europe had ever experienced.

Christmas brought no relief and the daily meal of bread and water for male vagrants was supplemented with gruel. The Town Council made it illegal for people to make slides on the icy pavements and a local doctor claimed that the practice of salting the pavements was causing people's shoes to rot and giving them pneumonia. One Derby vicar blamed the latest clothes fashions for bringing on a chill.

In the first week of 1876 horses could not stand up and beggars died in doorways. Then, on 7 January, more snow was followed by three days of torrential rain and Derby was awash with melting snow, a place of damp, filthy slush. But the month-long freeze was over.

There have been many severe freeze-ups within living memory, but perhaps none so harsh as the dreadful winter of 1946-47. With Britain still in the grip of severe post-war rationing, Arctic conditions and shortages combined to leave the entire country just a short step away from calamity.

Shortages in coal supplies saw the government enforce reductions in power across the land. Prime Minister Attlee appealed to the British people to

reduce their use of power as much as they could. Then an overall reduction meant that selected areas had to endure total power cuts that lasted up to an hour at a time. By mid-December came the first warnings of snow and freezing temperatures. Initially the crisis appeared to come to a head in the week leading up to Christmas. Ten degrees of frost were forecast for the Derby area and it was already possible to skate on the Mundy Paddling Pool at Markeaton Park. Mass powercuts were imminent. Housewives had problems enough with food shortages; now it seemed there might not be enough gas or electricity to cook the traditional Christmas dinner. As it turned out, Christmas itself passed without incident, although the weather was cold, foggy and rainy. New Year heralded something of what was to follow, though, with strong gales and a sudden drop in temperature, although quite how bad things were about to become was not yet clear.

Fuel shortages meant that large employers such as Ley's were unable to restart production after the Christmas shutdown. On 6 January a thick blanket of snow fell on Derby. As always, children managed to find time for fun – snowballing and skating on Derby's park lakes. But dreadful road conditions caused two lorries to collide on St Peter's Street. The resulting traffic jam only exacerbated the chaos. The next day the whole nation suffered a 10 per cent reduction in the electricity supply. To make matters worse, a week-long strike at Smithfields meat market in London, and another by haulage workers, threatened food supplies still further.

Tragically there were several casualties. Eight people were killed at Grindon Moor when an RAF Halifax bomber came down in poor visibility. The crew had been trying to drop urgently-needed supplies to villages cut off by snowdrifts. And two men were killed when a Trent bus carrying 34 Rams fans on the way to an FA Cup-tie at Stamford Bridge collided with a lorry. In Derby itself six people needed treatment when a double-decker bus toppled over into a ditch between Chaddesden and Morley.

The weather brought chaos to public transport right across the country. The Manchester to London train, which stopped in Derby, was more than 14 hours late in the capital.

Thousands of workers were forced to stay at home, some estimates quote 20,000 of them. House-holds were urged to switch off all non-essential power at peak times. When the people of Derby did not respond enthusiastically, the borough electrical engineer compulsorily shut off the supply to the entire town. He said, 'We have had to go to the extreme because the public has not co-operated.'

Only the town centre was spared, since it shared a grid with the Derbyshire Royal Infirmary and the telephone exchange. Ultimately, though, this action brought Derby to a standstill and it was decreed that such draconian measures would not be repeated.

Eventually Derbeians had no choice but to respond. When they heard that their weekly bread ration might be reduced, they resorted to baking their own until supplies of yeast ran out. Newspapers were reduced in size.

Derby power station announced it had only enough fuel to keep the town going for one more week, but housewives were assured there would be enough power to cook the Sunday dinner. By mid-February, and just in the nick of time, coal was taken from the pithead for the first time in weeks.

As the coldest February on record drew to a close, the snow returned with a vengeance. On the night of 22-23 February, ice floes formed on the Derwent as temperatures plummeted once more – this time to 17 degrees Fahrenheit (-8 degrees Celsius) – the town's coldest night for 80 years. Derby had seen sunshine on only six of the 28 days of February.

At the beginning of March, a thaw was predicted and whilst this did eventually arrive it was preceded by what the *Derby Evening Telegraph* called 'the worst all-night blizzard of winter'.

On 6 March queues formed at St Mary's Wharf off Mansfield Road when it was announced that up to 28lbs (12.7kg) of coal per household was to be released for sale. Two days later there was a nationwide relaxation in power restrictions, but warnings were issued that everyone had to agree to conserve energy, as much as one-third in the case of business users. Prosecutions were threatened against anyone ignoring the appeal.

By 10 March the much anticipated thaw had begun, but with it came terrible flooding. The deeply-frozen earth could not absorb the excess water from rain and snow melt. There was another blizzard on 14 March followed by even more serious flooding. On 17 March a 'hurricane' swept 98-mph winds across Britain, bringing more death and devastation to the nation, including the death of a Chellaston man.

Derby itself was severely flooded. Allestree and Little Eaton were submerged and the Evans cotton mill, which had been able to continue operations because it had an independent power source, was forced to close when water from the swollen Derwent broke into the boiler room. Neighbours at Darley Abbey used boats to check on one another. Workers at Derby Cables on Alfreton Road found themselves surrounded by 6ins (152mm) of water on all sides, but worked on, and a 200-yard stretch of Mansfield Road was under water. The Derwent was within a few feet of Exeter Bridge in the town centre and the ten-year-old Raynesway Bridge began to sag in the middle when water cracked the supports.

Gradually, the waters subsided and by 20 March the first snowdrops were sighted at the Arboretum. Spring arrived, but the power cuts that had so blighted townspeople were to carry on through to the autumn although, ironically, the summer of 1947 was one of the most glorious the country had ever enjoyed.

If the winter of 1946-47 was the snowiest on record, it was not the coldest. That dubious distinction fell to the severe winter of 1962-63, which was the coldest since at least 1740. Once again the town's streets disappeared for weeks under frozen snow and there was also dense fog to compound people's misery. ('Pea-soupers' had been a fact of life for years and only with the introduction of the Clean Air Act were Derbeians finally free of the filthy 'smogs' which enveloped all industrial areas of Britain.) Derby County, then playing in the old Second Division, went from 22 December 1962 to 23 February 1963 without playing a League game and the third-round FA Cup-tie against Peterborough United went ahead at the seventh attempt.

In December 1965 there was further serious flooding when the Derwent burst its banks at Darley. Although the town centre had been saved by improvements put in place after the 1932 floods, the residents of Alfreton Road, Mansfield Road and Chester Green were not so lucky. Their houses were inundated and many were rescued by policemen and firemen using rowing boats. Villages all around the town were severely flooded.

But the Derby climate is nothing if not varied and the extreme summers of 1975 and 1976 saw the town experience drought. Sandwiched between these two heatwaves was one of the driest winters on record, with only 61 per cent of the usual precipitation, leaving reservoirs seriously depleted. At first the heatwave seemed a blessing with days of reliable sunshine, one after another. Outings and picnics could be planned without fear of interruption from the weather. But then the drought conditions started to hit home. As the ground dried up and began to crack, water became more and more precious. Grass began to turn brown and pavements seemed too hot to walk upon. Bedrooms were stifling at night and by day all anyone could do was to find shelter from the relentless sun, to drink as much fluid as possible and – a blessing for children – consume as much ice-cream and as many ice-lollies as they could lay their hands on. The drought conditions of 1976 proved to be the worst for 300 years. The heatwave experienced in June and July of that year was the longest continuous period of hot, dry weather on record. During this time the temperature reached 80 degrees Fahrenheit (27 degrees Celsius) almost every day with less than half the average rainfall. Of course, Mother Nature has a knack for balancing things out and so she did once autumn came around. September and October 1976 were almost the wettest on record with more than twice the amount of average expected rainfall.

It was copious rainfall, once more, that brought the city to a standstill in 1981.

On the afternoon of 9 July 1981, the people of Derby had cause to wonder if day had turned to night. Everyone who was in the city on that afternoon remembers the day of the Great Derby Storm. The sky turned to pitch as the Sun was blotted out by clouds which were only 800ft (244m) above the ground (less than four times the height of the Cathedral tower) and which reached as high as 32,000ft (almost 10,000m, the average cruising height for a transatlantic airliner). Extreme humidity and high temperatures had caused a massive storm to form, the like of which had not been seen for generations. Three inches (76mm) of rain fell in only 70 minutes – the worst-hit areas being to the west of the city centre. Derbeians witnessed a spectacular storm with crashing thunder and lightning explosions that continued for well over an hour. There was widespread flooding across the city. In the city centre, shops and businesses were forced to close as drains could no longer cope with the inundation and water seeped inside premises. Many had lost power.

At the City Hospital dialysis patients had to be evacuated when the busy treatment room became flooded. At Littleover School, where afternoon lessons were being held, there was a torrent of water pouring into the hollowed-out school grounds from the surrounding high ground of Pastures Hill and Mickleover Golf Course. Classrooms shook as ever-nearing lightning approached. Traffic came to a virtual standstill as the storm continued well into rush hour and the schoolchildren set out for home. Buses stopped to pick up passengers wherever they could and more than 1,000 telephones were cut off.

The storm of 1981 had been a remarkable, almost unique meteorological event, but if the people of Derby had convinced themselves that flooding was now a thing of the past, they were to be proved wrong within 20 years. In November 2000, several weeks of heavy rain had left Britain in a state of saturation. The Derwent had been rising steadily for several days but nothing could have prepared the city for just how close it would come to another disaster. Towns and villages further up the Derwent were being swamped by the swollen river and, as the level of the Derwent rose within the city, all people could do was wait and see what would happen when the excess water from upstream arrived. On the Monday morning of 6 November, the Derwent had reached within four steps of the top of the River Gardens terrace and the Holmes Bridge weir was no longer visible. By 4pm it was within three steps, and by 6pm within two. The following morning the water was lapping over the top step, less than an inch away from breaching the bank. Fortunately, the level never rose above that point, but it had been perilously close. Just a few yards upstream the river had run over its banks and the Industrial Museum building, in the old Silk Mill, was several inches deep in water. What seemed remarkable was the roar of the water as the Derwent surged through the River Gardens, where the river's course is normally so languid.

Others were not so fortunate and several people had to be rescued from flooded homes, Darley Abbey again being one of the worst-hit areas. At Haslam's Lane livestock, most notably a water buffalo, had to be herded to safety. Roads within the city centre were flooded and a power failure to a pump under Eastgate meant that it was many days before that particular stretch of the inner ring road could be re-opened. Mother Nature continues to surprise us.

A PRINCESS COMES TO TOWN

THE final phase of the Central Improvement Plan was completed on 27 June 1949 when Princess Elizabeth and her husband Prince Philip visited Derby to officially open the Council House. Had the building not been in use by the RAF during the war, it would likely have still been the shell of its pre-war days. The foundation stone had been laid in May 1939 and only another four months' work had been possible before the outbreak of the war. In March 1940 work had resumed and in August 1942 the building had been requisitioned by the Air Ministry and the whole of the ground-floor accommodation, as well as some first-floor offices, had been used by the RAF. It was not handed back to the Council until April 1946, coincidentally the month Derby County won the FA Cup but too late for them to appear on the Council House balcony to receive their fans; the balcony of the police station and magistrates court opposite had to be used instead. And although the Roman numerals carved into the pediment are MCMXLI (1941) , the council was not able to meet in its new home until 1954.

The wartime hiatus had also seen changes to the original plans. Architect Charles Aslin had intended that an oval council chamber be built where the car park now stands, and a stone clock tower above entrance opposite Full Street was never completed. As is the case with almost every new building, the original budget had been exceeded and, according to the *Derby Evening Telegraph,* it was 'the borough's chief – and most criticised – civic building'.

On that June day in 1949, the royal couple, the focus of much media and public attention since their marriage two years earlier, arrived at Darley Park in sweltering sunshine.

The mayor in his scarlet ceremonial robes, accompanied by the mayoress and other dignitaries, took up his place in front of a row of halberdiers in their black tri-cornered hats and black cloaks. Around the corner came an open-topped car flying the Royal Standard, as excited crowds cheered. The *Evening Telegraph* reporter recorded the scene in great detail: 'Despite the brilliance of the Sun, she looked cool and at ease in her green and white checked taffeta dress with full skirt, attractive fitted bodice with bow at the waist and a bonnet-shaped hat of natural straw trimmed with lilies-of-the-valley.'

Eight trumpeters of the Royal Horse Artillery, in full dress uniform, added more splendour to an already colourful occasion as they sounded a fanfare. After chatting to the mayor, the princess and the duke were driven out of Darley Park on their way to Royal Crown Derby.

The *Evening Telegraph* again set the scene: 'Amateur photographers were out in their hundreds and as the car swept between the crowds surging from each side of the road, many forgot their cheers in their efforts to get a snap of Princess Elizabeth and her husband. Then came the schoolchildren – agog with excitement at seeing a real princess. Open-mouthed they waited and then shouted themselves hoarse for several minutes until the procession had passed. As the procession approached the town centre, the crowd thickened and even the police on duty could not prevent the cheering crowds from overflowing into the roads to get a close-up of the princess they had seen so often in pictures but never before in person. Every shop and office window was taken; all work had stopped.'

While Prince Philip continued on to Rolls-Royce, the princess toured the Royal Crown Derby factory, where she met some of the company's oldest employees, several of whom were in their 70s. She was presented with a special gift for her baby son, Charles. The princess then rejoined the duke at Rolls-Royce where they entered the reception hall to view the Battle of Britain Memorial Window. In the background, although out of sight, the Rolls-Royce Male Voice Choir sang *Crimond.* As the royal couple stepped out into the sunlit street again, they were cheered by employees leaning out of windows and by crowds thronging the streets outside the works. Every inch of the route between Nightingale Road and the Council House was packed with people waving flags. There were 150 St John Ambulance volunteers on duty and during the day 40 people fainted in the heat. Some early arrivals at the Council House thought they had found the perfect viewing position – and they could sit down too. Unfortunately their delight did not last long. Officials moved them on. They had been in special seats reserved for official guests. Again, the mayor was there to greet the princess and the duke. Alderman W. R. Raynes, the chairman of the Estates Committee, and Mr T. W. East, the borough architect, were presented and then Princess Elizabeth used a silver key to open the main doors. In the words of the *Derby Evening Telegraph*: 'The doors were thrown open and here indeed was a wonderful sight. Huge banks of flowers – miniature orchids in almost every colour of the rainbow and many other sub-tropical plants grown by the Derby Parks Department – welcomed the princess as she entered the main hall.

'At the top of the stairs, a glass panel, bearing an engraving of the borough coat-of-arms, had been erected and along the bottom an attractive arrangement of bright yellow and white flowers added a graceful touch to the scene.

'Inside the Council Chamber, royal blue and grey drapings presented a colourful sight and the princess accepted a bouquet of pink carnations from the mayoress.'

After signing the visitors' book the royal visitors were introduced to a number of local people before being entertained to tea in the panelled reception room with its magnificent chandelier. Then they stepped on to the Council House balcony to acknowledge the thousands of people gathered below. As the royal couple came into view, the cheering grew and the duke turned to give a special wave to those people in Corporation Street who were craning forward to snatch a glimpse of the couple. As they turned to return to the reception room, the duke and princess gave a last wave and the crowd responded with fresh cheers. A few minutes later they were walking down the steps to the royal car and their final engagement.

Towards the end of 1945, Derby Rotary Club had suggested to Derby Corporation that a fund should be set up for public subscriptions to provide a 'village' for the disabled. The Rotary Club offered, if the suggestion was taken up, to bear the cost of the first house. Public meetings were held and in April 1947 the mayor, Alderman C. R. Bates, had formed a committee, known as the Mayor of Derby's War Memorial Council, comprising service and ex-service organisations as well as the commercial and social sectors of the town. An appeal was launched in

Princess Elizabeth and Derby's mayor, Alderman Charles Frederick Bowmer, during the 1949 royal visit to officially open the Council House.

September 1947, to raise £100,000 to build some 60 houses and bungalows, a community centre, bowling green and children's playground on a 20-acre (8-hectare) site at Allenton. By the summer of 1947 the appeal had reached just over £47,000, enough for the first 20 houses. At 6.45pm on that special day, Princess Elizabeth arrived to lay the official foundation stone. The Bishop of Derby, Dr A. E. J. Rawlings, performed a service of dedication before the foundation stone was lowered into position and Princess Elizabeth tapped it on both sides with a silver-inscribed mallet and said: "I declare this stone well and truly laid."

Prayers were followed by the hymn *O God Our Help In Ages Past*. At around 7.20pm, the royal party left for Derby Midland station, the bells of St Andrew's, the 'railwayman's church' ringing out, and the people of Derby reflecting on a happy and successful day. They had entertained their princess, little realising that soon she would become their queen.

THE KING IS DEAD...

LATE on the morning of Wednesday, 6 February 1952, a class of children at Becket Junior School in Gerard Street were listening with their teacher to a BBC schools service broadcast when the programme was interrupted for a news flash. The announcer's voice was sombre and even the eight and nine-year-olds in the class, children normally too young to appreciate fully a world event, were shocked by the words they heard. From Sandringham had come news of the sudden death of His Majesty King George VI. The teacher said simply: "Wait there. I must tell the headmaster." It was a scene that was repeated right across the town, and indeed, throughout Britain. The country had a new young queen. Although the nation knew that the king was not in good health – he had not sounded well during the traditional Christmas broadcast only six weeks earlier, and he had looked tired and drawn as he waved goodbye to his daughter and her husband when they left London Airport at the start of their long Commonwealth tour just a week earlier – the suddenness of his death shocked everyone.

King George VI was held in great affection by the British people who he had led through some of the darkest days in the country's history. He had never wanted, nor indeed expected, to be king, but had fought against acute shyness and a speech impediment to accept his duty following the abdication of his brother, Edward VIII, later the Duke of Windsor. One woman summed up most people's feelings when she told a newspaper reporter: "I feel quite stunned." Meanwhile there was official reaction and Derby Town Council members stood in silence before agreeing to defer business to a date to be fixed by the mayor, the splendidly-named Councillor Zachariah Padgin Grayson. The Council decided to present an address of loyalty, which included an expression of sympathy on the death of her father, to Queen Elizabeth II. The Council also agreed to send its condolences to the newly-styled Queen Mother. The new queen, who had been in Kenya when the news broke, flew back to Britain immediately. British Forces Radio flashed the news to troops in Germany and then closed down in tribute. General Eisenhower ordered all the flags of the 12 NATO countries to be flown at half-mast at his headquarters near Paris. And in the Vatican, Pope Pius ordered a telegram of condolence to be sent to the Royal Family. Across Europe and the rest of the world numerous countries declared periods of official mourning for the late king. The Duke of Windsor, the man who wouldn't be king, announced that he would set sail for England aboard the *Queen Mary* the following day.

In Derby, events were following the national trend. Major J. W. Chandos-Pole, presiding at the Derbyshire Conservative Political Club lunch at Ramsden's Cafe in the Cornmarket, asked members to stand in silence, and an address by Peter Bailey, chairman of the Conservative Association's East Midlands Area Education Committee, was cancelled. Derby Borough Police's rugby match against Monmouthshire Police was cancelled, as was the dance which was to have followed at the borough police station. That evening's meeting at Derby's greyhound stadium was called off and so was the annual dinner and dance of Derby Chamber of Trade to have been held at the Assembly Rooms. There was some controversy, however, when the Rialto Ballroom announced that dancing would still be held there. Proprietor Mr J. Aldread explained: "It's a Forces invitation dance and I can't cancel it at such short notice. On the day of the funeral, though, I shall close the Ritz and the Rialto." Whilst the Derby public were prepared to accept that Mr Aldread had been placed in a difficult position, they were less convinced by Sam Ramsden who announced that his dance night at the Plaza the following evening would also have to go on 'because I'm under contract with a Birmingham band'. His decision brought intense criticism and several angry letters to the local paper. Elsewhere an evening theatrical performance at the Railway Institute went ahead after a minute's silence and the National Anthem. And that weekend, a minute's silence was held before the start of Derby County's game against Liverpool at the Baseball Ground.

As the nation mourned, one Derby man had special reason to be devastated by his king's death. Tom Jerram, the eldest son of Mr and Mrs Jerram of 35 High Street, Chellaston, had been the king's personal valet for more than 25 years – a role he had been fulfilling at the time of the king's accession in 1936. During the war he had served as a staff sergeant in the Grenadier Guards since George VI had felt it more appropriate that members of the Royal Household should not be exempt from military duty.

On Friday, 8 February 1952, the public proclamation of the queen's accession was made at St James's Palace at 11am. At the same time, the mayor of Derby read the proclamation from the steps of the Council House, when hundreds of people joined in singing *God Save the Queen*. Many people were in tears during the short ceremony carried out in crisp sunshine under a clear blue sky. It was a colourful occasion. The mayor was in his scarlet fur-trimmed robes of office and flanked by two mace bearers in navy, white and gold and cocked hats. All sections of the borough's municipal life were represented, together with members of the church, the law and the armed forces. A fanfare of trumpets heralded the proclamation and afterwards some of the crowd moved on to the County Hall in St Mary's Gate where the High Sheriff of Derbyshire, Mr G. C. M. Jackson, read again the proclamation.

Immediately plans were under way for the State Funeral to be held one week later. In Derby, it was announced, a civic procession and memorial service at the Cathedral would be held to coincide with the funeral procession and service in London. Two minutes' silence would be observed in all Derby factories, and all local markets would close for the duration of the service at the Cathedral. Eventually it was announced that the two minutes' silence would extend to the whole town and would be signalled by Civil Defence and local works' air-raid sirens at 2pm.The sirens would also signal the end of the silence. In London an estimated 4,000 people an hour filed past the king's coffin at Westminster Hall where he lay in state. Hidden from view at Westminster Hall was Derbyshire-born artist Frank Beresford, who was producing a painting of the lying-in-state, a service he had performed 16 years earlier at the lying-in-state of George V. On that occasion his work had been purchased by the king's widow, Queen Mary. Mr Beresford worked non-stop, wearing a black overcoat and with an oil heater to keep him warm.

Back in Derby one man found it all too much. Frederick Leonard Johnson, 73, of Strutt Street committed suicide by coal-gas poisoning. The Derby borough coroner was told that Mr Johnson, who was in poor health and already depressed, had become more so since the death of the king. The Derbyshire Assizes, which had been due to start on the day of the king's funeral, were postponed to the following Monday.

Edna Baker, Sylvia Trowell and Brenda Balson of T. Rowley & Sons were responsible for the creation of the funeral wreath that Derby would send to London. The 5ft (1.5m) wreath was too large for Rowley's Green Lane premises and had to be assembled elsewhere, watched over by the 83-year-old man who had made Derby's wreath for the funeral of Queen Victoria more than 50 years earlier. After completion the wreath was displayed at the Council House and a steady stream of Derby men, women and children filed past it.

On the day of the funeral the two minutes' silence brought the town to a silent and sombre standstill. Men, women and children in homes, schools, factories, offices, shops and in the streets stopped what they were doing, removed their hats and bowed their heads, to pay their personal tribute. Many schoolchildren listened to the wireless broadcast of the funeral. The rumble of traffic died and many shops were already closed and draped in black and purple cloth. Even the normal bustle of the Friday cattle market was stilled, punctuated only by the lowing of cattle and the bleating of sheep. At Normanton Barracks the two minutes' silence was heralded by Private J. Davis of the Sherwood Foresters sounding the *Last Post*, followed by *Reveille* to mark its end. At the Cathedral hundreds gathered. From Corporation Street began the slow procession to the Cathedral, accompanied by the strains of Handel's *Dead March* from *Saul*. The crisp, solid sound of marching feet and the faint whispers of the mourners were eventually joined by the solid tone of the Cathedral's minute bell.

Detachments of the Sherwood Foresters, the RASC, the Royal Navy and the RAF, many of them young National Servicemen, the police, the fire brigade and the ambulance service all passed by in the same dead silence. They were followed by representatives of the old comrades' associations and war veterans and even a Chelsea Pensioner in his bright scarlet coat. As it passed the Council House, the procession was joined by the mayor and

To coincide with the funeral of King George VI at St George's, WIndsor, a civic service was conducted at Derby Cathedral. Crowds lined the streets for the procession in which the Mayor, Councillor Zachariah Grayson, was preceded by the sword and maces.

civic representatives. Surely a striking and moving sight, it took no less than 20 minutes to file past the war memorial in the Market Place. So many had wanted to watch, and to attend that they stood four or five deep outside the Cathedral, held back by a line of policemen. The unexpected crush caused several contingents of the procession to be left outside the Cathedral as the service began at 2pm.

There were hymns and readings followed by prayers and words of thanksgiving for the departed king and the new queen. After the *Dead March* and the National Anthem, the procession emerged into the milky February sunlight and returned to the Council House. Elsewhere in Derby, more than 1,200 people,

many of them railway workers, attended a memorial service for the king at St Andrew's Church on London Road. Among the 200 people who were at a similar service at Normanton Barracks was a detachment of the Sherwood Foresters and members of Normanton and Pear Tree Branch of the British Legion.

That so many had chosen to mark the king's death in such a way illustrated the high regard in which he had been held by his people, and reflected the dignity with which he had lived his very public life. Such a sharing of public grief is, perhaps, now easier for modern Derbeians to understand, having not long ago mourned the sudden loss of a young and vibrant princess.

...LONG LIVE THE QUEEN

THE Coronation of Elizabeth II, set for Tuesday, 2 June 1953, would, in many ways, mark the beginning of the end of an era of austerity brought about by the second of two world wars. Coronation celebrations would be as grand as anyone in Derby could manage. From 29 May until 13 June, the Derby and County Coronation Year Exhibition took place on Bass's Recreation Ground. Some 400 stands were erected, staffed by 1,500 people representing organisations and businesses of all descriptions including Rolls-Royce and British Celanese, who presented their 'Court of Fashion'. This featured beautiful creations by top designers of the day, including Norman Hartnell who had designed the new queen's wedding dress six years earlier, all made from Celanese fabrics. The exhibition enjoyed an average daily attendance of 7,000 and several local businesses reported making important overseas trading contacts. On the Sunday of Coronation Week, a civic parade was planned, to be led by the Band and Drums of the Sherwood Foresters. Derby's schools would close from Monday lunchtime until Wednesday morning, the exception being the town's grammar schools where examinations meant that pupils there would have only Coronation Day off. On Monday morning some 23,000 pupils were presented with their Coronation souvenir, an inscribed spoon from the Derby Education Authority. At each school, according to age groups, an appropriate ceremony would be held 'to bring home to the children the meaning and significance of the Coronation'. And that morning people sitting in Derby's Riverside Gardens were startled by two loud explosions from across the river on waste ground near Exeter Flats. They came from armoured cars of the Derbyshire Yeomanry who were practising the 21-gun salute they were due to give at 10.26am on Coronation Day, at the exact moment when the queen would leave Buckingham Palace on her way to Westminster Abbey. For those who wanted to go to London itself for the historic occasion, there were plenty of special train services from Derby Midland station to St Pancras, and to St Marylebone from Friargate. And several Derby people had important roles in the day's events. Littleover's Stan

Bellaby, a 22-year-old lance-sergeant, was chosen as one of 52 men of the Queen's Company, Grenadier Guards, who would mount guard over the queen's crown and other precious symbols of the monarchy which would figure in the age-old ceremony. Lance-sergeant Bellaby had been on duty on the streets of London during the funerals of both George VI and Queen Mary, who had passed away the previous March. Another local man serving in the Grenadier Guards, 20-year-old Lawrence Lambert, whose family lived at Lord Street, Allenton, would be in the Coronation procession. Twenty-one-year-old Music-ian Eric Beardsall, from Allen Street, Allenton, would be playing the euphonium in the Royal Naval School of Music Band in the procession and yet another Derby representative would be 19-year-old Daniel Docherty of Brackens Lane, Alvaston, who was one of the Irish Guardsman chosen to line the route.

Back in Derby, at 10.30pm on Coronation Day, a rocket fired from the Derby and District Boy Scouts Association's Drum Hill camp site at Little Eaton would be the signal to Scouts at Allestree, Chaddesden and Locko Park, Spondon to touch off Coronation beacons, part of a chain extending throughout the British Isles.

The *Derby Evening Telegraph* had called for 'Royal weather to set the seal on the Coronation celebrations in Derby'. Sadly Mother Nature did not oblige and the day was cold and damp. Although the brightly-coloured bunting began to droop, spirits could not be dampened as people crammed into neighbours' front rooms ready to watch the Coronation procession and ceremony on small black and white television sets. Outdoor events did suffer, though. The fireworks display at Markeaton Park was cancelled – one held the previous Saturday had attracted 2,000 people who saw an image of the queen's face surmounted by a crown outlined in white and yellow fireworks – and at Normanton Park the Sherwood Foresters Band played as scheduled and the Middies managed a display of counter-marching before the rest of the programme was cancelled. The fair at the Racecourse did a little better with a steady stream of children enjoying the rides and sideshows, and local cricketers struggled gamely through their tournament in weather more suitable for football. Not surprisingly considering that most of the exhibits were indoors, the Coronation Exhibition on Bass's Rec attracted by far the most visitors.

On the day itself families celebrated at nearly 250 street parties. The Town Council had allocated 12 guineas (£12.60) as prizes to be awarded to the three best decorated streets in the borough. Imaginations were allowed to run wild in the design for the decorations, but there were restrictions. The police warned organisers that all garlands and bunting must be of sufficient height to allow vehicles to pass underneath. Motorists were warned, too, to take special care and be on the lookout for children and the elderly. The residents of Grey Street, off Gerard Street, had special reason to cheer for they had won first prize for the best-decorated of 56 streets, while Tewkesbury Street and Gisborne Street tied for second place and there were commendations for Winchester Crescent, Colombo Street, Norman Street, Birdwood Street, Harcourt Street (near-neighbours of the winners), St Luke's Street, York Street, Bath Street, Albion Street, Canal Street and Nelson Street. In Grey Street, the mayoress received a bouquet from five-year-old Valerie Wood, whose parents had organised the decorations and who were presented with a 'hall set' by grateful neighbours. The street certainly looked a picture: decorated tubs containing masses of flowers were set at regular intervals on the pavements down either side of the street, every window sill had a window box, and every one was the same with red, white and blue flowers. At the bottom of the street a large board proclaimed, 'God Save The Queen,' and naval signal flags spelled out the same message.

At Chaddesden, tables were laid in the open at Cowsley Road, and the children of Worcester Crescent enjoyed pony rides and races on the green opposite Roe Farm School. The school itself provided refuge for six crescents of the Roe Farm Estate and many public houses, like the Blue Boy on Wiltshire Road, opened their doors to crowds of children.

Almost every street leading from London Road, between The Spot and Bateman Street, held a party and many forms of alternative accommodation were negotiated in a bid to beat the elements as schoolrooms, garages, cycle sheds and the spare rooms behind pubs were utilised. Between the

A queue at the Spondon Sitwell for the film *A Queen Is Crowned*.

showers the children emerged to take part in races. Residents of Liversage Street and Hope Street found an unusual way of entertaining themselves. Before the rain started again they carried a three-piece band into the street – piano, drums and cymbals – and danced to the music. People from the four street parties held in Rose Hill Street, Grange Street, Alexandra Street and the combined Cambridge Street-Reeves Road party converged on St James's Church during the afternoon for a simple 15-minute service. Nearby Yates Street celebrated beneath a banner 116 years old which had hung over the same street on Queen Victoria's Coronation Day. The red banner was embroidered in gold with the words 'God Save The Queen' and a crown. It was owned by a licensee in the district. Where many parties were forced indoors because of the weather, 60 children from Osmaston Road refused to be daunted and donned raincoats to eat their tea in the open. In Harrison Street, too, scores of children ignored the rain and insisted on enjoying their tea in the street as planned. Residents of Underhill Avenue had also managed their tea and were about to embark on their sports when the rain came down again. There was a brief interval while mothers went to fetch raincoats and wellington boots, and then the festivities continued, although the participants in the ladies v gents cricket match got thoroughly soaked. Many communities arranged their own fancy dress competitions and in Etwall Street, one up-to-the-minute costume was that of a mountaineer, a tribute to the successful attempt on Everest which had been announced earlier that day.

It seemed that every neighbourhood had prepared its own special celebration. About 70 children from Haydn Road, Chaddesden, were treated to a Saturday afternoon trip to the Peak District where they received badges and sweets. Babies were given a souvenir mug and sweets in lieu of the bus trip. Children living in Greenwich Drive North had their party, held in the gardens of two houses on the drive, the day after the Coronation. At Chaddesden Park, Coronation Week got under way with a Sunday united religious service attended by more than 1,000 local people. There were also more than 1,000 people at International Combustion's Coronation Gala held at the Welfare Sports Ground on Sinfin Lane. About 500 children were entertained to tea and there was a full programme of sports for both adults and children with sideshows and 'an American tennis tournament'. The team from the firm's drawing office won the R. H. Gummer Trophy for the highest number of points in the adults sports. The event was organised by the Kiddies' Treat and Gala Day Committee.

For several Derby families Coronation Day would take on extra special significance. In the early hours of Coronation morning Mr and Mrs Geoffrey Ellis celebrated the birth of their baby son. One of the earliest arrivals on Coronation Day was a baby girl to be named Elizabeth June, born to Mrs Kathleen Storer at her home at Canalside, Siddalls Road. Other Coronation Day babies included a daughter to Mrs Betty Jackson, born at home in Curzon Lane, Alvaston; two babies born at the Queen Mary Maternity Home: Elizabeth Danuta Wasikowska and Jill Bennett; and six babies who arrived at the Nightingale Maternity Home: Hans Peter Foss; Neville William Hollies; Sarah Sherbrook; Michael Robert Poole; Philip John Hunkin; and Donald William Holmes. One boy – Anthony John Dakin – and one girl – Elizabeth Mary Snuggs – were born at the City Hospital.

For many Derbeians the day meant inclusion in the Queen's Coronation Honours list. Among those recognised were Arthur Adkins of Beaufort Street, the general yard foreman of Litchurch Gas Works who was awarded the British Empire Medal after 50 years' service in the industry, and Mrs Rene Holland, area canteen supervisor for Gee, Walker & Slater Ltd, was awarded the same honour. Mrs Holland had run a mobile canteen at Sutton-on-Sea, feeding the 100 men who, with bulldozers and other machines had been sent from Derby to battle against the East Coast floods earlier that year. Mrs Holland ("I was the only woman in Sutton") waged her own battle against a lack of such essential facilities as electricity. And although there was water all around her canteen, supplies of fresh drinkable water had to be brought to her each day from Derby.

Celebrations went on all week and, two weeks after the Coronation, there was an additional treat for 13,000 children from town and county who attended local cinemas to see film of the glorious event. The Gaumont on London Road showed both a newsreel and a 90-minute Technicolour film entitled *A Queen is Crowned*, which was narrated by Sir Laurence Olivier. Audiences at the Odeon in St Peter's Street and the Regal in East Street were treated to *Elizabeth is Queen*, a newsreel and a film about Westminster Abbey.

The flags which had been at half-mast were now flying high in recognition of the new queen, for the country knew that with the passing of one monarch, so began the reign of another, and with it a new era, and a new 'Elizabethan age'.

Flower arranger to the queen
Constance Spry OBE, florist to royalty and society, was born Constance Fletcher in Wilson Street, Derby, in 1886. Constance Spry developed flower arranging into an art form. She wrote, lectured and broadcast on her chosen subject. She owned a shop in London and became the expert in the field. All of society wanted Miss Spry to arrange their flowers and she lent her expertise to the weddings of Princess Elizabeth and the Duke of Gloucester, and at the 1953 Coronation. She wrote 12 books on the subject and was the classic flower arranger.

DERBY IN THE FIFTIES

CHARTER CELEBRATIONS

THE following year, 1954, was to become one of particular significance to the people of Derby. At last the Town Council was able to take up permanent residence in the Council House and the entire town participated in the Octocentenary Charter Celebrations. The special celebration was to mark the 800th anniversary of what was described as 'the first town charter'. It had been awarded to the town by Henry II and, although the exact date of the original charter remains unclear to within a few years or so, the town elected to hold its celebrations 800 years after the start of Henry II's reign. All manner of events were organised including a dinner-ball for 450 special guests in a 'monster' marquee at Markeaton Park. The main event, though, was a huge pageant, the Civic Cavalcade, which was watched by thousands of excited Derbeians. The parade route

Thousands lined the streets of Derby on Saturday, 2 October, 1954, for what was described as a giant cavalcade, the highlight of the charter celebrations. The Mayor swapped his stage coach for an open 1907, made-in-Derby, Rolls-Royce Silver Ghost to ride in the procession to Markeaton Park.

stretched from Bass's Rec to Markeaton Park and was led by the bands of the Borough Police and the Sherwood Foresters. Local businesses and organisations took part and dozens of colourful floats were paraded through the town. Derby Borough Fire Service exhibited no less than 10 appliances representing 200 years of firefighting. Firemen joined

in by wearing historical uniforms. The Borough Police also had its officers dressed in old-fashioned costumes and an old horse-drawn tram paraded alongside a modern diesel-engined bus that had only just entered service. There were also a horse-drawn street sweeping machine and as well as 'this year's model which collects the dust as it sweeps'. George Fletcher & Co Ltd displayed sugar machinery (weighing 7½ tons) and the Co-operative Society depicted Henry II and his court. At Markeaton Park a whole sheep was roasted, and Derbeians took full advantage of the lifting of wartime food rationing just three months earlier.

Babington Lane pictured in 1954. The old Midland Electric Theatre on the right was then the Picture House. On the left is the 'Benefit corner', home of a shoe shop. It is now the premises of Waterstone's booksellers.

ON THE STAGE

THE 1950s were a golden age in entertainment in Derby. On 10 October 1952 the Derby Playhouse opened in the former Baptist Church on Sacheverel Street. It moved there from a converted schoolroom in Becket Street where the town's first

The Hippodrome on Green Lane pictured in 1924. Originally a theatre, it was used as a cinema in the early 1950s before reverting to stage performances.

repertory theatre had opened in 1948. Known as the 'Little Theatre', it had featured a combination of professional and amateur performers in a wide selection of plays, in contrast to the new Playhouse which featured only professional performances. The Playhouse became a popular venue and many star names performed there in its early days, as well as several destined for later stardom such as Susannah York, and John Nettles of *Bergerac* and *Midsommer Murders* fame.

In March 1956 the theatre suffered a severe fire which gutted the interior. Just over a year later, it was reopened having been completely rebuilt. Just like the Phoenix, which it adopted as its symbol, the Playhouse rose from the ashes. The final curtain fell in May 1975, when the company transferred to the splendid new theatre within the newly-developed Eagle Centre, the Phoenix being replaced by the Eagle. The Sacheverel Street building was, for some years, a cinema showing Asian films, but was eventually demolished. The old Playhouse had been the scene of many popular pantomimes over the years, the last of which was *Cinderella*, where the audience were instructed to 'raise the roof – we won't be needing it much longer!'

One of the town's most popular pantomimes was that held at the Hippodrome on the corner of Macklin Street and Green Lane. The panto cast was usually packed with star acts and thousands of Derby children joined in with the traditional fun. In 1954 the production of *Babes in the Wood* had starred Stan Stennett and featured Morecambe and Wise, who were on the verge of stardom. The Hippodrome had opened in 1913 and had become recognised and well-loved for its popular music-hall and variety

shows. Between 1930 and 1950 it was also used as a cinema. Comedians such as Jimmy Jewell and Ben Warris, Jimmy James, Norman Evans and Frankie Howerd all appeared at the Hippodrome. Stage versions of popular radio programmes such as *The Billy Cotton Band Show* and *Over The Garden Wall* were also put on there. Between the wars the legendary duo Flanagan and Allen had appeared there and it was whilst staying in 'digs' nearby that they penned what was to become their theme tune *Underneath the Arches*, although claims that the song was inspired by the railway arches at Friar Gate have since been dismissed. For local families, particularly those living in Crompton and Wilson Streets, the Hippodrome brought in welcome income, as they rented out rooms to visiting 'theatricals'. For young Stuart Clay, growing up in such a house in Crompton Street meant a special treat of a trip to the Bass's Rec fairground for him and his brother and sister – their guardians for the day being Morecambe and Wise who were 'digging' with the family. And another Derby man remembers well his first introduction to the exotic delights of chewing gum, courtesy of the Canadian group, the Maple Leaf Four, who were lodging in Webster Street.

By the 1950s and into the 1960s, Derby had a burgeoning social scene with dance halls like the Locarno in the former Grand Theatre in Babington Lane, a bowling alley in Colyear Street and night clubs like the Curzon Club, also in Colyear Street, and the Windmill Club opposite the bus station. Derby, of course, also had its town centre pubs, many of which survive – albeit renamed in some cases – others having fallen victim to demolition.

Lady Docker – Derby's colourful socialite

Lady Norah Docker, one of the most colourful socialites of the mid-20th century, was born in Shaftesbury Crescent. Born Norah Turner in 1905, to a Derby shopfitter, she married three times but it was her life with Sir Bernard Docker, a wealthy financier, which caught the imagination of the public. Her flamboyant taste and flashy decadence ensured her almost constant appearance in the tabloids in the 1950s.

DERBY IN THE SPACE RACE

I T was only in the year 2000 that the people of Derby were let in on one of the city's best-kept secrets – Rolls-Royce's key role in the space race. Only when official papers recently became available to the public were workers on a top-secret project known as Blue Streak, able to speak out about their work. For many, it was the first time they truly understood the work they had been involved in. They had been carefully vetted by the secret service and were not permitted to discuss their work. Indeed, their knowledge had been limited to a small component of the project.

In the 1950s Blue Streak was a new weapons system and Royce's worked on the innovative rocket engines to power long-range ballistic missiles. Work had begun at Nightingale Road in 1954 and was nearly ready for testing when, in 1960, it was abandoned. The US and Soviet systems had outpaced the Rolls-Royce versions. The research completed at that point now forms the basis for the Ariane rocket systems employed in Europe, and instead of being used as a weapon the Blue Streak work has been adapted to peaceful purposes.

THE CARRIAGE AND WAGON FIRES

A FEROCIOUS fire in the early hours of 10 September 1957 was to devastate a large section of the Derby Carriage and Wagon Works. Emergency services had been called to the scene at 12.41am after four painters had noticed the blaze in the empty Y-H shop. One witness said: "The heat was terrific – you could feel it 50 or 60 yards away." According to the *Derby Evening Telegraph* the situation could have been much worse had it not been for the swift action of a number of C & W employees who 'worked heroically... They toiled desperately to get inflammable stuff away from the blaze.' In all more than 80 firemen fought the fire

with two miles of water hose. The blaze destroyed a 6,000sq ft (558m²) area of two adjoining repair shops, and 1,000sq ft (93m²) of roofing on nearby buildings was also damaged. Inside valuable equipment and 12 rail vehicles were severely affected.

By 2.33am the fire was said to be under control, but only when daylight came did the full extent of the damage become apparent. It was not clear how the fire had started. It appeared to have begun in one of the vehicles in the repair shop, but the sheds were closed at night and the cause remained a mystery. Firefighters would say only that arson was not suspected.

The Carriage and Wagon fire of 1957 had been dramatic and devastating, but remarkably, almost exactly a year later another fire broke out in the same shed. And it proved to be even more severe than the first.

On the evening of 8 September 1958, 19-year-old Brian Walker, an employee of the C & W, was playing bowls near his workplace. Interviewed by the *Derby Evening Telegraph* the next day he told his story: "I caught sight of what must have been the fire about 7.55pm. There was just a little wisp of dark smoke coming up and I didn't take any notice of it. About five or ten minutes later I happened to look again in the same direction and the top of the shed was all aglow. There were no flames."

With Brian was Gary Morton, one of the Carriage and Wagon firemen, who raced off to alert his colleagues. Witnesses reported several small explosions and a much larger one about an hour later. Again the fire was visible from a great distance away and so many spectators crowded on to the Long Bridge across the Derwent that the police were forced to first block and then clear it, fearful that any flying debris might land there. Although the fire was declared under control by 10.30pm, firefighters continued to pour water on the area for another hour or so. In all the fire service reported that 100 firemen had been involved using 22 jets, 1,000 gallons (4,546 litres) of water and three miles of hose to extinguish the blaze.

A PLAN TO CHANGE THE FACE OF DERBY

IN February 1963 a fire caused by an electrical fault in the amplification system at the Assembly Rooms on the Market Place had destroyed the roof of the old building. Immediate concerns were to safely remove the heavy ventilator, some 6ft (1.8m) in diameter, which was dangling precariously from the charred roof timbers. Initially it had been thought that this was the limit of the damage, but more detailed inspections revealed the entire structure to be unsound. It took several years for the authorities to decide precisely what to do with the building,

during which time it remained cocooned in scaffolding supports.

Over the centuries town planners have dreamt up numerous schemes to change the layout and appearance of the centre of Derby. None, however, were as dramatic as those presented in July 1963.

The perennial problem of increased traffic volume was presenting difficulties and it was announced that a new inner ring road would be formed to combat this. The implementation of the St Alkmund's Way section of the inner ring road meant the loss of the

The area to the top of this picture disappeared in 1967, to make way for the inner ring road. St Alkmund's Church and its Georgian churchyard were the main casualties.

St Alkmund's Churchyard some seven years before it was demolished. What would Derby now give for such a jewel?

The elevated road which would have taken traffic through the town centre past the old Northcliffe House, along Albert Street and Victoria Street and then turned up Green Lane.

beautiful Georgian square of St Alkmund's Churchyard and of the church itself, as well as much of the medieval layout of the northern town centre, a decision which still has its critics almost 40 years later.

The Nottingham Castle public house at the corner of Queen Street and St Michael's Lane, part of which dated to at least the 16th century. It closed in 1962 and was demolished two years later, another victim of 'improvements'.

The inner ring road itself was to become something of a local white elephant – the traffic problems seem just as bad today – and only in 2001 did the Council propose the completion of the 'ring' with a much amended plan. The loss of the old St Alkmund's area caused great consternation at the time and, if it was to contribute anything positive to Derby, perhaps it was to remind people of how precious is the city's heritage and that every effort should be made to prevent the loss of more historic buildings and streets.

It is probably also responsible in part for the more cautious approach adopted by developers in interceding years. Looking back now at those plans of 1963, rather than continue to mourn the loss of St Alkmund's we might well be thankful for the mercies afforded us when other major parts of the plan were not carried out. Architect's models show pedestrians on Victoria and Albert Streets and Green Lane carrying shopping beneath the hulk of a vast overhead road that was to begin in the Morledge, rising to first-floor level in Albert Street. A similar elevated road was designed for East Street and St Peter's Churchyard and would have obstructed buildings and completely transformed the town centre into an ugly and unrecognisable tangle of high-rise roadways. Ironically the citizens of Boston, Massachusetts, the city founded by a Derby man in the 17th century, are still trying to bury their roads underground and rid themselves of a similar 1960s

Derby power station between the Cathedral and the Silk Mill. In 1934 the organist at All Saints' complained that the Cathedral's windows 'had to show the sordid spectacle of a filthy electricity power station'. It remained so for almost 40 years, until the power station was demolished and the site landscaped.

system of elevated roadways that were thought at the time to be the answer to traffic congestion but instead simply scarred a beautiful city.

Another major feature of the Derby scheme was to be the redevelopment of the Market Place with first the removal of traffic – which did not come to fruition for more than 20 years – and then the construction of a very wide five-storey office complex to fill in the gap on the east side of the square, between the old Assembly Rooms, which it dwarfed, and the south side where the Guildhall stands. Had this particular aspect been completed, it would

surely have cut off much of the town from the River Derwent and certainly have masked the view of the Council House and Exeter Bridge from the Market Place and vice versa – two of the city's more attractive views.

Not all the scheme's proposals were negative. There were plans for a new pedestrianised shopping precinct around the Eagle Street area and a new and bigger home for the Morledge market, which became the Eagle Centre and Eagle Market respectively, and plans were also in hand to restore the Victorian Market Hall to something like its original appearance.

A City for the Seventies

ON 4 February 1971, the unthinkable happened. Rolls-Royce, so long the pride of Derby, and a business on which so many Derbeians relied for their income, was in dire financial trouble. The development of the RB211 engine had cost the company dearly. Rolls-Royce had undertaken to supply US aircraft manufacturer Lockheed with 600 RB211s for their Tri-Star jet fleet at a fixed price. But development costs had far exceeded original estimates and, despite the injection of tens of millions of pounds from the British Government, Royce's expected to incur losses of around £48 million on the deal. The Official Receiver had been called in and, despite his promises to save what he could, the situation appeared hopeless.

Derbeians waited and hoped, many tuning in to Radio Derby, a new local BBC station which had taken to the air early to provide up-to-date news for the town. It seemed the future of Derby hung in the balance, but perhaps it was Royce's national, rather than local, importance that was to ensure its survival. Dozens of businesses across Britain relied heavily on Rolls-Royce for work. It was even suggested that the RAF, who depended upon Rolls-Royce engines, would become unworkable should the company liquidate. The government elected to nationalise the business, and thus ensured the future of Rolls-Royce at Derby.

In contrast to the universal relief that came with the government's intervention, there had been panic just a short time before. Rumours that the Derbyshire Building Society had substantial investments in Rolls-Royce almost brought the town to a standstill. Many feared the building society itself was on the brink of collapse and, despite repeated assurances that these rumours were 'malicious and unfounded', scores of investors arrived, determined to withdraw their savings before the society ran out of money. Queues stretched from the Derbyshire's Irongate offices, across the Market Place. In a single day, £250,000 was withdrawn. Once the panic had subsided, most investors returned their money.

Confidence in the town had taken a serious set-back – but then there was the sudden and unexpected turnaround in the fortunes of Derby County.

The Legacy of Brian Clough

WHENEVER a new manager is appointed to their club, football fans everywhere are filled with renewed hope. But there can have been few Derby County supporters who dreamed of the dramatic change of fortune that was to follow the appointment of Brian Clough and his assistant Peter Taylor in July 1967. First, the new manager removed all reminders of previous successes. Gone were the photographs of Bloomer, the Goodalls, and the Cup Final heroes. According to Clough, Rams history started again here. And so it proved.

Despite an unpromising first season, Derby stormed back into the top flight in 1968-69, winning 13 of their last 15 games. Crowds of delighted supporters gathered outside the Midland Hotel where the team were celebrating their success. Hotel staff formed a guard of honour outside the dining room and waitresses wore black and white scarves and had Derby County motifs sewn on to their uniforms. In the town centre celebrations went on all night and at 9.30pm the Irongates Tavern had to close its doors due to overcrowding. Revellers spilled out on to the street and every pub and club was packed to capacity.

And it got better. Two seasons later Derby County were crowned League champions for the first time in the club's history. In May 1972, over 39,000 fans at the Baseball Ground saw a John McGovern goal beat Liverpool in the Rams' last game, but still the championship was not certain. Derby had finished the season earlier than their rivals; it would be a week before any celebrations could be confirmed. Peter Taylor took the players to Majorca, while Brian Clough took his family to the Scilly Isles.

In the event both Leeds and Liverpool failed to take the points they needed, the long wait for a League title was over and the party could begin. The players returned home to receive their trophy before a packed Baseball Ground – specially opened on a Sunday morning – and later paraded it through the streets on an open-topped bus. It seemed almost too good to be true, and so it was to prove.

The following year the Rams reached the semi-finals of the European Cup, but disaster for the fans was to follow. Both Clough and his chairman Sam Longson were blunt, outspoken men and it was only a matter of time before their relationship soured. Clough had been drawing attention for his often controversial comments whilst appearing as a pundit on television. Ultimatums were issued and Clough, followed immediately by Peter Taylor, resigned in October 1973. Longson denied that it was a clash of personalities. "It is a fight between right and wrong." Clough had another explanation. "I'll tell you why I'm going. My knees and elbows are sore from all the crawling Peter and I have been forced to do these past three months." The *Derby Evening Telegraph* declared: "While the Rams were successful and retained Clough and Taylor, there was no limit to the potential. Today Derby are a laughing stock." Rams fans were left reeling and mounted a mass demonstration with a march through the town centre to 'Bring Back Clough'. The players also sided with Clough and Taylor and attempted to have them reinstated.

When Dave Mackay was announced as Clough's replacement, the players asked him not to accept the position, and even discussed the possibility of striking. But no amount of posturing on either side was going to see a compromise and Clough and Taylor were consigned to Derby County's history, albeit a very big part of it.

Under former playing star Mackay the Rams won another championship, in 1974-75, and reached an FA Cup semi-final in 1976, but controversy was never far away and in November 1976, Mackay, stung by criticism of his managerial style, asked for a vote of confidence. It was not forthcoming and he left the Baseball Ground. The rot now set in and four years later Derby were back

Derby County captain Roy McFarland and the mayor, Joe Carty, on the Council House balcony after the club won the League championship in 1972, for the first time in its history.

in the Second Division. There were disasters on the field; and off it, police investigations into alleged corruption had made national headlines.

If playing success was now hard to come by, then financial stability seemed impossible. In 1984, now facing a return to the Third Division, the Rams were effectively bankrupt. In March, the Inland Revenue and Customs and Excise brought a winding-up petition against the club, but thanks to the continuing efforts of the board, most notably Stuart Webb, and the financial intervention of media magnate Robert Maxwell, an 11th-hour deal was struck to save the club from closure.

Three years later, following successive promotions under new manager Arthur Cox, the Rams were back in the top flight. With promotion came media attention and Robert Maxwell took centre stage. As the club and the city itself were to discover, life with Maxwell was nothing if not eventful. He posed happily with the players, team colours draped around his neck, a broad smile across his face – every bit the proud chairman. But when form began to slip and the inevitable relegation came, in May 1991, his enthusiasm evaporated overnight.

Later, of course, the world was to learn the truth about Robert Maxwell and Derby fans realised why he hadn't been pouring money into their club. Yet only after protracted negotiations could the club be released from his stranglehold. It was time to begin again – and build upon the legacy left by Brian Clough.

DERBY'S OLYMPIANS

THE 2001 World Athletics Championship saw Derby's Fiona May re-establish her place as the best female long-jumper in the world. Although born in Slough, May spent most of her formative years in Derby and from the age of 12 represented Derby Ladies Athletics Club, of which she is a life member.

Fiona May, who now represents Italy but who learned her athletics with Derby Ladies Athletics Club.

In 1988 she won the world junior championship, the same year she competed in her first Olympics. In 1995 she became world champion and the following year was silver medalist at the Atlanta Olympics. In 1997 she became world indoor champion and won the bronze at the outdoor level. The following year she narrowly and controversially missed out on the gold when her rival's winning jump was declared good, whilst television pictures suggested otherwise. After a period of disillusionment, during which she considered quitting the sport, May returned to take the silver medal at the Sydney Olympics and gold at the following year's World Championships in Edmonton. Her exceptional achievements have been all but overlooked in this country following her decision to represent Italy after her marriage to Italian pole vaulter Gianni Iapichino in the mid-1990s. That is an injustice as she remains one of the most successful British-born athletes in history. And she learned her sport in Derby.

Fiona May is not Derby's only Olympian. Others include Harry Sewell, who came fifth in the 3,000 metres steeplechase at the London Olympics of 1908. Boxer Donald Scott won the light heavyweight silver medal in the 1948 London Games. Arthur Keily ran in the marathon in the Rome games of 1960. At one time or another Keily was British champion in all distances from 10 miles to 40 miles and held 11 world records. Weightlifter Louis Martin won the middle heavyweight bronze in the Rome Olympics of 1960 and silver in Tokyo in 1964, as well as being crowned world champion on four occasions and British champion for 12 consecutive years between 1959 and 1970.

Other Derby sportsmen and women listed as having taken part in the Olympic Games include runner Ernie Barnes, who was the second British runner to finish the 1908 marathon, hurdler Phil Harris, cyclists Eric Thompson and Harry Wild, yachtswoman Sue Carr, Hallard Brittain, Mike Bullivant and Fred Attenborough.

Derby even had an MP who was an Olympian: Philip Baker (later Philip Noel-Baker) won a silver medal in the 1,500 metres at Antwerp in 1920.

THE JUBILEE CITY

MANY visitors to Derby in the 20th century may have been forgiven for assuming that the town was already a city. Travellers along Uttoxeter Road would pass a City Hospital, at Chester Green there was already a City Road, and during World War Two there was even an RAF City of Derby Squadron. But not until Queen Elizabeth II's silver jubilee celebrations in 1977 could the old town officially call itself a city.

There had been many attempts to obtain city status – in 1927 with the creation of the Diocese of Derby; in 1935 to mark the centenary of the Municipal Corporation Act; in 1954 during the charter celebrations; and in 1968 when the borough boundaries were changed. However, it had seemed that Derby was never to be a city when, under the 1972 Local Government Act, the town lost its borough status, becoming merely a district council and subject to the newly-empowered County Council. And although a short time later the borough title was restored, Derby's deferential status remained unaffected. Councillor Gerald Andrews decided to mount a new campaign, initially with little support. But in May 1976 the Council as a whole decided to make an official application for city status, to coincide with Queen Elizabeth's silver jubilee. This time the request was successful and Derby prepared to celebrate its new identity and, along with the rest of the country, the jubilee.

At 10am on 27 July 1977, Queen Elizabeth II arrived at Derby station to be greeted by hundreds of flag-waving Derbeians. She and the Duke of Edinburgh were driven through a town draped in red, white and blue, streets lined with row after row of happy, welcoming faces, an estimated 60,000 of them. At the Council House the royal couple were greeted by yet more crowds, with cheering children frantically waving flags and hoping that the queen would look in their direction. The official reception committee was led by the mayor, Councillor Jeffery Tillett, wearing his full regalia. The queen and her husband were escorted upstairs where they waved to the crowds from the small balcony above the main entrance. The queen returned to the Council House steps where the official ceremony was to take place. As the crowds watched in anticipation, the queen handed Councillor Tillett the Letters Patent which stated: 'We are graciously pleased to… direct that the BOROUGH OF DERBY shall henceforth have the status of a CITY and shall have all such rank liberties privileges and immunities as are incident to a City.'

Of course, a city has no greater power than a town, the title is purely honorific, but at that moment the townspeople of Derby became proud citizens of Derby. Jeffery Tillett echoed these feelings in an open letter to all Derbeians published in the *Derby Evening Telegraph*. He proposed a new 'motto' for the new city: 'Proud of our achievements of the past; Jealous of our fair reputation; and Determined to make our city a place worthy of its name.'

The Queen is greeted by young citizens of the new city of Derby.

THE PRIDE OF DERBY

ON 18 July 1997, Queen Elizabeth II and her husband Prince Philip once more visited the city of Derby. This time she was to open Pride Park Stadium, Derby County's new home. It had been just a few short weeks since supporters had waved a tearful goodbye to the Baseball Ground. Emotions had run high and fans had abandoned any pretence of doing anything other than soaking up the atmosphere long before the final whistle blew. That last season at the club's old home had been one of celebration rather than misery, since it had seen the Rams back in top-flight football, now the English Premiership. It had been a thrilling season. The Premiership was a glorious place to be, populated by some of the very best and most exciting players in world football, and just being there had given the whole city new prestige. Now the Rams could begin this second season in their splendid new home.

The Pride Park regeneration scheme had begun in 1993 with the cleansing of around 197 acres (80 hectares) of contaminated industrial wasteland. It was soon to become one of the most successful schemes of its kind and in 1999 it was recognised in the British Construction Industry Civil Engineering Awards for its 'exemplary environmental achievement'. Although most of the area had yet to be developed, there was little trace of its former identity when the stadium opened.

The royal couple toured the stadium before greeting the fans from the pitch, where the queen unveiled a special dedication plaque. The royal couple were then driven around the pitch with manager Jim Smith and chairman Lionel Pickering, the Derby fans cheering as much for their heroes as for their monarch.

It seemed fitting that the queen should be here on such an important day in Derby's footballing history, for she had been in attendance with her parents in 1946 when the Rams had won the FA Cup. Now here, too, were two heroes of that Cup Final - Reg Harrison and Jim Bullions, together with 'squad player' Angus Morrison – who were driven around the pitch in a vintage Rolls-Royce along with the FA Cup itself which they clutched protectively. They were part of a grand parade which also featured Disney

Queen Elizabeth II and Derby County owner Lionel Pickering at the opening of Pride Park Stadium in July 1997. Pickering, a multi-millionaire local businessman, had bought the club and pumped millions into it.

characters and marching bands. The occasion also saw army parachutists, even a Spice Girls 'tribute' act. In all it was an exciting day and as the crowds tumbled out of the ground, all fears about leaving the old Baseball Ground had been dispelled. And in 2001, news of plans to demolish the old ground to make way for housing brought some sadness but little anguish. The Baseball Ground's time had past, its job done. A century of ghosts and memories had travelled with the fans to Pride Park. And whilst nothing could ever replace the Baseball Ground in the hearts of the supporters, Pride Park Stadium was already carving its own special spot there.

Shopping in the city

Derbeians cannot fail to have noticed the dramatic improvements in the shopping facilities throughout the city over the last 25 years. The introduction of out-of-town retail parks made good use of former wasteland – the Kingsway Retail Park, for example, was built on the site of a former tip – but there were fears that these new retail parks would draw shoppers away from the city centre. Thankfully, this has not yet proven to be the case, the continued redevelopments and improvements to the central retail area ensuring that city centre shopping is more popular than ever.

The Eagle Centre was first opened in 1975 and provided Derby's first large indoor shopping mall. It has recently undergone a major renovation which has in effect given the city a brand new third millennium shopping centre, which must now be one of the premier city centre shopping malls in the country. Utilising a bright, warm colour scheme and incorporating plenty of light and fresh air, the Eagle Centre is in complete contrast to the closed-in corridor feel of older shopping centres such as the Victoria at Nottingham. With a host of stores, many new to the city, a more pleasant and secure basement car-park and, for the first time, automatic doors to keep out the cold and damp, or allow fresh air to flow freely, the Eagle Centre is drawing people into the city. And yet outside of the city centre there remain a number of neighbourhood shopping precincts, many dating from the second half of the 20th century. While many of the traditional corner shops have been forced out of business by the recent proliferation of supermarkets, others continue to serve the community as they have done for a hundred years or more. And many of the suburban 'village' shops are flourishing, although a few seem in danger of being swamped by fast food outlets.

Sadler Gate, another of Derby's ancient thoroughfares now given over to shops and bars.

There are other popular shopping areas on the edge of the city centre, such as Normanton and Pear Tree Roads which are particularly renowned for the concentration of Asian and Caribbean grocers, as well as fabric shops, which continue to thrive there. And back in the city centre, Sadler Gate, which has been pedestrianised for more than 30 years, remains one of the city's most popular shopping zones with its array of funky boutiques selling designer labels. An area which has benefited enormously from recent redevelopment has been the once-dreary Albion

Street. This is now a vibrant and pleasant shopping area featuring trendy high street stores. The face a city presents to the outside world is often reflected in the calibre of retailers which choose to open there and Albion Street's Gap, Virgin Megastore, HMV and Disney Store, hint of a city which is attracting some of the world's biggest retail corporations.

The Co-op

Much of the Albion Street-Exchange Street area was, until the 1990s, occupied by the various departments of the Derby Co-operative Society and its successor, and the society's main department store remains in Albion Street. In 2001, work was under way to transform part of the complex into a shopping mall featuring well-known names and a cafe or coffee shop belonging to a major high street chain.

Founded in 1849 by 12 members of the Carpenters and Joiners Society, led by Jonathan

Albion Street, once the home of the Co-operative Society's offices, now leading into the refurbished Eagle Centre and itself having undergone a remarkable transformation in recent years.

Henderson, Derby's 'Co-op' was only the second co-operative society in the world, closely following the ideals laid out by the 'Rochdale Pioneers'. Initially selling just flour, from a hayloft in the George Yard off Sadler Gate, the Co-op soon expanded both its range of products and its premises. Goods were bought wholesale and then sold on to members at a low price. The store operated for the convenience of working people and opened each evening between 7pm and 9.30pm. Just eight years after its opening, the Co-op had to move to larger premises on Victoria Street, before settling in Exchange Street. It seemed as if every neighbourhood had its own branch and by 1900 there were no less than 60 separate stores and departments in the town. At its height the Co-op sold everything from groceries and clothing to furniture and electrical goods. It had its own building department, bakery, drapery, butchery, delicatessen, tobacconist and chemist and also had special departments which sold sports goods, cosmetics, school uniforms, bridal wear, hats and shoes. There was a restaurant and customers could also take advantage of a wide range of services from dry cleaning and laundry to wedding car hire, and the Co-op also offered a delivery service for groceries, coal, bread and, of course, dairy produce. Its own garage in Woods Lane serviced the fleet of vehicles.

The Co-op could also custom-make curtains and there was even a painting and decorating department, as well as the undertaker, travel agency and department stores of today.

The Co-op was very much a part of daily life for all Derbeians. The famous 'divi', where shoppers received a dividend of the profits, is remembered with particular fondness.

Many Derbeians can still remember their own, or their parents' divi numbers. The divi was eventually replaced by a savings stamp system and younger Derbeians will also remember the treat of sticking those into special books. Fondly remembered, too, is the complicated system of payment where money was placed into a brass or steel tube which was then shot through the store to a central point, either along a cable or via a vacuum tube. This survived well into the 1970s, as did some of the old lifts which featured folding inner screens and which had to be operated by a lift attendant.

Most of these premises were built at the start of the 20th century when the Co-op chose to redevelop

An unusual 'icon' but a favourite with many Derbeians – the 'Co-op Cow'.

an area of land near the Morledge. Known as 'Olympia', it had housed a development of shops and a small fairground. The Co-op had a far more grandiose scheme for the land. Here they intended to build a modern complex consisting of shops at ground-floor level with offices above. But the main feature was to be an enormous hall, with a balcony, which could be used for meetings and concerts. Completed in 1917, the Central Hall was capable of catering for 1,200 people and in 1919 the Co-op in Derby had the great honour of hosting the TUC conference. Delegates came from far and wide and among the many dignitaries in attendance was the Prime Minister of Australia.

The famous 'Co-op Cow' was erected on the roof of the Central Hall in the mid-1950s. Illuminated and visible at night from the railway lines coming into Derby station, it has welcomed home generations of Derbeians with that kind of comfortable familiarity that is unique to home, and has become an unofficial icon for the town. The cow was much missed during its removal due to redevelopment of the Central Hall in the summer of 2001. Developers promised to return the Co-op Cow to its rightful place once work on the roof had been completed.

Ever more cosmopolitan

The atmosphere of the city centre is changing. More leisure time and more expendable income has seen an upsurge in the number of restaurants, clubs and bars. Restaurants in particular have both contributed to, and reflected, the greater sophistication of modern Derby and attest to the dramatic lifestyle changes of the last few years. There are now eating establishments to suit all ages, tastes and wallets.

Derby Market Place in 2001. In the background is Franceys's House, the late 17th-century home of Alderman William Franceys, whose son, Henry, was apothecary to the town's gentry.

Derby has long enjoyed a deserved reputation for some of the tastiest Indian food in the country, and the city now boasts a wide variety of other cuisines. Visitors can already choose from Thai, Chinese, Italian, French, Greek, Caribbean, and Mexican restaurants along with traditional and non-traditional English and Continental food. The introduction of stylish coffee houses such as the award-winning Caruso establishments in the Eagle Centre, has given the city centre a more European and North American feel, yet remarkably there is still the atmosphere of the market town which was Derby for so long.

The transformation of deserted shops and offices into chic cafe-bars has proved popular with all age groups. Catering for all tastes, the laid-back contemporary feel of daytime gives way to a more hip and upbeat mood after dark.

By the 1990s a pedestrianised zone had been completed in the middle of the city centre stretching the length of St Peter's Street, through the Cornmarket and along Irongate. Also included in the scheme was St James' Street and the Market Place. The pedestrianisation meant the diversion of all traffic, including buses and taxis, and, whilst initially inconvenient for some, the move drastically reduced city centre traffic fumes and noise pollution and made for a much more pleasant shopping environment.

The Market Place was completely re-landscaped and returned to its role as a public space. Many small trees and plants were added and this has softened the square somewhat. The trees look particularly pretty at Christmas time, when decorated with twinkling lights, creating a magical mood. The War Memorial has been given more prominence in its new site at the entrance to the Guildhall.

Pride Park Stadium in 2001, home of Derby County and host to the full England international team. In four years the whole Pride Park area has undergone a breathtaking change.

Less popular has been the addition of the 'waterfall fountain' at the Cornmarket side of the Market Place. Whilst many Derbeians agreed that, in principle, the addition of a water feature to the Market Place would be an asset, the rather stark and industrial structure that was created has won few fans. The only exceptions to this seem to be the small children who love to splash about underneath the cascade, and late-night revellers who are tempted to do the same. Quite out of place in its elegant surroundings, it appears somehow incomplete, and has earned many unflattering comparisons.

Modern Derby
The City of Derby, a unitary authority since 1997, now covers an area of some 30 square miles (78km²), has 2,000 acres (809 hectares) of parkland and a population of around 218,000.

In contrast, the modern statue of the Ram at the corner of East Street and Albion Street, erected in 1995, is an interesting tribute to the city's mythical symbol. It was completed in situ by sculptor Michael Pegler and measures approximately 6ft 6ins x 7ft 10ins x 5ft 6ins (2m x 2.4m x 1.7m) and was carved from 18 tons of millstone grit. The completed sculpture weighs approximately 10 tons. The Derby Ram manages to combine both tradition and modernity and has become a popular meeting point for weekend shoppers. Another, much smaller, statue of a ram stands in the Main Centre. Unveiled in 1963, the statue is cast in bronze and depicts the figure of a boy riding on the ram's back. Elsewhere, in Museum Square and the River Gardens, there are a few statues of Derby notables, but these excepted, there are few examples of public art in the city. Successive councils have shown a reluctance to remedy this and even the impressive statue of Bonnie Prince Charlie in Full Street owes its existence to private subscription. Erected in 1995, it was sculptured by Anthony Stones and was awarded a Special Award by Derby Civic Society in 1996. It is claimed to be the only such statue in the world, although there is a famous monument at Glenfinnan near Fort William, where the prince began his rebellion. On top of that 60ft (18.3m) structure is an 8ft-tall (2.4m) statue which was intended to be of the prince. The sculptor made an error, however, copying the face from the portrait of a young Jacobite soldier rather than one of the prince himself. Although it does bear a striking resemblance to the Young Pretender, it is known by the name 'The Highlander'.

Derby has plenty of open spaces which would benefit from statuary and it seems a pity that opportunities continue to be missed to rectify the situation. There are many historical figures, such as Cotton and Flamsteed, Whitehurst and Wright (commemorated by a monument in Irongate, but not by a statue), Spencer and Darwin, who could be remembered in this way, providing a lasting tribute to their contributions as well as adding an ornamental touch to the city landscape.

Derby has also acquired a more cosmopolitan edge, thanks in part to the greater experience of world travel of many Derbeians, and to the University which has brought into the city young people from across the country and farther afield. Major international companies have chosen Derby as their headquarters. Toyota UK is based at nearby Burnaston on the site of the former Derby Airport, and Prudential chose Pride Park for the location of the national call centre for their Egg internet banking service.

LARA CROFT – WORLD-FAMOUS CYBERBABE

ACCORDING to her official biography, gun-toting, artefact-hunting adventurer Lara Croft, was born to Lord Henshingley Croft in 1967 at Wimbledon in Surrey. But Derbeians know that the world's favourite cyberbabe has roots much closer to home. For Lara Croft, heroine of the *Tomb Raider* series of computer games, was Derby born and bred. She was created in a Derby design studio by Toby Gard, then a key member of the Core Design workforce, and she went on, quite literally, to conquer the world. The *Tomb Raider* game itself was a ground-breaker, but it was the sexy and gutsy heroine Lara Croft who captured the imagination of the public and propelled *Tomb Raider* to international success. Blessed with good looks, intelligence, agility and courage, Lara has appeared on the cover of mainstream style magazine *The Face*; has featured in *The Sunday Times*; modelled aquatic wear; secured a lucrative contract endorsing Lucozade; has been the subject of comics; has her own action figures and collectable cards; and, in 2001, became the subject of a blockbusting movie with Angelina Jolie in the title role. Her fans range from grown men and women, to teens and children, who write fan letters and send drawings to the offices of Core Design. There are dozens of fan clubs and webpages devoted to Lara, detailing her history and even her favourite food and her blood group. Obsession with *Tomb Raider* and Lara has even been blamed for a slump in form of former Liverpool and England goalkeeper David James, and a delay in the release of an album by the Prodigy. Worldwide more than 28 million copies of the various versions of the game have been sold and helped to make Core Design, who have created more than 50 successful games, into one of the world's leading computer games developers. Now occupying purpose-built premises at Pride Park, Core Design is part of the Eidos Interactive company.

DERBY OF THE FUTURE?

AS Derby settled down to the 21st century, plans to demolish Aslin's 1930s bus station to make way for a state-of-the-art replacement is surely one of the most contentious issues to have faced Derby's city planners. They could not have imagined the fierce opposition that was to rise up in a city normally content to sit back and let matters take their course. Any new proposal will always find opponents, but the bus station issue seemed to galvanise opposition like nothing else. Petitions were gathered, established environmental groups like Friends of the Earth criticised the scheme, and a local Bus Station Action Group was formed. Perhaps it was merely the reflection of a general mood of local protest which had been sweeping the country. Or perhaps it was the inevitable reaction of generations who in recent years had witnessed the destruction of so much of Derby's heritage.

Initial plans had also called for restructuring of the traffic system in the Morledge-Cockpitt Island area of the city centre. Plans to drive a roadway across part of Bass's Rec and the historic mill fleam soon led to the establishment of an encampment of 'eco protesters' who built treehouses in some of the threatened trees. Plans had to be changed when it was discovered that such redevelopment was prohibited by the terms under which the land had been donated to the town.

The huge car park which was built on the former Cockpitt Island dominated the skyline so much that it only increased the concerns of those opposed to the scheme. Total costs were expected to exceed £30 million and a completion date of 2003 was set. Amended traffic proposals and the establishment of a European-style piazza overlooking the River Derwent were met with mixed responses. The River Gardens had been laid out as part of the 1930s Central Improvement Plan, but many of its original features, the formal lily ponds and giant tortoise sculptures for example, had already been removed. Opponents were fearful that what remained would also be lost beneath a proposed hotel, health club and multiplex cinema. But the inclusion of the piazza, which would make good use of the riverfront with bars and cafes, showed greater promise.

Derby has long neglected the potential of its long and lovely river front and, with almost two thirds of the city concentrated on one bank, it is possible at times to forget that Derby has a river at all. Perhaps if this scheme – called Riverlights – could make use of the beauty of the Derwent, whilst preserving its natural state, it could be another asset to the city and even attract visitors.

With the eventual abandonment of the police station and magistrates' court on Full Street, the council also announced plans to redevelop that site and create an £11 million complex to house an arts centre and provide a new home for the Metro Cinema, as well as a modern library to replace the one on the Wardwick, presumably then allowing the expansion of the ever-cramped Derby Museum.

> **The best city...**
> In September 2001, the city of Derby was fifth out of 376 local authority areas in a list of the top places to live in England and Wales. The survey, carried out by Experian, took into account factors such as education, shopping, crime levels, green spaces and the cost of housing. The first four in the list were all rural areas, making Derby, quite literally, the best city in which to live.

Elsewhere in the city, plans which have been floated included one to regenerate the area behind the Debenhams department store. The 'Becket Well' scheme suggested the redevelopment of the long neglected, almost deserted and always ugly Duckworth Square shopping precinct into a variety of retail units, as well as providing space for leisure usage.

Becket Well would be linked to St Peter's Street by an enclosed walkway and would include the redevelopment of the area between St Peter's Street, Colyear Street, Macklin Street and Victoria Street, necessitating the compulsory purchase of around 85 shops and properties. Various options were discussed, from the simple renovation of Duckworth Square to a complete rebuilding of the whole area. Costs of around £100 million had been suggested and included the possible extension of Debenhams itself.

But with the Riverlights scheme, and plans to extend the Eagle Centre to fully incorporate the Main Centre on London Road, one wondered if the Becket Well scheme could proceed. Indeed, in the autumn of 2001 it was announced that the company which had bought Duckworth Square in 1997 had put it back on the market for £1.5 million. The council had already decided that no work would be carried out on the Becket Well site while the Eagle Centre extension was operative.

Architect's model of the proposed £2.5 million multi-faith centre at the University of Derby.

Multi-faith Centre

It seemed that new proposals for improvements and developments were being registered weekly. In the summer of 2001 it was announced that a new Multi-faith Centre was to be opened at the Kedleston Road campus of the University of Derby. Believed to be the first such centre of its kind in the world, it had been in the planning and fundraising stages for some time and the initial costs were estimated at £2.5 million. The University of Derby has boasted a flourishing Religious Resource and Research Centre for several years and also produced what has come to be regarded as the definitive guide to religion in the UK. The Multi-faith Centre would be available to all faiths for meetings, for prayer and meditation. The University also hoped it would promote cultural exchange and increased understanding and tolerance between faiths. Featuring a unique architectural style reflecting the infinite diversity of world culture and religion, the centre would have three Congregation Rooms for meetings and mass worship; a Meditation Area and offices. The design and concept were the result of collaboration between seven of the UK's major religious groups. Amongst those who have officially lent their support are: His Holiness the Dalai Lama; His Grace the Most Reverend Rt Hon Dr George Carey, Archbishop of Canterbury; Dr Jonathan Sacks, Chief Rabbi of the United Hebrew Congregations of the Commonwealth; Dr Manazir Ahsan, Director General of the Islamic Foundation; Wendi Momen, Chairman of the National Spiritual Assembly of the Bahá'í's of the UK; Dr Indarjit Singh, Chairman of the Network of Sikh Organisations; Mr Sharma, President of the National Councils of Hindu Temples; Dr Natubhai Shah, Chair of the Jain Academy; and Dorab Mistry, President of the Zoroastrian Trust Funds of Europe (Inc).

In addition to the Multi-faith Centre, the University of Derby proposed an £8 million extension to Britannia Mills and a £12 million viewing tower and space study centre at Kedleston Road.

Among other recent proposals are the following:

- A major shopping and leisure development linking Sadler Gate and St James's Street by way of a trendy new thoroughfare for bars and restaurants, with a European-style piazza as its centrepiece.
- A £12 million shopping and leisure complex on the former site of Mackworth College
- The £4 million restoration of the Arboretum.
- The renovation of the neglected Roundhouse, near the railway station, for use as a restaurant.
- A £1 million expansion and redevelopment of the Industrial Museum
- A controversial £10 million recycling centre on Sinfin Lane to convert household rubbish to energy for the National Grid.

Whichever of these schemes comes to pass, over the last 2,000 years, and without ever losing its friendly county town feel, Derby has evolved from a range of tiny agricultural communities to a thriving, vibrant city. Confident of its identity, protective of its heritage and proud of its achievements, Derby Our City stands ready to greet the next 2,000 years.

BIBLIOGRAPHY

A Cinema Near You, Ashley Franklin (Breedon Publishing)

Derbeians of Distinction, Maxwell Craven (Breedon Publishing)

Derby County: A Complete Record, Gerald Mortimer and others (Breedon Publishing)

The Franklin Papers Collection, The American Philosophical Society

Hanged for Three Pennies, Edward Garner (Breedon Publishing)

A History of Derbyshire County Cricket Club 1870-1970, John Shawcroft (Derbyshire CCC)

I'll Sing You a Thousand Love Songs, Mike Carey (Pinnacle Printing)

Regency to Golden Jubilee, Harry Butterton (Breedon Publishing)

Roman Derby, Maurice Brassington (Breedon Publishing)

Melville's Derby Legacy, Harry Greatorex (Breedon Publishing)

Newspapers

Various editions of the *Derby Evening Telegraph* and the *Derby Mercury*

INDEX

Abbey Inn 23, 101
Abbey Lane 23
Abbey Street 24, 91, 94, 101
Abingdon Street 148
Adams, Chris 115
Adamson, Arthur 147
Adkins, Arthur 164
Agard Street 71, 91, 150
Albert Street 27, 98-100, 107, 169
Albion Street 18, 22, 151, 163, 176, 178
Alderman, Albert 114
Alexandra cinema 109
Alexandra Street 163
Alfreton 82
Alfreton Road 155
All Saints' Church (see also Derby Cathedral) 16, 19, 24, 33, 35, 38, 41-2, 44-5, 50, 53, 118-19, 138-9, 170
Allen Street 162
Allenton 9, 158, 162
Allestree 25-6, 101, 110, 140, 155, 162
Allestrey, William 43
Allestrey family 33
Almond Street 25
Alvaston 23, 25, 28, 109, 140, 147, 150, 152-3, 162, 164
Alvaston Lake 150
Ambrose Street 25
Andrews, Annie 145
Andrews, Councillor Gerald 174
Arboretum 7, 25, 85, 103-5, 118, 147, 150, 155, 181
Arboretum Field 105, 118
Arboretum Place 105
Arkwright, Richard 67, 70
Art Gallery 69, 98
Ascot Drive 140
Ashbourne 51, 62, 73, 118
Ashbourne Road 52, 72, 88, 94-5
Ashbourne Road Methodist Church 110
Ashgate School, 94
Ashover 138

Aslin, Charles 142-3, 157, 180
Assembly Rooms 41, 54, 71-2, 106, 159, 168, 170
Assizes 32, 85, 87, 160
Athenaeum Society 97-8
Attenborough, Fred 173
Auckland Close 25
Auxiliary Fire Service 146
Babington, Sir Anthony 25, 36
Babington Hall 25, 36
Babington Lane 25, 36, 107-9, 165-6
Babington Plot 36
Bacon, Arthur 148
Bailey, Peter 159
Bainbrigge, William 33
Baine, Bishop Ralph 35
Baker, Edna 160
Baker, William 78
Bakewell, Robert 70, 100, 139
Balaclava Road 25
Ballard, Father John 36
Balson, Brenda 160
Bancroft, William Henry 129
Barlow, Eddie 115
Barnes, Ernie 173
Barnett, Kim 115
Base, Arthur Frederick 148
Baseball Ground 117-18, 141, 144, 146, 159, 171-2, 175
Bass, Michael Thomas 98, 136
Bass Street 25
Bateman Street 163
Bates, Alan 110
Bates, Alderman C. R. 158
Bates, Doug 147
Bates, Olive 147-8
Bath Street 163
Battle of Britain Memorial Window 157
BBC Radio Derby
Beardsall, Eric 162
Beare, Ellen 90
Becher Street 25
Becket Junior School 159
Becket Street 100, 165
Becket Well 180-1

Becket Well Lane 95
Bell, Alexander Graham 95
Bell, Richard 135
Bell, Tom 132
Bell Hotel 116
Bellaby, Stan 162
Belper Road 11
Bemrose, Arnold 9
Bemrose, William 127
Bemrose Corporation 127
Bemrose School 96, 110, 112
Bennet, Gervase 44
Bentley, Doris 145
Bentley, Sheila 145
Beresford, Frank 160
Binge, Ronald 111
Birdwood Street 163
Birkdale Close 25
Bishop Lonsdale Teacher Training College 95
Black Death 30-2
Blackfriars 33
Bloomer, Steve 116-18
Bloor, Robert 58
Blount, Walter 32
Blue Boy public house 163
Blue John 66
Blunt, Canon Alfred 135
Board Schools 94
Bolam, James 112
Bold Lane 24, 106
Bonnie Prince Charlie 50-4, 138, 179
Boott, Kirk snr 75-6
Boott, Kirk jnr 75-6
Borough Fire Service 165
Borough Military Band 150
Borough Police 85, 159, 165
Boulton, Matthew 60-1, 65
Boulton Moor 9
Bowmer, Alderman C. F. 158
Bradshaw Hay 88, 90
Bradshaw Street 122
Bradshaw Way 89, 122
Bradstreet, Dudley 53
Brandreth, Jeremiah 90

Breadsall 64, 114
Breadsall Priory 64
Brewster, Florence 146
Brick Street 31
Bridge Gate 24-5, 27-8, 52, 83, 133
Bridge Street 27, 71, 153
Brisbane Road 25
Britannia Mills 96, 181
British Celanese 162
Brittain, Hallard 173
Britton, Elenor 38
Brook Street 71, 150, 153
Brookside 99, 153
Brown, Joshua 79
Bullions, Jim 175
Bullivant, Mike 173
Bulwell 91
Burdett, Peter Perez 69
Burnaston 179
Burton Road 24-5
Bus Station Action Group 180
Busby, George 50
Buxton 37, 101
Cade, Dr James 70
Cade, Rowena 70
Cadeby Main Colliery 134
Caesar Street 24
Cairns Close 25
Calke Abbey 72
Cambridge Street 163
Cameron Road 130
Camp Street 24
Canal Street 91, 163
Canal Tavern 81
Canberra Road 25
Canning, George 62
Cannon Street 25
Carnegie, Andrew 93
Carnoustie Close 25
Carr, Donald 115
Carr, Sue 173
Carrington Street 137
Carter, Raich 152
Cartwright, John 114
Carty, Councillor Joe 172
Castle Mill 22
Castlefields 22, 82, 84
Cavendish, The 107, 109
Cavendish, Elizabeth 37
Cavendish, Henry 37, 96, 140

Cavendish, Mary 37
Cavendish, William 37, 41
Central Hall 177
Central Improvement Plan 141, 143, 157, 180
Central School 96
Centurion Walk 24
Chaddesden 8, 25, 27, 109, 114, 133-4, 146, 154, 162-4
Chaddesden Hall, 78 133
Chaddesden Park 164
Chaddesden Wood 8
Chain Lane 11, 25
Chaleybeate mineral water 101
Champion, Charles Henry 129
Chandos, Major J. W. 159
Chapel Street 94
Charles I 39-41, 43
Charles II 34, 45-6, 49-50
Charter Celebrations 165, 174
Chatsworth 37-8, 104, 140
Chatterton, William 114
Chauncey, Dr William 101
Cheapside 15, 24, 27
Chellaston 8, 27, 70, 149, 155, 159
Chelsea Close 25
Chesapeake Road 25
Chester, Earl of 22
Chester Green 24, 120, 151, 155, 174
Chesterfield 82, 86, 91, 138
Chesterfield, Earl of 114
Cheyenne Gardens 25
Church Farmhouse 28
Church Lane 27
Church Street 28
City Hospital 102, 145, 148, 156, 164, 174
City Road 11, 126, 174
Civic Society 179
Clay, Stuart 166
Clough, Brian 171-2
Cluniacs 23
Cocklayne, Matthew 90
Cockpitt Car Park 22
Cockpitt Island 180
Cockpit Hill 22, 81, 106
Codnor 37, 91
Coffee, William 58, 76
College of Art 70, 95-6, 110

College of Further Education 95-6
College Place 33
Collins, John 102
Colombo Street 163
Colyear Street 166, 180
Condor engine 124
Congregational Church 132
Conroy, Frank 112
Copecastle 22
Copson, Bill 114
Core Design 179
Corn Exchange 107-8
Cornhill 26
Cornmarket 10, 24, 37, 50, 55, 61, 72, 79, 82, 85, 97-8, 100, 132, 153, 159, 178
Coronation Exhibition 163
Coronation Gala 164
Corporation Street 158, 160
Cosmo cinema 109
Cotchett, Thomas 55
Cotton, John 74
Council House 99, 142-3, 152, 157-8, 160-1, 165, 170, 172, 174
County Ground 83, 113-18
County Hall (see also Shire Hall) 73, 160
Cowsley Road 163
Cox, Arthur 172
Crapper, Thomas 101
Croft, Lara 179
Cromford 67
Crompton Street 25, 166
Cromwell, Oliver 43-5
Crooks, Sammy 152
Crosthwaite, Joseph 49
Crown Courts 87
Royal Crown Derby 57-9, 70, 136, 157
Crown Hotel 9
Crown Inn 90
Crump, Thomas 101
Crystal Palace 25, 104
Cumberland, Duke of 54
Curzon Club 166
Curzon Lane 164
Curzon Street 92, 108
Dakin, Anthony John 164
Dale Abbey 24
Dale Road 24

Danelaw 18

Darley Abbey 27, 33, 68, 80, 103, 155-6

Darley Fields 14-15

Darley Grove 10

Darley Park 7, 103, 157

Darnley, Lord 36-7

Darwin, Charles 64, 92-3

Darwin, Erasmus 25, 60-1, 63-4, 66, 73, 101

Darwin, George 62

Darwin Place 25

Darwin Road 25

Davis, Private J. 160

Dawkes, George 115

De Ferrers family 25

Deadman's Lane 24, 31

Deeley, Richard Mountford 9

Defoe, Daniel 101

DeFreitas, Philip 115

Degge Street 25

Denby 46

Dennis, Denny 111

Depot Street 24

Derby Airport 179

Derby, Bishop of 138, 158

Derby Canal 80-1

Derby Castle 22, 41-2

Derby Cathedral (see also All Saints' Church) 15-16, 33-4, 38, 50-1, 127, 138-40, 144, 151, 156, 160-1, 170

Derby City Church 27, 43, 108

Derby County FC 110, 112, 114, 116-17, 141, 145-6, 148, 152, 155, 157, 159, 171-2, 175, 178, 182

Derby and County Athletic Club 141

Derby Daily Telegraph 108-9, 116, 119-20, 122, 128, 130, 132, 133

Derby, Diocese of 138, 140, 174

Derby Evening Telegraph 140, 155, 157-8, 162, 167, 172, 174, 182

Derby Gas Company 101

Derby Heritage Centre 27, 33

Derby Independent Grammar School for Boys 34

Derby Junction FC 105

Derby Junction Railway 82

Derby Ladies Athletics Club 173

Derby Mercury 52-4, 67-8, 91, 100, 182

Derby Museum 6, 9-10, 12, 16, 19, 21, 53, 69-70, 87, 98, 180

Derby Pavilion 107

Derby Philosophical Society 61-2, 64-5, 67, 70, 75, 94, 98

Derby Playhouse 110, 165

Derby Racecourse 11, 146

Derby Road 94, 131, 149

Derby School 33-4, 46, 48, 69, 74, 92, 94, 96, 112, 137

Derby School Board 94

Derby Shakespeare Company 112

Derbyshire Association for the Deaf 95

Derbyshire Building Society 171

Derby Canal 80-1

Derbyshire Conservative Political Club 159

Derbyshire Constabulary 85

Derbyshire County Cricket Club 113-114, 116, 182

Derbyshire County Council 174

Derbyshire Football Association 116

Derbyshire Flying Squad 102

Derbyshire Regiment 51

Derbyshire Royal Infirmary 60, 100, 101, 102, 132, 141, 155

Derbyshire Yeomanry 130, 140, 149, 162

Derventio 11-15, 18, 24

Derventio Court 24

Derwent, River 8-11, 15, 23, 27, 33, 42, 51, 55, 61, 68, 71, 80-1, 120, 124, 144, 148, 153-6, 167, 170, 180

Derwent House 27, 33

Derwent Navigation 80

Derwent Valley 10, 148

Devonshire, Duke of 51, 61, 104

Devonshire, Earl of 50

Devonshire Almshouses 38

Devonshire House 37, 72

Dickens, Charles 76, 96

Dilkes, Mary 87

Diocesan School 92, 127

Docherty, Daniel 162

Docker, Lady Norah 166

Doggrell, Vera Mabel 148

Doherty, Peter 152

Domesday Book 16, 21-2

Dominican Friary 24, 32-3

Draycott, Dr Anthony 35

Drewry Lane 25

Dryden Street 25

Duckworth Square 180-1

Duesbury, Henry 99, 105

Duesbury, William 25, 57, 76

Duesbury Close 25

Duffield 111

Duffield Bank 138

Duffield Road 11, 102

Eagle Centre 142, 166, 170, 175-6, 178, 181

Eagle Market 143, 170

Eagle Street 170

East, Mr T. W. 158

Eastgate 156

Eastwood 91, 110, 126

Eastwood, James 126

Edge, Joanne 140

Edinburgh, Duke of 95, 174

Edward I 22

Edward III 32

Edward IV 32

Edward VI 34

Edward VII 107, 119-20

Edward VIII 34, 159

Eliot, George 87, 93

Elizabeth I 34, 36-8

Elizabeth II 102, 159, 174-5

Elliot, Harry 114

Ellis, Mrs Geoffrey 164

Elm Cottage 28

Elvaston 28, 32

Elvaston Lane 28

Erewash Canal 80

Essex, Lord 41

Essoldo cinema 109

Etruria Hall 73

Etruria Works 73

Etwall Street 163

Evans, Elizabeth 145

Evans, Mrs Ada 68

Evans, Thomas 67-8

Exchange Street 107, 176-7

Exeter, Earl of 25

Exeter Bridge 25, 142, 155, 170

Exeter Flats 162
Exeter House 25, 52-3
Exeter Street 25, 80, 92, 125
Fallowes, William 84
Farmer, Dorothy Lena 148
Farmer, Sylvia Mary 148
Farrington, Victor Rutherford 146
Ferguson, James 65, 69
Fern Bank 134
Ferrers Way 25
Finan, Margaret Eileen 148
Finchley Avenue 25
Findern 23, 67
Fish Market 24
Fitzgerald, Thomas Gerald 147
Flamsteed, John 45-50, 55, 65, 179
Fletcher, Constance 164
Fletcher, George 165
Florentine Boar 7, 104
Ford Street 27
Foresters Leisure Park 121
Foss, Gladys Emily 146
Foss, Sidney 146
Foster, George 90
Fox, Dr Douglas 96
Fox, George 44
Fox, Roy 111
Fox, Sir Charles 25, 104
Fox Street 25
Franceys, Alderman William 178
Franceys, Henry 106, 178
Franklin, Benjamin 60, 62, 65-6
Franklin, Elizabeth Helen 148
Fretwell, John 45
Friar Gate 23-7, 31-3, 42, 45, 52, 71-3, 78, 83-8, 90-2, 94-5, 126, 143, 153, 166
Friar Gate Bridge 25, 83
Friargate station 83
Friary Hotel 23
Frost, Ralph 79
Full Street 52, 60-1, 63-4, 85, 90, 106, 110, 142-4, 152, 157, 179-80
Gallows Baulk 89
Galton, Francis 64
Gard, Toby 179
Garlick, Nicholas 34, 36
Gaumont cinema 109-10, 164
Gell, Sir John 40-1, 43, 45
Gell, Thomas 43

General Strike 135, 137
George Hotel 54
George I 50
George II 50, 54
George III 57, 61
George V 120, 135, 140, 160
George VI 134, 145, 152, 159-62
George Yard 177
Gerard Street 159, 163
Gerard Street School 94
Gibb, James 139-40
Gifford, Fred 146
Giltbrook 91
Gisborne, John 72
Gisborne Street 163
Gladwin, Cliff 115
Gleneagles Close 25
Glossop 8
Gloucester, Duke of 164
Glover, Stephen 85, 96, 98
Goodall, Archie 117
Goodall, John 117
Goodwin Street 151
Gower, Catherine 42
Grand Junction Canal Company 81
Grand Theatre 107, 166
Grange Street 163
Gratton, George Henry 148
Gray, Barry 111
Gray, Simon 110
Grayson, Councillor Zachariah 159, 161
Great Northern Railway 83
Greatorex, Dora 148
Green Hill House 102
Green Lane 94-5, 102, 110, 120, 140, 160, 166, 169
Gresley, Cuthbert 70
Gresley, Frank 70
Gresley, J. S. 70
Gresley, John 32
Grey, Lord 32
Grey Street 163
Greyhound Inn 78
Grimmer, Francis Robert 148
Guildhall 26, 35, 55, 65, 87, 99-100, 114, 119, 135, 170, 178
Habershon, Matthew 99
Haden, Ann 76
Haden, Henry 78

Hague, Robert 51
Halley, Edmund 48-9
Hallows, Arthur George 146
Halton, Immanuel 46
Hamer, Arnold 115
Handyside Street 25
Hann, Judith 112
Hann, Ralph 112
Harcourt, Rt Hon Sir William 136
Harcourt Street 25, 163
Hardwick, Bess of 37-8, 140
Hardy, James Gibbs 129
Harris, Phil 173
Harrison, Corporal 'Sid' 150
Harrison, Reg 152, 175
Harrison, Thomas 65
Harrison Street 163
Hartington Street 122
Harvey Road 25
Haslam, Sir Alfred Seale 119
Haslam's foundry 126
Haslam's Lane 156
Hawthorn Street 145, 148
Haydn Road 164
Hayley, William 70
Headless Cross 31
Heanor 82, 125
Heath, John 68
Heathcote, Alderman Samuel 53
Helliwell, Barry 149
Hendrick, Mike 115
Henry II 165
Henry V 32
Henry VII 32, 34
Henry VIII 25, 33-4, 36-7, 138
Henson, Elsie May 145
Heritage Gate 23, 143
Hertford, Marquess of 38
Hewitt, Hannah 90
Hewitt, Henry 134
Heyworth Street 25
Higgins, Sidney 148
High Street 159, 176
Hill, Joe William 148
Hilton, Colonel Sir Peter 29
Hinds, Arthur 25
Hippodrome theatre 166
Hithersay, Henry 129
Holland, Mrs Rene 164
Hollies, Neville William 164

Holmes, Donald William 164
Holmes Aqueduct 81
Holmes Bridge 156
Home Guard 7, 144-8
Hope Street 163
Horn, Charles Levi 148
Howard, Mary 60
Howard Hotel 86
Howe, Sir Robert George 137
Hudson, Charles 134
Hudson, Thomas 69
Humpston, Private Robert 133-4
Hunkin, Philip John 164
Hutton, Margaret Agnes 145
Hutton, William 25, 56
Hutton Street 25
Hyde, Ann 50
Ilkeston 82
Improvement Commissions, 96, 99-101
Industrial Museum 55-6, 156, 181
International Combustion 164
Irongate 10, 16, 20, 24, 26-7, 33, 54-5, 65-6, 69, 106, 127, 171, 178-9
Irongates Tavern 171
Isaac, Frederick Cecil 148
Isleworth Drive 25
Jackson, Dundonald 145
Jackson, Les 115
Jackson, Margaret Ann 146
Jackson, Mr G. C. M. 160
Jackson, Mrs Betty 164
Jackson Avenue 145
Jacobean House 100
Jacobites 50-4, 179
James I 38-9, 50
James II 50
James IV 38
Jenkins, Doreen Cecilia 148
Jerram, Tom 159
Jervis, Hon W. M. 114
Jessop, William 80
Johnson, Claude 123
Johnson, Dr Samuel 57, 59
Johnson, Leonard 160
Jones, Dean 115
Jones, Christine Elsie 146
Jones, Elsie May 146
Jury Street 22, 24

Kedleston Road 94-6, 148, 181
Kedleston Road Technical College 95
Kedleston Street 79
Keene, Richard 83-4
Keily, Arthur 173
Kenilworth Avenue 146
King Alfred Street 151
King Alfred of Wessex 18
King Cnut 19-20
King Guthrum 18
King Harold 21
King John 26
King Penda 16
King Stephen 23
King Street 25, 27, 58, 72-3, 75, 79, 82
Kingsway Hospital 102
Kingsway Retail Park 175
Kirsten, Peter 115
Knowles, Michael 112
Knox, John 35
Kuiper, Adrian 115
Lafferty's public house 52
Lambert, Lawrence 162
Lancastrian School 94
Lander, Eric 110
Lansing Gardens 25
Lawrence, Ethel Esther 148
Lea Hall 101
Leacroft, Mr Becher 25
Leacroft Road 25
Lennox, Countess of 37
Lennox, Earl of 37
Leonard Street 30
Ley family 141
Ley's foundry 154
Ley, Sir Francis 118
Lichfield 42, 60
Lichfield, Bishop of 95
Lichfield, Diocese of 140
Lilly, Colonel Harold 134
Linacre, Thomas 34
Litchurch 30, 77, 84, 145
Litchurch Gas Works 164
Little Chester 11, 15, 17
Little City 25
Little Eaton 80, 155, 162
Little Theatre 166
Littleover 9, 11, 27-8, 34, 112, 145, 156, 162
Littleover School 156

Lloyd, Kevin 110-11
LMS 111, 145-6, 149-52
LNER 84
Locarno dance hall 166
Locko Park 162
Loco Works 82, 129-30
Lodge Lane 144
Lombe, John 55-7
Lombe, Thomas 55, 57
London Road 31-2, 53, 109-10, 120, 122, 146, 161, 163-4, 181
Long Bridge 81, 167
Long Eaton 73, 147
Longford, Nicholas 32
Longford Hall 72
Longson, Sam 172
Lonsdale, Bishop John 95
Lord Street 162
Loudon, John Claudius 103
Loudon Street 25, 88, 103
Louise Greaves Lane 30
Lowe, Cyril Leslie 148
Lowe, Mary 75
Lower Dale Road 24
Ludlam, Robert 34, 36
Ludlam, William 90
Lunar Society 60-2, 65, 70
Mackay, Dave 172
Macklin Street 166, 180
Mackworth 25, 112
Mackworth College 181
MacManus, Arthur 132
Madeley Street 146
Main Centre 179, 181
Maine Drive 25
Malcolm, Devon 115
Manor Hospital 102
Manor House Farm 14
Mansfield Road 11, 155
Marcus Street 11, 14, 24
Markeaton Brook 8, 15, 22, 24, 27, 71, 81, 85, 97, 99, 142, 153
Markeaton Hall 72, 78
Markeaton Lane 52
Markeaton Park 154, 162, 165
Market Hall 24, 99-100, 170
Market Place 20, 23-4, 26-7, 32, 41, 50, 52, 55, 72, 78, 82, 85, 87, 99-100, 106, 119, 131-2, 140, 142, 150-1, 161, 168, 170-1, 178

Marlborough Road 148
Martin, Louis 173
Mary I 34
Mason, Alfred 131
Masters, Baden Marples 141
Mather, Cotton 74-5
Matlock 36, 82, 101
Maxwell, Robert 172
May, Fiona 173
McCluskey's night club 107
McFarland, Roy 172
McGovern, John 171
McMillan, Stuart 152
Mechanics' Institution 96
Mead, Thomas 79
Melbourne Street 151
Mellor, Robert 43
Melville, Andrew 107
Merlin engine 124, 147
Meteor Centre 110
Metro Cinema 96, 110, 180
Michigan Close 25
Mickleover 25, 28, 55, 95-6, 102, 109, 145, 156
Middies marching band 162
Middleton Street 150
Midland Counties Railway Company 82
Midland Electric Theatre 108-9, 165
Midland Hotel 82, 119, 122, 132, 171
Midland Railway 77, 82, 104, 132-3, 137
Midland Road 151
Mill Hill Lane 34
Miller, Geoff 115
Mitchell, Tommy 114
Monk Street 24
Monmouth, Duke of 50
Moor Lane swimming baths 141
Moore, Ambrose 25
Moore Street 25
Moorway Lane 34
Moorways sports centre 141
Moot Hall 26, 106
Moreton, Susannah 87
Morgan, Derek 115
Morledge 27, 81, 87, 100, 142, 154, 169-70, 177, 180
Morris, John 115

Morrison, Angus 175
Morritt, Charles 108
Morrow, Eliza 91
Mortensen, Ole 115
Morton, Gary 167
Moult, Ted 112
Muirfield Estate 25
Mundy Paddling Pool 154
Municipal Corporation Act 174
Municipal Sports Ground 141
Murray, Lord 53
Murray Road 25
Museum Square 179
National Schools 92
National Tramway Museum 71-2, 106
Nelson Street 163
New Normanton 24-5, 84, 107
Newcastle, Duke of 41, 66
Newsum, Henry 33
Nicholas, Jack 152
Nield, Doris 148
Nightingale, Florence 101
Nightingale Maternity Home 164
Nightingale Road 123-4, 147, 157, 167
Noel Baker, Philip 137, 173
Norman Street 163
Normanton 17-18, 24-5, 57, 84, 88, 107, 109-10, 121-2, 130, 150-1, 160-2, 176
Normanton Barracks 110, 121-2, 151, 160-1
Normanton Enclosure Act 57
Normanton Park 150, 162
Normanton Picture House 109
Normanton Road 88, 121, 151
North Midland Railway 82
North Street 102
Northampton, Earl of 41
Northcliffe House 169
Northworthy 15, 17
Nottingham 17-18, 27, 41, 51, 90-1, 176
Nottingham Castle Inn public house 169
Nottingham Road 57, 80, 83, 113, 117
Nuns Green 45, 50, 53, 71-3, 85, 87, 90, 106, 113

Nuns Green Acts 72, 85
Nuns Street 23, 27
Odeon cinema 109-10, 164
Offerton Avenue 146, 148, 151
Old Chester Road 11, 14, 27, 33
Old Dolphin public house 27
Old Institute public house 96
Old Mayor's Parlour 28-29
Old Spa Inn public house 91, 101
Old White Horse public house 26-7, 83, 90
Oldham, John 74
Oldham, Lucretia 74
Oliver, William 90
Ollerenshaw, Rosamund 90
Orchard Street School 94, 133
Oregon Way 25
Osmaston Hall 140
Osmaston-by-Derby 31
Osmaston Park 140-1
Osmaston Park Road 83
Osmaston Recreation Ground 144
Osmaston Road 105, 122, 150
Osnabruck Square 67
Outram, Benjamin 80
Overdale Road 24
Padley 34, 37
Padley Martyrs 37
Parker, Mrs Mary 60
Parkfields Cedars School 96, 112
Pastures Hill 11, 156
Pastures Hospital 102
Paxton, Sir Joseph 104
Payne, Edna May 146
Peach, James 148
Pear Tree 25, 83-4, 121, 131, 161, 176
Pearce, Dr Edmund Courtenay 138
Pegler, Michael 178
Pemberton, John 35
Pentrich Revolutionaries 90
Percival, Brenda Ellen 146
Percival, Rachel Ellen 146
Perth, Duke of 53
Pickering, Lionel 175
Pickford, Joseph 37, 71-3, 106
Pierrepoint, Henry 86
Plaza ballroom 150, 159
Plimsoll, Samuel 25, 136
Plimsoll Street 25

Pole, Mrs Elizabeth 60
Poole, Michael Robert 164
Pope, Alf 114
Popular cinema 109
Post Office Hotel 97, 99
Pountain, Eric (see Gray, Barry)
Pountain, Ronald (see Denis, Denny)
Poynton, Bill 130
Pride Park 77, 118, 129, 175, 178-9
Pride Park Stadium 175, 178
Priestley, Joseph 62
Priestley, Ruby Manifold 146
Prince Rupert 42
Princess Aethelflaeda
Princess Elizabeth 157-8, 164
Princess Royal 85
Prince of Wales 107
Public Health Act 85, 100-1
Pulvertaft Hand Clinic 102
Purser, Cecil Edward 146
Pym, John 39-41
Quakers (see also Society of Friends) 44, 92, 137
Queen Anne 48
Queen Mary 25, 33-4, 36-9, 140, 159-60, 162, 164
Queen Mary Maternity Home 164
Queen Mother 159
Queen Street 16, 25, 27, 65-6, 70, 72, 169
Queen Victoria 58, 95, 102, 119-20, 133, 160, 163
Radbourne Street 110
Ragged School 94
Railway Cottages 82, 84
Railway Institute 159
Railway Orphanage 136
Ramsden, Sam 150, 159
Rawlings, Dr A. E. J. 158
Raynes, Alderman W. R. 25, 158
Raynesway Bridge 155
RB211 engine 124-5, 171
Red Lion public house 98
Reeves Road 163
Reform Bill Riots 78
Regan, Dennis 148
Regent Street 145
Regent Terrace 137
Reginald Street 105

Reigate School 112
Repton 16, 19, 94, 137
Rhodes, Harold 115
Rialto ballroom 159
Richard III 32
Richards, Ceri 139
Richardson, A. W. 114
Richardson, Samuel 114, 116
Ripley 85
Riverlights scheme 110, 180-1
Rivers, Charles 74
Rivers, Private Jacob 133-4
Riverside Gardens 81, 154, 156, 162, 179-80
Rivett Street 151
Roe, Sir Thomas 135
Roe, William 94
Roe Farm Estate 163
Roe Farm School 163
Roe Memorial Home for the Adult Deaf 95
Rolls, Hon C. S. 123-4
Roosevelt Avenue 25
Rose Hill Methodist Church 151
Rose Hill Street 24, 105, 163
Rossington, Jane 112
Rotton Row 55
Rowditch 84, 109
Rowland, Ronald 146
Rowley, Frank 111
Rowley, Thomas & Sons 120, 140, 160
Royal Crown Derby 57-9, 70, 136, 157
Royal School for the Deaf 94-5
Royal Show 140
Royce, Sir Henry 105, 123-4
Rykneld Street 11-12
Sacheverel Street 165-6
Sacheverell, Dr Henry 50
Sacks, Dr Jonathan 181
Sadler Gate 20, 24, 27, 52, 82, 116, 153, 176-7, 181
Sadler Gate Bridge 27, 52
St Alkmund 15-16, 33
St Alkmund's Church 16, 19, 21, 132
St Alkmund's Churchyard 168-9
St Alkmund's Well 16
St Andrew's Church 158, 161

St Augustine 16
St Helen's House 23, 34, 72-3
St James's Street 130, 178, 181
St Luke's Street 163
St Mary's Bridge 36, 42
St Mary's Bridge Chapel 16, 27, 150
St Mary's Church 15-16
St Mary's Gate 16, 50, 85-7, 160
St Mary's Wharf 85, 143, 155
St Mary de Pratis priory 23, 27
St Michael's Church 16, 31, 42, 55-6, 76, 140
St Michael's Lane 169
St Peter's Bridge 27, 95, 99-100
St Peter's Church 16, 31
St Peter's Churchyard 33, 46, 169
St Peter's Street 10, 24, 27, 36, 100, 109, 130, 154, 164, 179,
St Thomas's Church 121
St Thomas's Road 132
St Werburgh's Church 15-16, 59, 132, 135, 138, 153
St Werburgh's Churchyard 91
St Werburgha 16
St Wystan' Church 16
Sandby, Paul 69
Sanders, Thomas 42-3, 45
Sandiacre 80
Sawley 80
Schweppe, Mr Jacob 126
Scott, Donald 173
Scott Street 25
Searchlights Concert Party 150
Seven Stars Inn public house 27
Sewell, Harry 173
Seymour, William 38
Shaftesbury Crescent 166
Sharp, Abraham 48-9
Shaw, Lt Gen Rt Hon Sir Frederick 137
Shaw, Sir John 137
Shepherd Street 27, 145
Sherbrook, Sarah 164
Sherwood Foresters 121-2, 130, 133-4, 137, 140, 149, 151, 160-2, 165
Shire Hall (see also County Hall) 50, 86-8

Shore, Sir John 34
Shot Tower 142
Shrewsbury, Countess of 140
Shrewsbury, Earl of 34, 36-8
Siddalls Road 130, 164
Silk Mill 25, 55-6, 72, 79, 127, 156, 170
Silk Mill Lock Out 79
Simpson, Arthur 127
Simpson, Dr George Clarke 127
Sinfin Lane 127, 164, 181
Sinfin Moor 113, 149
Sinfin Moor Lane 149
Sitwell cinema 109, 163
Sitwell Street (Spondon) 70
Slack, William Edward 86
Smith, Denis 114
Smith, Edwin 115
Smith, Harry James 146
Smith, Jim 175
Smith, Thomas 33
Snailham, Christopher 146
Snuggs, Elizabeth Mary 164
Society of Friends 44
Sorocold, George 55
South Avenue 149
South Derbyshire Cricket Club 114
Southern Derbyshire Acute Hospitals NHS Trust 102
Southwell, Diocese of 138, 140
Spencer, Herbert 92-3, 153
Spencer, Matthew 62, 94
Spofforth, F. R. 114
Spondon 28, 30, 70, 109, 134, 162-3
Spot, The 10, 24-5, 109, 163
Spry, Constance 164
Stamps, Jack 145, 152
Stanley, Fred 112
Staveley 116
Stevens, Harry 77
Stevens, James 77
Stillman, Les 115
Stockbrook Street 150
Stone House Prebend 33
Stonehill Road 24
Stones, Anthony 179
Storer, Harry 114
Storer, Mrs Kathleen 164
Strand Arcade 100
Strutt, Jedidiah 67-8

Strutt, Joseph 25, 96-8, 103, 105
Strutt, William 76, 101
Strutt Street 25, 160
Swarkestone 81
Swarkestone Road 27
Swinburne Street 145
Sympson, Richard 34
Talbot, George 37
Taylor, Ann 83
Taylor, Bob 115
Taylor, Gwen 112
Taylor, Joseph 148
Taylor, Peter 171-2
Temperance Hall 108
Tenant Street 24, 27, 29, 90
Tenant Street Bridge 27
Tewkesbury Street 163
Theatre Royal 106
Thomas, Jimmy 135-6
Thompson, Eric 173
Thorley, Richard 91
Thorn Street 25
Thorntree House 104
Ticknall 112
Tillett, Councillor Jeffery 174
Tomlinson, Samuel 102
Townsend, Ernest 144
Townsend, Leslie 114
Trafalgar Street 25
Traffic Street 92
Trent Bus Company 147
Trent, River 80-1
Trent Valley 11, 14, 70
Trowell, Sylvia 160
Trowells Lane 134
Turner, William 90
Tutbury Castle 37, 41
Underhill Avenue 163
Union Workhouse 59, 102
University of Derby 23, 95-6, 181
Upperdale Road 24
Uttoxeter New Road 95
Uttoxeter Road 25, 96, 102, 134, 174
Vauser, George 80
Vernon, Lord 35
Vernon Gate 24, 86, 89
Vernon Street 78, 86, 89, 91-2, 110
Vickars, Mrs Mary 90
Victoria cinema 109

Victoria Street 97-9, 132, 169, 177, 180
Walker, Brian 167
Walker, Matthew 125
Wallace, Robert 97
War Memorial 131, 158, 161, 178
Ward, Alan 115
Wardwick 15-16, 24, 96, 99-100, 104, 153, 180
Wardwick Tavern 153
Warner, Alan 115
Warsi, Mrs Perween 126-7
Waste, Joan 34-5
Waterloo Street 25
Watson, Julia 111
Watt, Alexander 59, 61
Watts, Arthur Geoffrey 146
Webb, Stuart 172
Webster Street 166
Wedgwood, Josiah 59-61, 66, 73
Welbeck Abbey 37
West, Sir Thomas 33
West End 71, 83, 107, 109-10, 150, 153
Westbourne Park 112
Westleigh Estate 151
Wheeldon, Alice 131-2
Wheeldon, Hettie 131
White, Colonel Charles 45
White Bear Lock 80
White Hall cinema 109
White Lion public house 98
Whitehurst, John 25, 61-2, 65-7, 69-70, 94, 127, 179
Whittle, Sir Frank 124
Wibberley, Charlie 91
Wild, Harry 173
Wilkinson, Tom 58
William of Orange 50
Willoughby, Percival 29
Willow Row 85
Wills, Tom 114
Wilmot, Sir Henry 114, 133
Wilmot, Sir Sacheverel 133
Wilmot Street 92
Wilson, Lucy 86, 91
Wilson Street 164, 166
Wiltshire Road 163
Winchester Crescent 163
Windmill Club 166

Windmill Pit 34-5
Wirksworth 41, 127
Wolfa Street 117
Wood, Barry 115
Wood, Valerie 163
Woodley, Vic 152
Woods Lane 177

Woollatt, William 67
Woolley, William 33
Wooster, Edward 76
Worcester Crescent 163
Worthington, Stan 114
Wright, Anna Romana 70
Wright, John 115

Wright, Joseph 60, 65, 69-71, 76
Wright, Mrs Ethel 151
Yates Street 163
Yeaveley 14
York Street 163
Young, Gwendoline Bertha 146
Young Street 25